TREATING
POSTNATAL
DEPRESSION

TREATING POSTNATAL DEPRESSION

A Psychological Approach for Health Care Practitioners

JEANNETTE MILGROM, PhD
Austin & Repatriation Medical Centre, Melbourne, Australia

PAUL R. MARTIN, DPhil
University of New England, Armidale, Australia

LISA M. NEGRI, DPsych
La Trobe University, Melbourne, Australia

JOHN WILEY & SONS, LTD

Chichester · New York · Weinheim · Brisbane · Singapore · Toronto

National   01243 779777
International   (+44) 1243 779777
e-mail (for orders and customer service enquiries): cs-books@wiley.co.uk
Visit our Home Page on http://www.wiley.co.uk
or http://www.wiley.com

Other Wiley Editorial Offices

John Wiley & Sons, Inc., 605 Third Avenue,
New York, NY 10158-0012, USA

WILEY-VCH Verlag GmbH, Pappelallee 3,
D-69469 Weinheim, Germany

Jacaranda Wiley Ltd, 33 Park Road, Milton,
Queensland 4064, Australia

John Wiley & Sons (Asia) Pte Ltd, 2 Clementi Loop #02-01,
Jin Xing Distripark, Singapore 129809

John Wiley & Sons (Canada) Ltd, 22 Worcester Road,
Rexdale, Ontario M9W 1L1, Canada

Library of Congress Cataloging-in-Publication Data

Milgrom, Jeannette.
    Treating postnatal depression : a psychological approach for health care practitioners /
Jeannette Milgrom, Paul R. Martin, Lisa M. Negri.
        p. cm.
    Includes bibliographical references and index.
    ISBN 0-471-98645-3 (paper : acid-free paper)
    1. Postpartum depression—Treatment.   2. Puerperal psychoses.   I. Martin, Paul R.   II.
Negri, Lisa M.   III. Title.

    RG852.M54 1999
    618.7'6—dc21
                                                                        99–045635

British Library Cataloguing in Publication Data

A catalogue record for this book is available from the British Library

ISBN 0-471-98645-3

Typeset in 10/12pt Palatino by Dorwyn Ltd, Rowlands Castle, Hants
Printed and bound in Great Britain by Bookcraft (Bath) Ltd, Midsomer Norton, Somerset
This book is printed on acid-free paper responsibly manufactured from sustainable forestry,
in which at least two trees are planted for each one used for paper production.

To the Infant Clinic staff who developed a vision and pursued it and to the mothers, fathers and babies who have told us their stories, each in their own ways. Lastly, to our own infants and children, Natalie, Joshua, Kathryn, Richard, Natalie and Shona who have taught us a lot.

CONTENTS

ABOUT THE AUTHORS

Professor Jeannette Milgrom
Department of Clinical Psychology, Austin & Repatriation Medical Centre, Heidelberg West, Victoria 3081, Australia

Professor Paul Martin
School of Psychology, University of New England, Armidale, New South Wales 2351, Australia

Ms Lisa Negri
School of Psychological Science, Psychology Clinic, La Trobe University, Bundoora, Victoria 3083, Australia

Jeannette Milgrom is Professor of Psychology, School of Behavioural Science, University of Melbourne, and Director of Clinical and Health Psychology at the Austin & Repatriation Medical Centre, Melbourne, Australia. She has been involved in research on mother–infant interactions and studies of psychiatric disorders since 1978, and has held a Harkness Fellowship in the USA as well as an O'Rourke Fellowship in Paris for work with families and infants. She developed a model for clinical psychology in hospitals, and pioneered the 'Infant Clinic'. For over 15 years she has been centrally involved in the development of a number of postgraduate training programs, including in infant mental health, and in research evaluating and developing interventions for postnatal depression. She now spends a significant proportion of her time in teaching, clinical practice and research. She is also active professionally, having recently held the positions of Scientific Director of the Australian Association for Infant Mental Health (Victorian Branch), and Secretary of the College of Health Psychologists of the Australian Psychological Society.

Paul R. Martin is Professor of Psychology and Head of the School of Psychology at the University of New England. He is also Director of Scientific Affairs of the Australian Psychological Society and was National President of the Australian Behaviour Modification Association. He has previously held positions in the University of Oxford, Monash University and the University of Western Australia, including being Director of the Adoption Research and Counselling Service at the latter university. Authored and edited books include *Clinical Psychology* (with J. S. Birnbrauer), *Psychological Management of Chronic Headaches*, and *Handbook of Behavior Therapy and Psychological Science*. He has been involved in postnatal depression services and research for a number of years, and his particular interests in this field include program evaluation and rural issues. In addition to his research and teaching roles, he is a practicing clinical and health psychologist.

Lisa M. Negri is a psychologist in private practice. She has recently completed her doctoral thesis on the Screening and Treatment of Women with Postnatal Depression. This was a groundbreaking study in which she developed a community screening program, and Version 1 of the cognitive-behavioural group intervention program for depression. Her approach has been further developed by the Infant Clinic and forms the basis for the group program in this book. Lisa has worked extensively in the area of child, adolescent and family psychology within a variety of settings over the past 10 years. Her experience includes working with children with intellectual disabilities and learning difficulties; adolescents within the Juvenile Justice System; as well as mothers and babies in a mother–baby unit, the Infant Clinic, and via the Management Committee of La Trobe University Children's Centre. She is also a consultant/lecturer at La Trobe University and supervises Master of Clinical Psychology students.

ABOUT THE CONTRIBUTORS

Ms Jennifer Ericksen
Department of Clinical Psychology, Austin & Repatriation Medical Centre, Heidelberg West, Victoria 3081, Australia

Ms Carol Richards
Department of Clinical Psychology, Austin & Repatriation Medical Centre, Heidelberg West, Victoria 3081, Australia

Jennifer Ericksen is Coordinator of the Infant Clinic and a psychologist experienced in early childhood assessment, parent support and skills training, cognitive behaviour therapy, service planning and implementation in the public sector. She has worked in a variety of specialist children's services targeting difficulties in children's development in social, emotional, intellectual and motor areas. Currently, she coordinates a three-year screening and intervention study for women with postnatal depression.

Carol Richards is a Maternal and Child Health Nurse with 30 years' experience working with mothers, babies and families. As founding Director of Canterbury Family Centre, she developed a program using a multidisciplinary team of professionals to work with high-risk families, children and infants. Work with mothers in the area of adoption has made her a strong proponent of the need for early intervention in the mother–infant relationship, and the essential role of treating the mother and infant as a unit.

FOREWORD

It is fully appropriate with the approach of a third millennium that women's mental health, and postnatal depression in particular, is at last achieving a more global priority which could lead to improved services.

In Westernised countries it is known that at least one in 10 women will suffer from a pervasive mood disorder after childbirth. In situations of deprivation, poor social support, families in transit and young parents dug up from their cultural roots, this figure is, however, a conservative estimate. Childbirth is *not* always followed by a time of peaceful tranquillity and recent studies suggest that for a third of mothers with severe postnatal blues, possibly triggered by neuroendocrine changes, this emotionalism does not remit but instead merges into a more prolonged depression. The duration of such depression is linked closely to the status of childbearing within our societies and to the availability of family support whether transmitted by traditional custom, as in Japan, China or Malta, or by enhanced welfare provision and more sustained parental responsibility as found in Sweden.

Greater geographical mobility, equal opportunities for men and women with regard to work and domestic responsibilities and more widespread family planning are changing the micro—and macro—social context within which children are born and raised.

Although Louis Victor Marcé in the middle of the last century, and his teacher Esquirol, were aware of the devastating effect of puerperal psychosis as well as the depression 'not appearing in hospital statistics', it is a tribute to the international inspiration of the Marcé Society that the knowledge reviewed in this book has now increased to the extent that the readers could include both distressed parents and health care professionals.

Furthermore this book is not just a scholarly text but is also a 'hands on' manual—and therefore represents a particular pinnacle of Australian achievement within this field. It is also timely. Jeannette Milgrom, Paul Martin and Lisa Negri have written a lucid text which the academic and self-help communities have been waiting for far too long.

The full understanding of postnatal mood disorder and postnatal depression in particular can indeed only be approached comprehensively from within a biopsychosocial perspective—yet no lone clinician or researcher can possess all these clinical and research skills derived from the biological, social and psychological sciences. It is, for example, a plausible hypothesis that postnatal depression is sparked off by neuroendocrine changes (perhaps conditioned by antenatal stress and personality predisposition) and yet its duration is determined more by so-ciocultural factors such as the self-esteem of the parturient mother, the status of childbirth and of infants within society, the availability of support as well as by the wish of service planners to make available local services.

Within this global context it is not surprising therefore that the Edinburgh Postnatal Depression Scale has been translated into over 15 languages and that studies on postnatal depression now achieve a priority for research funding not anticipated 30 years ago. Furthermore, as the contributors to this book know well, the causes and consequences of postnatal depression can only be grasped by a multi-professional team which straddles the individual contribution and training of psychologists, doctors, social workers and nurses—as well as paediatricians, obstetricians, occupational therapists and midwives. Can the tardiness to develop appropriate perinatal services for young families be partially explained by the multi-professional morass where responsibility for a total service is passed from one professional to another—and nothing therefore achieved? A comprehensive perinatal service may span an acute hospital service provision as well as a community base, and includes psychiatrists, psychologists and nurses who must bridge the primary and secondary care interface.

The authors are strongly within the tradition of distinguished clinicians and researchers who have understood this subject from the inside—partly through personal experience but mostly through face-to-face contact with infants and their distressed parents—and are cognisant of the international literature and the implications of others' findings for optimum perinatal services. Furthermore, and above all, they are aware of the need to stop only talking about their findings unless they can also demonstrate the way in which these findings improve mental health services.

Indeed, as this book amply illustrates, it *is* time for clinicians and researchers to listen to the narratives of users; and then to influence health policy at a governmental level.

The authors are altruistic in their goals and they have hidden nothing—including their awareness that their outcome studies have yet to be completed. They are also aware that the cognitive-behavioural treatments which they so cogently advocate are labour intensive and costly, and that there is a need for more information about which parents, with which types of perinatal problems, benefit from this particular approach. This they know.

They also know that giving details of their treatment procedures, including model 'Overheads' about how to run a cognitive-behavioural therapy group or a parenting group, could ensure that postmodern families, who may lack cultural cohesion and lack continuity with their own past, can yet receive assistance from a postmodern society.

The work of the Transcultural Unit has shown abundantly how the break in the transmission of knowledge and beliefs between generations about parenting, particularly for Cambodian refugees and for parents in the fast-changing modern society, can leave mothers bereft of advice and support—precisely at a time when they are most needed.

Psychiatrists need to share their skills and experience with other colleagues and to recognise fully the major contributions from developmental and clinical psychologists to this field. Jeannette Milgrom and her colleagues are correct in suggesting that many women prefer a psychological approach to their problems; yet as they point out it is also necessary at times to overcome the reluctance of mothers to take medication, and for antidepressant medication to be administered within the context of a supportive treatment alliance.

The authors have correctly also described postnatal depression as a 'devastating' illness and appropriately have included 'missing voices'. Parents and professionals will therefore welcome this scholarly and humane book from Melbourne, which will enhance so visibly the welfare of women and their families.

John Cox
Keele University
Royal College of Psychiatrists

PREFACE

This book has evolved over a number of years and is the culmination of our experiences as clinicians and researchers with women suffering from postnatal depression.

In 1992, one of us (Jeannette Milgrom) completed a four-year longitudinal study (funded by the Victoria Health Promotion Foundation) that had followed 60 women after their admission for postnatal depression to various mother–baby units in Melbourne, Australia. The results of our findings were devastating. Four years later, the majority of women were still clearly differentiated from non-depressed women in terms of their mood state, self-esteem, attachment to their infants, marital breakdown and parent–infant relationships. The behavioural profiles of their children were also clearly different. Whilst we did not have comparison prenatal data, it was clear that this was a group of women who needed more help than what was traditionally offered as best practice.

Out of this experience grew the Infant Clinic, a development that has inspired, frustrated and made us believe in the difference that health care practitioners can make to the future of countless families in formation.

One of the most moving memories was watching the love affair that developed between a mother of three and her new infant. This young woman, who had experienced institutionalisation herself and a difficult childhood, had found a new experience. With tears in her eyes, she turned and said, 'I never knew it could be like this.' With her first two children, postnatal depression and inadequate parenting skills had meant years of disrupted relationships and, sadly, her two children now had significant developmental delays. With this new infant, early intervention was initiated from the first few weeks, with a radically different outcome.

The Infant Clinic developed out of a group of dedicated professionals who recognised that traditional intervention approaches needed to be modified to help women with infants. We developed innovative approaches to deal with parent–infant bonding difficulties and a multidisciplinary team. We searched the literature and put together knowledge from the fields of developmental psychology, infant mental health, depression and psychiatry. We experimented with Selma Fraiberg's approach of being in the kitchen, at home with women, and we got down on the floor to play with babies. We fought with funding agencies who argued that this did not fall within strategic funding plans, and despite enormous difficulties continued to survive, sustained by our successes and learning all the time, how to improve what we did. Burn-out, budgeting on a shoestring, escalating referrals and changing student populations all added extra challenges. We accepted a wide range of infant-centred difficulties (such as failure to thrive, severe sleeping problems) and parent-centred difficulties (postnatal depression, attachment difficulties).

Our interest in postnatal depression remained paramount. We asked ourselves, how can we best intervene with a problem that is so widespread? Too often research and practice are not integrated: academics do research, practitioners administer treatment packages. We felt that we were in an ideal position to use our knowledge in the two areas, to inform each other. We therefore embarked on a large screening and treatment trial for postnatal depression (funded by the Research and Development Grants Advisory Committee, Commonwealth Department of Human Services and Health) to identify and help with the hidden distress of depression, so commonly masked by women with newborn infants. We started our interventions with cognitive-behavioural therapy, as to date evidence-based practice suggests that these techniques have proven validity for helping with depression. We needed to modify this approach, however, to take into account the needs of women with infants and to make the program gender sensitive. Our findings were encouraging and we found that our detailed manual could be applied by a range of practitioners, mostly trained in psychology, with successful results. This book is the product of our experience.

Our treatment trial continues, and we have screened more than 4000 women. We are now searching for adaptations of the structured cognitive-behavioural therapy approach to explore whether less costly interventions, or those that require less training, can be equally effective for a problem of this magnitude. In the meantime, we offer a sound management approach for the treatment of postnatal depression.

ACKNOWLEDGEMENTS

First and foremost, our thanks to Barbara Frazer, without whom this book would never have come together. Barbara painstakingly typed, checked, retyped, pointed out errors and inconsistencies, chased contributors and references and, in short, made it happen.

To members of the Infant Clinic team, two of whom have contributed directly: Jennifer Ericksen (without whose organisational skills we would have floundered) and Carol Richards (without whose care, enormous empathy and practical approaches we would have risked becoming technicians). They were key innovators in the development of the individual approaches and fathers' packages and painstakingly wrote and rewrote them based on their extensive understanding of women with depression. The third founding member of the team, Elizabeth Loughlin, brought creativity and dance therapy to us and always reminded us that the non-verbal relationship between mothers and infants underpins their interactions. Our thanks also to Rachael McCarthy, always cheerful and hardworking, who tested and retested the packages, giving us thoughtful and useful feedback. To Jan Tonkin for her help in trialing our early approaches and thoughts on cognitive interventions. To Vanessa Heinze, who helped us refine our diagnostic criteria for postnatal depression and assessed many, many women always with care and compassion. To Meg McNeil for her help in treating women while completing her thesis and her persistence in seeing her project through. To Kerryn Burrows for her contribution to understanding the impact on fathers (and to the many students who have rotated through our clinic). To our tireless research assistants Alison Pearce initially and now Caroline De Paola.

We are grateful to our collaborators, Maternal and Child Health Nurses in northeast Melbourne, especially those in the Banyule, Nillumbik, Darebin and Whittlesea regions and particularly to Marita van Gemert, Coordinator, Banyule region. These nurses helped set up the screening of mothers and supported all the women we have treated with their care and wisdom, and without whose help we could not have mounted a project of this size. More recently, the Post and Ante Natal Depression Association (PanDa) who joined our project team with their experience of self-help.

Also thanks to Dr Lyn Littlefield, La Trobe University, for her contribution to the development of the original cognitive-behavioural group intervention. And finally, to those individuals and bodies who helped us with funding, without which this work would not have been possible. Paulin Walter, our brilliant manager to whom we owe our survival, and Eril Deighton and Rae Anstee who helped us start. We are grateful for funding from the Commonwealth Department of Human Services and Health Research and Development Grants Advisory Committee (RADGAC), Victorian Health Promotion Foundation, Austin Hospital Medical Research Foundation, North Eastern Health Care Network and Healthier Outcomes Network, Sussan Corporation (Aust.) Pty Ltd, Austin Hospital Auxiliary, HBA (Dr Bert Boffa in particular) and the 3Rs.

PS: To those who have inspired us—Professor Russell Meares and Professor Serge Lebovici.

Part I

Understanding Postnatal Depression

INTRODUCTION

Traditionally, childbirth is viewed by society as a joyful event, not only in Westernised countries, but also in other cultures. It is a time for celebration, fulfilment and hope. The private experience of childbirth is often in stark contrast to this idealised image, with a daunting number of women experiencing low mood and emotional lability. Instead of the expected tranquillity, many women struggle with: the new set of demands a baby brings, for which they have inadequate preparation and support; the loss of order and routine; the sleepless nights; the changes in their role, including career decisions; the relationship with their partner; and their partner's possible adjustment difficulties to parenting, or his absence due to work demands or relationship breakdown. Concurrently, stresses in their lives may include isolation, financial difficulties or an unexpectedly difficult birth. This emotional upheaval in vulnerable women can lead to a depressive experience of varying degrees.

A small proportion of women enter a full psychotic depressive episode. A more staggering 10–20% experience postnatal depression (PND), a condition characterised by: feelings of sadness, guilt, worthlessness and anxiety; thoughts about suicide and death; difficulties in concentration and decision making; disturbances of appetite and sleep; and lack of interest and energy. These symptoms are not transitory and can persist in varying degrees for a number of years.

One of the most striking features of PND is the impact it has, not only on the woman, but also on her infant and her partner. The difficulties that arise in these relationships, often triggered by the depressive episode, mean that the adverse effects of PND may persist even after resolution of maternal symptoms.

Despite widespread ramifications for all the family, it is only recently that attention has been paid to the emotional upheaval arising from childbirth rather than just focusing on the pain associated with delivery. Health professionals have become aware of the importance of early intervention in PND, yet most of the information available is descriptive of the condition, with few detailed programs to guide professional intervention. This book provides a handbook for management of PND, involving the woman, her partner, and if needed, her infant.

Listening

On the outside looking in
You see a smile and all is well
Yet if you look a little closer
You'd see the pain in which I dwell.

You ask me how I am
But the truth you do not seek
For if I show you my pain
You do not let me speak.

On the inside looking out
I see the joy in others' lives
I wonder where my joy has gone
Its absence hurts my eyes.

Through the haze I see the days go by
And I watch my child grow
I fear my acts will scar her
Or is she just too young to know.

My child is so precious to me
The most beautiful thing I've seen
I love her more than life itself
And yet sometimes I'm so mean.

I don't know why I get so angry
When her cries are just her speech
She does not deserve my anger
Or my attitude of defeat.

You tell me she's a good baby
Don't you think I already know?
Your words just drive the pain harder
When all I want is to let go.

Why are you so scared to hear
The truth behind my smile?
I need for you to understand
To listen for a while.

It is the illness that I suffer
A bad person I am not
As a mother I do my very best
I give it everything I've got.

In time I will be well again
But for now I need you here
For a shoulder just to cry on
Or an understanding ear.

Sherri Hardy 30 May 1996
Client of the Austin & Repatriation Medical Centre
Infant Clinic

Chapter 1

POSTNATAL DEPRESSION IN THE COMMUNITY

SYMPTOMS AND EXPERIENCE OF POSTNATAL DEPRESSION

The introductory poem 'Listening' described a woman's experience of being 'on the inside looking out'. The personal experience of depression is often devastating and has been vividly captured in accounts and poems. These are often written after the woman has recovered and attempt to convey how much she felt alone, describing the feeling of depression with emotive phrases such as being 'in a dark tunnel' or 'black sunshine'. These experiences, together with illustrations of women's stories, are further described below.

Symptoms of postnatal depression

Postnatal depression (PND) is accompanied by a range of symptoms that women often cannot make sense of and find overwhelming. Typically, they report a number of distressing symptoms:

Symptoms	Words women use
• Lowered mood, sadness	*'The colour has gone from everything.'*
• Tearfulness or crying uncontrollably	*'I want to cry all the time . . .'* *'I don't seem to be able to do anything . . .'*
• Feeling worthless	*'People are only interested in the baby—not in how I feel.'*
• Anxiety or even panic attacks	
• Self-blame or guilt	*'How can I feel so bad when I've got this beautiful baby?'*
• Worries about health, and their baby	
• Lack of energy and feeling exhausted	*'I'm tired . . . so tired.'* *'Everything is an effort.'*

- Slowed speech and movements

- Alternatively, agitation or feeling hyperactive

  'Am I going mad?'

- Loss of interest in activities, including sex

  'I don't want to see anyone.'
  'I can't bear to be touched.'

- Feeling irritable

  'I feel like exploding.'

- Appetite disturbance, eating too much or too little

- Reduced concentration and decision-making ability

  'I have trouble deciding.'

- Sleep disturbance, not being able to sleep even when the baby does

- Confused thought and becoming more forgetful

  'I'm confused and my thinking seems foggy.'

- Feelings of hopelessness, inadequacy and constantly thinking in a pessimistic way

  'The baby's crying again: I've only just sat down.'

- Emotional lability with oscillating moods

  'One moment I feel great and the next I'm really down again.'

- Thoughts about death and, at times, suicide

  'Sometimes I think everyone would be better off without me.'

The experience of postnatal depression

Symptoms of depression during the postnatal period take on a particular significance not only because of the need to recuperate physically from childbirth, but also because of the presence of an infant. Inability to sleep due to depression compounds the problems of being woken by a hungry baby. Sleep deprivation is further complicated sometimes by being woken by an infant when sleep is finally achieved. Difficulties in concentration and decision making can become accentuated by the many demands a baby makes and, not uncommonly, depressed women feel overloaded and unable to make the simplest decision—for instance, about whether to dress or not dress. A woman's irritability and lability may also have a spiralling effect on her infant, and possibly other toddlers, who can then become more difficult to manage. Many women experiencing PND become preoccupied with negative thoughts about their feelings of failure as parents and the vulnerability of their baby (Olioff, 1991). Anxiety is often pronounced, and sometimes focused on the baby's welfare. In this context, marital difficulties often become entrenched and women commonly perceive a lack of support from their partners, who in turn may be having difficulty adjusting to their newborn.

BOX 1: 'OUR STORIES'

Excerpts of letters from women who have written to us at the Infant Clinic

The slow development of PND often makes it confusing for mothers to gauge how badly they are coping:

'Looking back now, I realise my depression had been gradually building up. However, at the time, I felt that one day things were okay but that the next day I'd lost control of my life and would never be able to regain it.

I spent a lot of time in tears. I wasn't able to feel happy about anything. I felt inadequate—a failure as a mother and a partner. I was reluctant to tell people how I was feeling—I've been able to cope well in life so far, so why not now? Besides, I could always think of others I knew who were in worse situations and they were coping, so what right did I have to be falling apart? I felt more tired each day. The list of jobs I needed to get done was getting longer. Sometimes, I'd motivate myself to start something but I'd lose interest shortly after. Making decisions, even trivial ones such as whether or not it was warm enough for the children to wear short sleeves, were too hard. I couldn't understand where the organised, methodical and self-sufficient individual I used to be had gone to.

My mind was such a muddle of confused thoughts, that I was frightened to talk to anyone in case they would guess what was going on—but at the same time I was yearning for someone to realise I needed someone to talk to without me having to initiate it.'

The guilt: how hard it is for some mothers, when depressed, to cope with a crying baby and then the unbearable feelings that follow:

'When Jodie cries it makes me angry, I don't know why. Sometimes I feel like she does it just to get to me. I know that's not true but that's how it feels. I get frustrated because I can't make her stop. I get so angry with her, then I cry because I feel so guilty, so horrible, because I'm her mother and I can't comfort her when she needs me because I can't stay calm within myself. I am unable to appreciate her. She is so beautiful and I feel so inadequate. I feel like I don't deserve to have a child because I don't appreciate her.

I don't understand why her crying affects me so much. If she's happy, then I'm okay. I wish I could cope. I want to be a good mother but I don't know how. I'm scared that one day I might hurt her. If I do, I'll never forgive myself. Other people cope, why can't I? My mother-in-law told me that the way I was with Jodie scared her. I scare myself, but having someone tell me that hurt me like nothing I have ever known. I felt like a bad mother. I don't want Jodie to suffer because of me. I love her more than anything in the world and I don't want her to grow up hating me. I want her to love me but I'm so scared she won't.'

The recognition that dealing with baby management difficulties is only a first step:

'I recall quite vividly a certain scepticism I felt when first referred to the 'Infant Clinic' but I also recall a certain despondency that urged me to pursue this avenue . . . I explained my situation: my eight-month-old baby was not sleeping properly. She would wake every night four or five times, and her daytime sleeps consisted of thirty minutes here and there! . . .

I put into practice all of your suggestions, starting with eliminating all night feeds, some controlled crying, I even 'roomed in' with the baby at one point. After much perseverance, Olivia's sleeping pattern began to improve. I remember feeling encouraged with just a slight change in her behaviour and that made it so much easier to continue with the suggestions you had given me.

With the sleeping problem almost under control, you encouraged me to attend the clinic again (I wasn't certain why, but it soon became clear), and in doing so you instigated much

Box 1 continued

conversation that prompted me to speak about many things that were troubling me. Whether or not you were aware of it, I did benefit a great deal from those sessions. It amazed me that mere conversation could be so productive although it was more than simple conversation.

In the months that followed, life got back on track. A confidence which had been lost for a while slowly began to reappear, a loneliness I have previously felt began to disappear . . .'

Thanks, Lina

The difficulties some mothers undergo to find health professionals who recognise PND:

'I had a wonderful pregnancy. I fell pregnant a little earlier than expected, but I was over the moon. I kept a diary of my pregnancy, concerns and feelings—all for my baby to read in the future. My little girl arrived five days late, and the labour went well, although it was rather long.

All I can say is that for the first couple of weeks I was on cloud nine. I felt fantastic and energetic. I couldn't believe how well I was coping. Come week four and things came to a head. My baby had very bad colic, wouldn't sleep longer than ten to fifteen minutes at a time and she just seemed to scream, or shrill, all the time. When she was six weeks I admitted myself to casualty at the local hospital. They told me I was okay and that I was suffering from severe stress. I had been having panic attacks, tingling in my arms and legs, felt nauseous all the time, and had two severe bouts of vomiting and diarrhoea complete with the shivers and shudders. After going to visit two doctors, they informed me it was gastro; I told them it wasn't and that it was my nerves. Prior to going to hospital, I went to a number of different doctors, who performed a ridiculous number of tests on me (all of which were normal) . . .

This went on and on, visiting doctors and them telling me there was nothing wrong and me just getting worse and worse. The butterflies in my stomach were there constantly, the heart palpitations were out of control, and I developed new and strange phobias and became obsessed in really strange ways with different things. I thought I was going mad. 'Something' was coming between my daughter and me preventing the developing of a bond, and occasionally now I still get the odd day when I feel like this. I don't know why, maybe it's a mechanism in me that blames her for how I feel and what I've been through. There was an overwhelming feeling that something terrible was going to happen and this was an all-consuming twenty-four hours a day thought. It would be my last thought as I dropped off to sleep and the first thought on awakening . . .

The amazing thing is that throughout all of this I never neglected myself or my baby and I looked rather well at most times. This, I believe, hindered me from receiving the help from the professionals I needed . . . As my illness developed I then became unable to sleep, sometimes getting an hour's sleep in twenty-four hours. This made me incredibly depressed and unable to cope with the baby or my thoughts any more. Finally, when my baby was five months old my husband contacted a local doctor who dealt with postnatal depression' . . .

Thanks, Jenny

This mother went on to receive a variety of interventions, including an Infant Clinic mother–baby intervention, antidepressants and a day-stay program setting for babies. She also found self-help material very useful.

The gratitude mothers feel at being heard:

Box 1 continued

'When I came to see you . . .

I was tearful, dragged down by daily activities and had very little hope for the future. You helped me overcome these problems to a large degree.

Once contact was established the support and guidance through the weeks of misery were exceptional in that I felt I could contact you at any time, discuss anything with you (about me, the baby, relationships, work, even shopping) and always feel supported. The sessions we had at the Infant Clinic were a pillar every week. They were time for me (as opposed to the mother, wife and working woman who I also am) to tell my story and, with you, work towards recovery from my postnatal depression.

Gradually the realisation came that (me as a person) was as important as the million other things I do for the million other people and that there is in fact life after new motherhood . . .

Now I'm better, and though I visit those dark days in my memory with trepidation, I know that if it happens again I'll be welcome at the Infant Clinic. The rapidity of response and access to help in the early days of parturition were key, I feel, to my recovery . . .'

And poems that express so much:

Black Sunshine

No one told me it was going to be like this
No one said it would be so hard
Black mornings, grey days, no appetite and so much
sleep I miss.

I used to just keep smiling and say I'm
fine thanks, just tired,
But now my face won't move to do that
and it's just too hard to lie.

I've tried snapping out of it and pulling
up my socks that's the advice that well
meaning people give me
But all I can do is stare at the clock
trapped in darkness and isolation.

My baby doesn't need a mother like this
sad, gloomy and unattentive
My partner doesn't need a burden like this
I'm not who I used to be, no warm words
no cuddles no caresses.
No one told me it was going to be like this
No one said it would be so hard.

It's sunny outside today, my baby smiled and my
partner bought me flowers and cooked the tea
But all I feel is profound sadness that won't shift
and all I do is drift from room to room and
have this sense of impending doom.
No one told me it was going to be like this
No one said it would be so hard.

Box 1 continued

I found a place where I could go and stay
have time out, nurture, take my baby and
not have to worry about the day.
I don't feel so alone now and I see I'm not
the only one that feels like this and I'm
not the only one who is finding things hard.

Four weeks I stayed until one day my baby
smiled and I smiled back
Someone asked—how are you? and I said I think
I'm going to be fine thanks and I wasn't lying.

It was then I realised it isn't always going
to be like how it's seemed and it isn't going to
be so hard anymore
and no one needed to say 'it's going to be okay'
because I knew I wasn't going back to where I'd been.

DIAGNOSING THE PRESENCE OF A DEPRESSIVE DISORDER

The presence of the symptoms listed previously does not necessarily mean that a woman is suffering from clinical depression. One of the difficulties with the term 'postnatal depression' is that it has been used to describe a range of distressing symptoms following childbirth. Some clinicians and researchers describe women as suffering from PND mainly on the basis of the symptom of lowered or depressed mood. More commonly, a clinical diagnosis has been made on the basis of the pattern and severity of symptoms. The *Diagnostic and Statistical Manual of Mental Disorders* (DSM-IV) (American Psychiatric Association, 1994) describes a range of diagnostic categories that are indicative of a depressive disorder.

Depressive symptoms that lead to a diagnosis of major depressive disorder

Women who experience the symptoms described previously can be diagnosed as suffering from a major depressive disorder, depending on the severity and number of symptoms. DSM-IV criteria for a major depressive disorder require the presence of either (1) depressed mood most of the day, nearly every day with self-reports of sadness, emptiness or observation of appearing tearful, *or* (2) markedly diminished interest or pleasure, *plus* five (or more) of the criteria listed below for at least a two-week period, nearly every day:

1. Markedly diminished interest or pleasure in all, or almost all, activities.
2. Significant weight loss when not dieting, or weight gain, or decrease or increase in appetite.
3. Insomnia or hypersomnia.
4. Psychomotor agitation or retardation (observable by others, not merely subjective feelings of restlessness or being slowed down).

5. Fatigue or loss of energy.
6. Feelings of worthlessness or excessive or inappropriate guilt.
7. Diminished ability to think or concentrate, or indecisiveness.
8. Recurrent thoughts of death (not just fear of dying) or recurrent suicidal ideation.

DSM-IV recognises PND as a form of general depression with a specifier coded 'postpartum depression', if its onset is within the first four weeks postpartum.

Depressive symptoms that do not lead to a diagnosis of major depression

Women who present with some of the symptoms described previously may not be suffering from a major depressive disorder, but fall into a range of other diagnostic categories recognised by the DSM-IV, including:

- minor depressive disorder (depressive disorder, not otherwise specified), which is similar to major depression but requires the presence of only two of the additional criteria;
- adjustment disorder with depressed mood, which is characterised by marked distress and impaired functioning over what would be expected, in response to an *identifiable stressor*. However, bereavement is not included in this diagnosis;
- dysthymic disorder, which refers to chronic depressed mood over two years, accompanied by a number of the symptoms that we described for PND. It is arguable whether this would be considered as PND unless symptoms worsened following pregnancy or delivery;
- mixed anxiety–depressive disorder, which is currently a research category in the DSM-IV and refers to the presence of both depressive and severe anxiety symptoms, which may be generalised or associated with panic attacks.

Women who become depressed postnatally and meet the criteria for either a major depressive disorder or the above diagnostic categories are considered, for the purposes of this book, to be suffering from PND.

It is recognised that some women present with a number of the symptoms described earlier, but do not fit a diagnostic category for a depressive condition of any type. Rather, they may have transient low mood in response to a particular event. Distress in the immediate postnatal period can occur as a brief situational reaction to the demands of the infant or others (e.g., a mother-in-law visiting). These difficulties are generally transient and do not normally require intensive intervention. For example, in the first two months women may be having difficulty adjusting to their baby, and brief information, reassurance and listening are sufficient intervention. Alternatively, difficulties in concentration, decision making and sleep disturbance can be due to severe anxiety. Unless a mixed anxiety–depressive disorder is diagnosed, these women are not generally considered to have PND, but do need appropriate intervention for a possible anxiety disorder. Some degree of anxiety in addition to a depressive disorder, however, is a common feature of PND and physical symptoms such as excessive perspiration, hyperventilation and muscle tension may be present.

Distinction from postnatal blues and postpartum psychosis

PND is distinguished from postnatal or maternity blues by the greater severity and longer duration of depressive symptoms in the former. Postnatal blues are extremely common, with up to 80% of women experiencing emotional lability in the first two weeks postpartum. It is not clear if women who experience severe postnatal blues in the days following childbirth are at increased risk of subsequently developing PND. Lane, Morris, Turner and Barry (1997) found recently that maternal mood within three days of delivery was the best predictor of later PND, in a study of 370 women.

Postnatal or 'postpartum' depression is also distinguished from postpartum psychosis which is a rarer phenomenon (two in 2000 births) and more severe. The treatment approach described in this book is not directed at women who are diagnosed as suffering from a major depressive disorder if they also have a descriptive specifier of 'severe, with psychosis'. These women require immediate psychiatric management. Women with postpartum psychosis have severely disturbed mood and behaviour and typically present with confusion, agitation, hallucinations, delusions or extreme disorganisation. Onset is usually abrupt, in the first week postpartum, and requires psychotropic medication and hospitalisation (Buist, 1996).

ONSET

Clinically, we find that most women develop symptoms of depression in the first three months postpartum, although a second peak has been observed at six to eight months postpartum. Cooper, Campbell, Day, Kennerley and Bond (1988) reported that 50% of cases of PND start within the first three months, and 75% of cases by six months postpartum. Other research into the onset of depressive episodes in the first year postpartum has confirmed that the majority of episodes occur in the first three months (Kumar & Robson, 1984; O'Hara, 1997), with a significant number of episodes in the first five weeks after delivery (Cox, Murray & Chapman, 1993). Interestingly, the DSM-IV 'postpartum onset' specifier for major depression is four weeks postpartum, similar to the definition of puerperal disorders as commencing within six weeks of delivery by the International Classification of Diseases (ICD-10, World Health Organization, 1993b). Cox (1986) discusses this dilemma, which reflects a difference between clinical practice and standard diagnostic criteria for onset of PND. Clinical practice allows for a longer period of symptom development, and clinicians report that an onset after six weeks is not uncommon, and may be preceded by dysphoric mood.

Controversy also exists about whether depression beginning in the antenatal period should be distinguished from PND. In this book, depression with an onset during pregnancy will be considered as PND, but not depression with an onset prior to pregnancy.

INCIDENCE

At least one in 10 women suffer from PND without psychotic features. Prevalence rates have varied depending on the population studied, the assessment method used and the length of the postpartum period under evaluation (O'Hara & Swain, 1996). It appears that the more stringent the diagnostic criteria for depression, the lower the prevalence rate. Prevalence figures of less than 8% have resulted from sampling women who seek psychiatric treatment in the first postpartum year and are therefore likely to be severely depressed (Dalton, 1971). Intermediate figures of 8–20% have been reported from samples of women who meet standard diagnostic criteria for clinically significant depression (Cox, Connor & Kendell, 1982; Cutrona, 1983; O'Hara, Schlechte, Lewis & Varner, 1991; Paykel, Emms, Fletcher & Rassaby, 1980). Elevated figures of up to 35% have been the product of studies which have utilised symptom checklist data only and have not employed specific diagnostic criteria (Campbell & Cohn, 1991; Cutrona, 1982). By contrast, prevalence rates differ by only a small (but statistically significant) amount depending on the method of assessment. In a meta-analysis of 59 studies, self-report methods yielded a 12% rate compared to interview methods reporting a 14% rate (O'Hara & Swain, 1996).

Confounding factors in studies of prevalence include the significant number of women who hide their mood disorders and do not respond to community surveys or seek assistance. In addition, not all studies of PND specify if women are primiparous, and once a woman has experienced PND the risk increases significantly with subsequent births. Another controversial issue is whether the incidence of non-psychotic PND is higher than that of depression in the general population. The postpartum period has been described as a high-risk period for the mental health of women, but the evidence relates mainly to the increased probability of developing a first episode psychosis following childbirth compared to other times (Kendell, Chalmers & Platz, 1987). Women are between 20 and 30 times more likely to be hospitalised for a psychotic episode following childbirth (O'Hara, 1997). The true risk of non-psychotic major depression following childbirth, however, appears to be not much higher than for non-childbearing women (Cooper et al., 1988). Four major controlled studies in the UK and the USA reported trends suggesting differences, but these were non-significant (O'Hara, 1997). While the current evidence suggests that the prevalence rate of depression is only marginally elevated in the postpartum, the nature, severity and chronicity of symptoms of depression, with and without postpartum onset, may differ.

Depressed women with infants compared to non-childbearing women have been reported to have more symptoms consistent with minor (but not major) depression, agoraphobia and anxiety disorders (Nott, 1987). O'Hara, Zekoski, Philipps and Wright (1990) also reported that women who became depressed following childbirth experienced higher levels of distress, in terms of the level of depressive symptomatology and social maladjustment, particularly marital maladjustment, compared to depressed non-childbearing women. For instance, self-report questionnaires such as the Beck Depression Inventory (BDI) showed these women to have more severe somatic symptoms. Patterns of sleep difficulties may also differ in the two groups since depressive sleep patterns are complicated by sleep disruption caused by an infant waking in the night. Finally, PND appears more long lasting and debilitating than depression at other times. While O'Hara (1997) argues that the actual length of episodes of a full clinical depression may not be longer postnatally, ongoing symptoms at subclinical levels may be more severe in the puerperium. We found that 50% of women with PND remained symptomatic for up to 24 months, and this has also been reported by others (Dennerstein, Varnavides & Burrows, 1986; Milgrom & McCloud, 1996). By contrast, naturalistic studies of depression without postpartum onset have described a lower rate of ongoing symptomatology one year after diagnosis and indicated that in a majority of cases there is a complete remission of symptoms (American Psychiatric Association, 1994). In addition, women who have suffered PND are twice as likely to experience future depression over a five-year period, compared to women who have an episode of depression unrelated to childbirth (Cooper & Murray, 1995).

In summary, while the incidence of depression postnatally may be similar to that in the general population, depressive symptomatology, chronicity of symptoms and increased risk of future depression after childbirth may be worsened. It is possible that this is the result of the interaction between depression and factors such as the need to recover physically from a complicated labour, the transition and stressors associated with early parenthood, personal vulnerability factors, changing demands on the marital relationship and the presence of an infant. This view is discussed further below with our development of a biopsychosocial model of PND, described after a consideration of the long-term consequences and risk factors associated with PND.

LONG-TERM CONSEQUENCES

Longitudinal studies of women with PND suggest that the chronic effects are threefold: long-term effects on the woman's mental health, the mother–infant relationship and its influence on child development, and the marital relationship.

The woman

In a 12-month follow-up longitudinal study, we found that postnatally depressed mothers ($n = 38$) continued to rate themselves as being more tense and anxious, more depressed and dejected, more angry and hostile, more fatigued, more confused and bewildered, and less vigorous and active, than a control group of 46 non-depressed mothers (Milgrom & McCloud, 1996). The highest levels of disturbed mood occurred at entry into our study, at three months postpartum. These women had been admitted to mother–baby units as suffering from severe PND and on discharge the majority were treated with antidepressant medication. Levels of disturbed mood reduced at six and 12 months but remained elevated well above control levels. At 24 months, negative mood symptoms still differentiated depressed and non-depressed women, and a small proportion were classified as still having a major depressive disorder according to DSM-IV criteria (Milgrom, 1998a). Pitt (1968) reports that without treatment 30% of women suffering from severe PND are still ill at one year postpartum.

Her infant

Evidence of a diminished quality of mother–infant interaction is accumulating, with depressed mothers showing less responsivity and sensitivity, not only during their depressive illness, but also to their toddlers at 19 months postpartum (Stein, Gath, Bucher, Bond & Cooper, 1991). Long-term effects of maternal depression on the child are beginning to be identified, particularly for mothers whose depression is long lasting and when associated with social adversity and marital conflict. These effects include cognitive and social difficulties (Murray & Cooper, 1997a), difficulties in infant attachment (Murray, Fiori-Cowley, Hooper & Cooper, 1996) and infant development (Murray & Stein, 1989). In addition, parental feelings of attachment towards their infant seem compromised (Milgrom & McCloud, 1996). Parental relationships with other children in the family have not been the subject of research but clinical experience shows that these are often in difficulty. Severe PND has also been claimed to contribute to child abuse and neglect (Scott, 1992).

As the effect on the infant has such widespread implications, this consequence of PND is expanded further in Chapter 8, and specific mother-child interaction intervention strategies will be provided.

Her marriage and her partner

Postnatally depressed mothers consistently rate their relationship with their partner as poor on a number of dimensions, including consensus, satisfaction and support. In many cases, it appears that PND exacerbates problems that existed before the pregnancy, since a poor marital relationship has been described as a risk factor for PND. The stress of PND often means that marital difficulties become more salient, long lasting, with significant deterioration over time. In addition, partners of women with PND show increased mood difficulties over a 12-month period (Milgrom & McCloud, 1996; Areias et al., 1996a). Many couples cannot negotiate the added difficulties that accompany PND, including loss of interest in sex, irritability and inability to cope with the infant. A significant proportion of partners of depressed women also experience psychiatric morbidity such as generalised anxiety disorders or even major depressive episodes, often occurring shortly after the acute onset of the woman's depression (Lovestone & Kumar, 1993; Harvey & McGrath, 1988; Ballard, Davis, Cullen, Mohan & Dean, 1994). These difficulties are described more fully in Chapter 3 in the section dealing with the assessment of partners and marital relationships.

PSYCHOSOCIAL RISK FACTORS FOR POSTNATAL DEPRESSION

As described above, the impact of PND on infants and partners is elaborated later in this book. The focus of this chapter is understanding both the symptoms and experience of PND and the factors that predispose women to develop depression after childbirth. In this section, we will describe the maze of psychosocial factors that have been found to be associated with PND. Current research does not clarify which of these factors have a direct effect in producing depression or how they interrelate. In the next section, we will present a biopsychosocial model of PND that proposes a link between psychological, social and biological risk factors in the context of cognitive-behavioural theories of PND.

Psychosocial risk factors described in the literature have covered a wide range of variables, including: the newborn's temperamental characteristics (Cutrona &

Troutman, 1986; Hopkins, Campbell & Marcus, 1987; Mayberry & Affonso, 1993); social isolation, social status, young age or lack of support (Cox, 1988; O'Hara & Swain, 1996; Raphael-Leff, 1991); past stressors including labour and birth (Paykel et al., 1980; Whiffen & Gotlib, 1989); previous history of depression (O'Hara, 1986); marital conflict (Holmes & Rahe, 1967; Kumar & Robson, 1984); personality characteristics such as immature defensive style and external locus of control, and use of irrational beliefs (Annakis, Milgrom & Stanley, 1998; Beatrice & Milgrom, 1999); punitive child-rearing attitudes, poor maternal self-efficacy and anxiety in pregnancy (Field et al., 1985; Fleming, Flett, Ruble & Shaw, 1988; Kumar & Robson, 1984); difficult experiences in early life such as a hostile or uninvolved parent, especially when coupled with subsequent multiple stressors or sexual abuse (Raphael-Leff, 1991); current interpersonal difficulties such as a poor relationship with their mother, or life stressors including reproductive loss (Elliott, Sanjack & Leverton, 1988; Kumar & Robson, 1984, O'Hara, 1995).

A typical presenting case

The impact of these risk factors is often brought alive by the personal history of women who present with PND. For instance, a young woman described to us how profoundly isolated she felt from family supports, both due to distance and as a result of disrupted relationships. She found it impossible to turn to her mother, as her relationship with her mother had always been troubled. When asked about the birth, she told us that she experienced it as traumatic due to an unexpected caesarean, and had difficulty coping since the birth. She believed that everyone expected her to hide how she really felt, and that she had not really told anyone how very bad she felt. She had difficulty managing her baby's constant crying and felt a severe sense of failure as a mother. These feelings were linked to low self-esteem, which was a long-standing problem.

She also had a strong preference for order and predictability but this had been disrupted by her newborn and she struggled to cope with the 'chaos'. She experienced her husband as unsupportive, and was resentful of his work commitments and of their changed relationship. Often, she felt a despairing sense of loss of her past lifestyle as the exclusive couple relationship was changed and the demands of early parenting were constant (Milgrom, 1998b).

As the literature on psychosocial factors and PND is so vast, the major categories of psychosocial risk factors will be considered and some of the most clinically relevant factors will then be expanded in this section. We have found it useful to categorise the range of psychosocial risk factors found in PND in the following way:

(a) *Stressors*
- Negative life events including birth complications, loss of employment of partner or health difficulties.
- Previous miscarriage or stillbirth.

(b) *Family and marital difficulties*
- Poor marital relationship.
- Conflict between the woman and her parents.

(c) Inadequate levels of perceived social support
- Poor family support.
- Social isolation.

(d) Personality factors, attitudes and skills
- Personality factors, including a strong need for order, control or perfectionism.
- Cognitive style such as an external locus of control and dysfunctional negative thinking.
- Low self-esteem.
- Poor social skills.
- Negative maternal attitudes towards child rearing.

(e) Mood during pregnancy
- Anxiety.
- Hostility.
- Depression.

(f) Personal or family history of depression
- Previous episode of postnatal or major depression.

(g) Infant temperament and mother–infant difficulties
- Difficult infant temperament.

(h) Early experiences
- Difficult relationship with one's own mother.
- History of sexual abuse.

(i) Societal expectations of the joys of motherhood
- Myth of serenity after childbirth.
- Cultural influences.

Life events and stress

The birth of a child, with the associated demands on newly acquired skills, is a significant stressor in the lives of parents (Watson, Elliott, Rugg & Brough, 1984). Additional life stresses occurring after the birth, or which existed prior to the birth, can have an additive effect and contribute to the development of PND (Cutrona, 1982; Hopkins, Marcus & Campbell, 1984).

Over the past decade, an increasing interest in the association between life stress variables and PND is evident in the research literature. Paykel et al. (1980) interviewed 120 women with mild clinical PND regarding stresses experienced from the beginning of the pregnancy until the date of the interview. They found a strong association between recent stressful events, in addition to the birth of the child, and PND. This was replicated by O'Hara, Rehm and Campbell (1982), who subsequently reported that stressors prepartum were not as strongly correlated with depression as stressors postpartum (O'Hara, Neunaber & Zekoski, 1984). A sharp accumulation of life stresses over a relatively short time period, rather than a gradual accumulation, is also associated with PND.

Hopkins et al. (1987) caution against generalising research findings from heterogeneous samples to all postpartum women, however, as they found that there was no relationship between PND and life event stress in a sample of married, middle-class, primiparous women. In addition, depression may be particularly associated with certain types of stressors, such as loss events and undesirable events (Finlay-Jones & Brown, 1981; Lloyd, 1980).

It has also been suggested that life stress and vulnerability interact. Only one in five women who experience a severe event at any stage of their lives go on to experience depression. By contrast, 84% of cases of depression have experienced a recent severe event or difficulty (Brown, 1993). O'Hara, Schlechte, Lewis and Varner (1991) found support for the vulnerability–stress model of PND, and concluded that life events were predictors of PND when they interacted with subject vulnerability to depression. It is interesting to note that the most significant life stressor variables in this interaction were those related to care of the infant. This is an important consideration in the development of treatment programs for PND, as mothers' concerns in the area of infant care and interaction need to be addressed, as well as mothers' specific needs in relation to dysphoric mood. Finally, Brown (1993) emphasised that vulnerability and protective factors must be considered separately and are not just mirror images of each other.

Marital discord

Life stress variables account for only about 10% of the variance in depression measures (Hopkins et al., 1984). Researchers have therefore looked to the moderating effect that marital and social support may have on the ability of the woman to cope with added life stress. Paykel et al. (1980) found that poor marital support was a vulnerability factor that affected postpartum adjustment only in the presence of stressful life events.

A positive relationship between marital satisfaction and postpartum adjustment has also consistently been reported by others (Atkinson & Rickel, 1984; Merchant, Affonso & Mayberry, 1995; Schweitzer, Logan & Strassberg, 1992; Zelkowitz & Milet, 1996). Campbell, Cohn, Flanagan, Popper and Meyers (1992) found that spouse support, together with positive mother–child interaction at two months postpartum, differentiated between those women with relatively short-lived depressive episodes (less than six months) and those with more chronic episodes of depression (six months to two years).

Schweitzer et al. (1992) suggested that women in marriages that are characterised by low levels of care and high levels of control by their husbands are at greater risk of developing PND. However, a number of questions remain unanswered by current research. Which elements of marital support are most important? Is perceived marital support an accurate measure of actual support in depressed subjects? Is there deterioration in the marital relationship due to the mother's depression (Cox et al., 1982), or does a pre-existing poor marital relationship contribute to the depressive episode? Some of these questions are discussed in Chapter 3 in the context of assessing the marital relationship.

Social support

The extent and quality of support offered to the new mother may also moderate the effect of life stress variables. Women are more likely to turn to family and friends for support in the first postpartum months. Taylor (1989) found that at six weeks postpartum the incidence of PND among mothers with family support was 20%, while the incidence for mothers without family support was 38%. Conflict between married mothers and their parents during pregnancy has been found to be correlated with PND (Ballinger, Buckley, Naylor & Stansfield, 1979; Kumar & Robson, 1978). Lack of a close confidante other than the husband (Paykel et al., 1980) has also been reported to be a factor in PND, although the quality of the support may be a significant factor rather than the number of confidantes available (O'Hara et al., 1982).

Cutrona (1984) found that the most strongly predictive components of social support for PND were deficiencies in reliable alliance and social integration; that is, the lack of someone on whom the mother can rely for help under any circumstances, and the absence of a group of friends with whom the mother shares common concerns and interests. Other features of social support related to PND include the need for: assistance with problem solving; opportunities for positively reinforcing activities; normative information provision with regard to infant care; and affirmation of worth. In a later study, Cutrona and Troutman (1986) used path analysis to demonstrate that the impact of social support was mediated through a cognitive variable, namely self-efficacy in the parenting role. Women who reported high levels of support prenatally had higher levels of self-confidence to perform well as mothers and less depression postpartum. These studies provide us with some clear positive implications for the inclusion of these targets in a treatment program for PND.

It may also be the case that strong social support networks prevent depressive reactions. Further research into this possibility is required, as is research into the supportive role of extended family and friends rather than sole reliance on the nuclear family (Atkinson & Rickel, 1984).

Cognitive style

Hayworth et al. (1980) investigated whether there was a higher risk of depression in women who have an external locus of control (i.e., those who believe that they have little or no control over events in their lives) compared to those with an internal locus of control (i.e., those who believe that they can control events in their lives). In a sample of 166 pregnant women, those who had an external locus of control were found to be more likely to rate highly on depression postpartum. O'Hara et al. (1982) reported that attributional style was a significant predictor of postpartum depression, together with prepartum depression, delivery stress and stressful life events. However, in a later study, O'Hara et al. (1984) found a low correlation between attributional style and depression in a sample of 99 women followed from the second trimester of pregnancy until six months postpartum. It may be that cognitive factors are not always sufficient to predict depression unless they interact with other risk factors, such as previous episodes of depression. In a study of 85 primipara women, Cutrona (1983) reported that prenatal attributional style predicted level of depression following childbirth as well as speed of recovery from the depressive episode only for women who were *not* depressed during pregnancy. The association was lost in the subgroup with depression in pregnancy.

In addition to the possible role of attributional style in depression, cognitive distortions (such as catastrophising) and negative thought patterns (including poor self-efficacy) have been identified as significant predictors of PND (Cutrona & Troutman, 1986; O'Hara et al., 1982). Boyce (1994) has also reviewed the evidence for personality differences in PND, such as neuroticism and interpersonal sensitivity, and suggested that these may be either causal or consequent to depression.

Maternal attitudes

Maternal attitudes to pregnancy and child rearing have been examined, to a limited extent, as a vulnerability factor for PND. For instance, Davids and Holden (1970) found that maternal hostility towards their family and negative child-rearing attitudes during pregnancy were positively associated with anxiety and depression ratings at eight months postpartum.

Social skills

Surprisingly few studies have examined the relationship between PND and the mother's social and child-rearing skills. It is possible that poor parenting self-efficacy associated with PND is partly a function of inadequate social or child-rearing skills. Anxiety during pregnancy and depression in the postpartum months may be accentuated when skill levels become open to scrutiny by professionals, family and friends. O'Hara (1986) administered a self-report social skills questionnaire to a sample of women during pregnancy. He found that scores on this questionnaire were predictive of PND. A possible mechanism may be that women who lack skills in eliciting positive reinforcement from others, including their infants, through poor social skills become susceptible to developing depression (Lewinsohn, 1974).

Anxiety

Severity of anxiety during pregnancy is strongly associated with depressive symptomatology in the postpartum period (Dennerstein et al., 1986; Grossman, Eichler & Winickoff, 1980; Hayworth et al., 1980; Hopkins et al., 1984), but is not sufficient to predict the likelihood of PND (Atkinson & Rickel, 1984). It is possible that anxiety is a consequence, rather than a cause, of the numerous stressors and vulnerability factors found to be present in women who later develop PND.

Previous psychiatric history

There is considerable support for a strong correlation between a previous history of a depressive episode and PND (O'Hara et al., 1982, 1984; O'Hara, Schlechte, Lewis & Varner, 1991; O'Hara & Swain, 1996). There is also a significant relationship between a prior history of all types of psychiatric disorders and PND (Elliott, 1984; Paykel et al., 1980; Watson et al., 1984). This correlation is even stronger for the development of depression during pregnancy (Cutrona, 1982). It is important to recognise, however, that many women who develop PND do not have a prior psychiatric history (Atkinson & Rickel, 1984; Cutrona, 1982; Richards, 1990).

O'Hara, Schlechte, Lewis and Wright (1991) studied the interrelationship between psychiatric, social, cognitive and life stress variables and maternal depression. They found that previous history of depression, particularly when combined with negative life events during pregnancy, a number of child-related stressors, and depression during pregnancy, were highly predictive of PND. This again provides support for a vulnerability–stress model of PND and is consistent with the development of depression in general, since a previous episode of depression at any stage of life has been found to be predictive of a further episode of depression (Lewinsohn, Hoberman & Rosenbaum, 1988).

Infant temperament

Few studies have examined the relationship between infant temperament and PND. The existing studies report that mothers of babies who cry or vomit more than average, or are more difficult, will be more likely to be depressed (Mayberry & Affonso, 1993; Dalton, 1971). Milgrom and McCloud (1996) reported that depressed mothers perceived their infant as more demanding, less adaptive and less reinforcing than their non-depressed counterparts. While it is not clear whether infants are actually more difficult temperamentally or perceived as such because of maternal depression, the daily experience of a mother who experiences her infant as more difficult to manage will have negative consequences. She is likely to experience less positive reinforcement from the mother–child interaction than mothers who perceive their child as manageable, and this puts her at greater risk of depression. In this way, infant temperament is postulated to have both a direct effect on the level of PND as well as influencing parenting self-efficacy (Campbell et al., 1992; Cutrona & Troutman, 1986; Hopkins et al., 1987).

As outlined in Chapters 3 and 8, interventions targeted at increasing positive behavioural feedback from the infant towards its mother, or influencing maternal perception of infants, may impact significantly on depressive symptomatology.

Societal pressures: a sociological view of depression

The transition to motherhood involves adapting to huge physical, emotional and social changes. Particularly with a first child, the transition to becoming a mother involves a review of her identity and a need to respond to the constant demands of a newborn infant. This experience often revives feelings about her family of origin and childhood. It also brings with it physical stresses such as breastfeeding and the endless routine of nappy changing, burping and settling of an infant. New motherhood can also result in frustration associated with not being able to complete activities such as cleaning, washing or tidying to the schedule that the woman would like, particularly if previously she was perfectionistic or had a strong preference for routine and order. It is therefore not surprising that a large number of mothers have difficulty adjusting to the mothering role and that they feel insecure, and at times overwhelmed, by its many demands and expectations. Nicolson (1998) criticises the scientific literature for not sufficiently taking into account women's stories of why they feel as they do about the complexities in their lives when they have babies.

The mythologies in our culture include widespread beliefs in the 'joys' of pregnancy and of 'perfect' motherhood. Not infrequently, the picture of a smiling, rested mother and her angelic infant is depicted as the norm. These images have a powerful influence, often creating unrealistic expectations about pregnancy, birth and motherhood. Mothers who hold these expectations and beliefs often feel like 'failures' when they experience problems coping, and depression is a common outcome.

Some cultures have structures in place that are supportive of new parenthood, but generally in Western society mothers are given little preparation, and are not asked what sort of support they need, for their challenging new roles (Brown et al., 1994).

Cox (1996) describes childbirth as a significant life event, permanently changing the status and responsibility of the mother. Many cultures mark such events with rites of passage, characterised by rituals and taboos that ensure social support, and sustain self-esteem by enhancing the status of parenting and providing acknowledgement of this life transition. He observes that these rituals are more lacking in the West compared to non-Western traditional societies, and suggests that this may contribute to the higher number of reports of PND. Furthermore, Cox argues that current changes in Western society, including delayed childbearing, smaller families and the changing role of women, result in a cultural disruption in women's and men's knowledge about parenting. Changes in the structure of family life, with an increased divorce rate and less evident support systems, bring added pressures to new mothers (Cox & Holden, 1994). All these factors may lead to ambivalence about the maternal role as well as lowered self-esteem, and result in depression. Whether this occurs in all cultures has been the subject of research.

O'Hara (1994) provided a comprehensive review of cross-cultural research in depression. He pointed out that characteristic features of depression have differed across cultural groups that have been studied. In Nigeria, there is a predominantly somatic presentation, whereas in Ghana self-accusations of witchcraft are common. This makes it difficult to develop instruments for cross-cultural comparisons of prevalence rates, as symptoms that form the core of the disorder and cultural meanings of symptoms may vary. These complexities also make it difficult to assess the controversy about whether PND exists in all cultures. A number of anthropologists have described the absence of PND in countries such as Kenya (Harkness, 1987) and Nigeria (Kelly, 1967), concluding that PND is a culture-bound phenomenon peculiar to the West. They have argued that these findings support a sociological, rather than psychological or biological, aetiology of PND, and point to the importance of the protective customs in some cultures designed to protect the vulnerability of new mothers. The customs include mandated rest, assistance, seclusion and social recognition (Stern & Kruckman, 1983).

By contrast, Cox (1988) concluded that PND is not purely a cultural phenomenon and cited his own observations in Uganda, where he identified 10% of women as depressed. It may be that the experience of depression manifests itself differently in different cultures rather than being totally present or absent. For instance, in a more recent study in Nigeria there was a reported high incidence of symptoms such as 'heat-in-the-head' after delivery (Jinadu & Daramola, 1990).

While the authors claimed that other psychological symptoms reported in the West, such as insomnia and anxiety, were less frequent in Nigeria, it remains debatable whether 'heat-in-the-head' may be a culturally acceptable form of distress that is the equivalent of a major symptom of depression.

Evidence that PND is to some extent unaffected by cultural factors also comes from the reported similarity in prevalence rates of PND around the world. Comparisons of prevalence rates of PND in Great Britain (Appleby, Gregoire, Platz, Prince & Kumar, 1994; Murray & Carothers, 1990; Cox, Holden & Sagovsky, 1987; Cox et al., 1993; Murray & Carothers, 1990), South America (Reighard & Evans, 1995), Africa (Cox, 1983), Chile (Jadresic, Araya & Jara, 1995), Portugal (Areias et al., 1996a), New Zealand (Webster, Thompson, Mitchell & Werry, 1994) and Australia (Boyce, Stubbs & Todd, 1993) reveal similar rates of 10–20%.

The controversy about whether or not PND is apparent in all cultures extends to the varying approaches used to prevent PND. Oakley, Rajan and Grant (1990) emphasise that within our culture we have paid too little attention to the capacity of social support to promote health. In a study of 509 women with a history of low-birthweight babies, supportive intervention improved birth outcome and most women singled out the fact that the midwife 'listening' was important. Romito (1989, p. 1443) advocated more strongly: 'because many of the social factors leading to postpartum unhappiness are rooted in society's expectations of new mothers, the solutions lie mainly in social changes'. Sheila Kitzinger (1989) similarly examined patterns of care common to different cultures after childbirth and her anthropological analysis led her to question some of our practices such as a woman feeling 'depersonalised through . . . donning of hospital garments and plastic identification bracelet; and socially isolated from friends and family'. She concluded we needed to review 'the status and identity of a woman giving birth, the care given her, the way in which the newborn baby is treated, the quality of relationships between those who share the birth experience and, indeed . . . power and powerlessness'.

In conclusion, it seems important to develop an integrative model of PND to take into account the importance of both psychological and biological risk factors as well as a sociological understanding of the aetiology of depression following childbirth.

DEVELOPING A BIOPSYCHOSOCIAL MODEL OF POSTNATAL DEPRESSION

In order to develop a model of PND we reviewed not only psychosocial risk factors that have emerged as important, but also relevant theoretical frameworks. These are briefly described and together with our knowledge of biological correlates of depression (see Chapter 2) suggest a biopsychosocial model of PND which is then presented.

Theories of stress and coping

The list of risk factors described above suggests that there are a number of vulnerability factors (such as difficult childhood experiences) that interact with stressors (such as the demands of looking after a newborn) and result in depression. In addition, a woman's coping repertoire will further influence her ability to deal with vulnerabilities and stressors. The model shown in Figure 1 depicts a stress and coping perspective which postulates that stress (including depression) arises as a result of an imbalance between perceived demands and perceived resources, both personal and social (Lazarus & Folkman, 1984). O'Hara, Schlechte, Lewis and Varner (1991) provide support for this model in PND. Stressful life events will be experienced and reacted to differently, depending on the maternal coping style (e.g., problem-focused versus avoidance). As described earlier, maternal cognitive style including her beliefs about her competence as a parent or how she appraises existing stressors has been posited as a mediating factor of the effects of stresses on postpartum adjustment (Cutrona & Troutman, 1986). Other perceived resources include factors such as inadequate social support which may also accentuate difficulties. Perceived demands may include the infant. Difficult infant temperament or infants who are unresponsive and do not initiate overtures towards the mother may be particularly demanding. Depending on how infant cues are appraised, increased maternal feelings of lowered competence and subsequent depression may result (Jernberg, 1984).

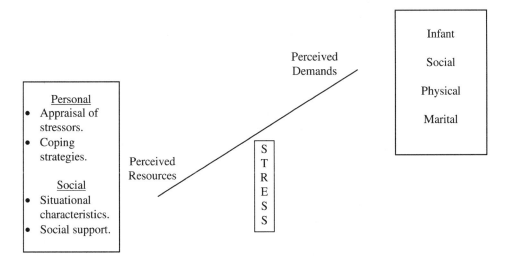

Figure 1 A model of stress and coping

Cognitive-behavioural theories of depression

Cognitive and behavioural theories of depression are outlined more fully in the next chapter but are summarised below to highlight the importance of these theories in formulating a model of depression in terms of the impact of a person's style of thinking and behaviour, as precipitating, exacerbating and maintaining factors.

Depression has been described by cognitive theorists as being caused, and maintained by, dysfunctional thoughts or cognitions about external events. Beck (1967) proposed that consistently negative expectations about one's self, the world and the future (the negative cognitive triad), lead to feelings of depression. In a related theory, Abramson, Seligman and Teasdale (1978) described persons with depressive attributional styles as reacting to negative external events with a belief that these events will always continue to happen and that they will happen in many circumstances. These individuals are therefore more likely to become depressed when faced with life events that are perceived as uncontrollable. In this way, distorted cognitions act as a filter for information and result in a depressive experience.

Behavioural theorists have in addition proposed that depression is the result of insufficient rewarding experiences and increased unpleasant events. This can occur as a result of lack of environmental opportunities or because of inadequate social skills to increase positive events (see Chapter 2).

Biological theories of postnatal depression

Many researchers have postulated a biological model for postpartum depressive disorders, given the profound hormonal and biochemical changes which accompany pregnancy and the postpartum period (Hopkins et al., 1984). Research to date has focused on three major perspectives. One perspective considers that significant hormonal changes, triggered by parturition, may be responsible for dysphoric mood and may result from changes in oestrogen, progesterone, cortisol or prolactin (Glover, 1992; Harris et al., 1989; Nott, Franklin, Armitage & Gelder, 1976). Given the dramatic hormonal changes that take place in the immediate postpartum period, it is possible that mood disturbances in the first week following delivery are due to biological changes (Nott et al., 1976). It is unclear, however, why women develop depressive symptomatology later in the first postpartum year, usually more than six weeks after delivery. Nevertheless, recent studies are finding support for the effectiveness of transdermal oestrogen as an effective treatment for PND (Gregoire, Kumar, Everfill, Henderson & Studd, 1996). A second important perspective that has received considerable attention recently is the link between disorders of the thyroid gland and thyroid antibody status as contributors to the onset of PND. This is believed to be a factor in some women who develop depressive symptomatology around two to five months postpartum (Harris, 1993). The third major perspective suggests that disturbances in the postpartum period, in neurotransmitters such as noradrenalin, are similar to those in mood disorders at other times (Bonnin, 1992; Handley, Dunn, Waldron & Baker, 1980; Taylor, Dore & Glover, 1996).

Unfortunately, biochemical studies to date have been restricted to the immediate postpartum period and are therefore not easily generalised to all forms of PND and future research is necessary on biological variables correlated with PND presenting in different ways (Hendrick, Altshuler & Suri, 1998; Hopkins et al., 1984). At this stage, support for biological theories of postpartum depressive symptoms remains equivocal (Cutrona, 1982; Hopkins et al., 1984; Ussher, 1992). The most common viewpoint is that these biological factors must coexist with other psychosocial factors to produce depression (Harris, 1993, 1994, 1996). However, the importance of retaining biological factors in a model of PND is exemplified by growing research on the role of the neuroendocrine system as a putative mediating pathway between prenatal psychosocial factors such as stress, and birth outcome such as low birthweight or fetal/infant brain development (Wadhwa, Dunkel-Schetter, Chicz-Demet, Porto & Sandman, 1996).

The biopsychosocial model

This model was developed by the physician George Engel (1980). Engel contended that traditional biomedicine was in crisis because of its adherence to a model of disease that was no longer adequate for the scientific tasks and social responsibilities of either medicine or psychiatry. According to Engel, the biomedical model was based on three outmoded concepts: (a) a reductionistic premise that complex phenomena are only derived from molecular biology, which can ultimately explain all biological events; (b) mind–body dualism, or the doctrine that the mental is separate from the physical; and (c) exclusionism, or the omission of whatever cannot be explained by the underlying molecular biology concept. Such a model, Engel contended, resulted in unfortunate attitudes toward patients as well as expensive practices such as unnecessary hospitalisation, overuse of drugs, excessive surgery and inappropriate use of diagnostic tests.

In contrast, the biopsychosocial model is based on a general systems theory that incorporates natural hierarchical systems ranging from the minute—molecules, cells and tissues—to the complex—the person and his or her experiences, other people, family, community and the surrounding culture. The basic premise is that the systems are interdependent, so that an event at one level potentially affects systems at other levels. Most of the research on postnatal depression, by contrast, has focused mainly on the effects of risk factors rather than on specific interactions between them or the moderating role of factors such as cognitive appraisal mechanisms (Olioff, 1991). In order to provide intervention most effectively, biological, psychological and sociological aspects of care must be acknowledged, addressed and interrelated.

A biopsychosocial model of postnatal depression

Our reading of the research literature and clinical experience has led to the development of a biopsychosocial model of PND as shown in Figure 2. The diversity of factors considered to play a role in PND on the one hand, and the limited empirical findings from methodologically sound studies on the other, makes such a model speculative and incomplete. Nevertheless, we believe that the model has heuristic value both for research and clinical practice.

On the left of the model are 'vulnerability factors' reflecting the findings that some women are more susceptible to developing PND than others. These factors include ones present from an early age, such as personality traits, through to others that have come into play more recently, such as psychiatric disorders and negative life events.

Immediately to the right of 'vulnerability factors' are the 'precipitating factors' that may trigger PND. Three broad classes of factors are identified: stress levels that reflect stressful events occurring just prior to the onset of PND, the stress-moderating variables of social support and coping skills, and biological factors

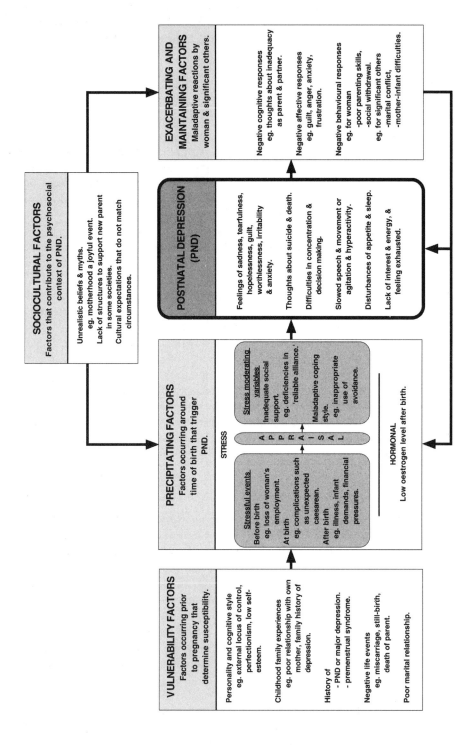

Figure 2   The biopsychosocial model of postnatal depression

such as the abrupt decrease in oestrogen following delivery. The model suggests that precipitating factors often trigger PND in vulnerable women but other factors are also important. Stress-moderating variables influence the impact of a given stressor. We would like particularly to emphasise the importance of cognition at all stages of the model, as it is the cognitive appraisal or perception of negative life events, social support, cultural expectations and so forth that is important rather than the 'objective reality'.

In addition, women and their significant others (partners, relatives, friends, etc.) may react to her PND in ways that exacerbate and maintain the disorder. Negative feedback loops or vicious cycles can become established whereby the reactions feed back directly to the PND, or feed back to the precipitating factors that trigger PND. It is understandable for a woman to respond to PND by thoughts of personal inadequacy and by feeling guilty, anxious and frustrated. Such reactions will only make the emotional experience of PND more intense, however. In addition, marital conflict and social withdrawal arising from her PND may lead to reduced social support, consequently decreasing the buffering effect that social support can provide against stress.

Sociocultural factors impact on PND via the pathways of precipitating and exacerbating factors. The lack of support provided to some mothers in Western societies, for example, results in no protective buffer against the stress occurring in association with the birth. Guilt, loss of self-esteem and feelings of inadequacy arise in response to PND as cultural myths falsely imply that the motherhood experience should be exclusively positive.

Our model is consistent with the emerging biological correlates of depression, suggesting that some individuals are particularly vulnerable to stress, possibly owing to genetic factors. There is also increased evidence that stressors are accompanied by biochemical changes, including changes in central nervous system neurotransmitter levels. When a precipitating stressor occurs, individuals experience neurophysiological changes, although these reactions may also be mediated by cognitive appraisal of the stress. Depression is then exacerbated or maintained by changed brain functioning.

Thus the model is referred to as 'biopsychosocial' as it includes: biological factors, such as genetic influences on personality or a predisposition to premenstrual disorders and marked hormonal changes; psychological factors, such as childhood family experiences and coping style; and social factors, such as the role of marital relationships and societal expectations.

Finally, multiple stressors are likely to aggregate together, making PND more probable. A trade-off between vulnerability and precipitating factors seems plausible, whereby a relatively low level of precipitating factors would trigger PND in highly vulnerable women, whereas a more elevated level of precipitating factors would be necessary to trigger PND in less vulnerable women. Women may therefore enter at different points in the model, depending on their personal history. One woman may be particularly vulnerable as a result of the loss of a previous infant; this circumstance then interacts with a precipitating factor such as a particularly difficult subsequent birth, to influence PND onset. The depressive episode is exacerbated by both her unresolved grief for her first baby as well as her cognitive style, whereby she tends to feel she has no control over her life anyway. In addition, her sociocultural milieu which has little support available may contribute to her depression. Another woman may have few vulnerability factors but experience severe multiple stressors concurrently, increasing the likelihood of depression.

PREVIEW: TOWARDS A TREATMENT OF POSTNATAL DEPRESSION

Our research and clinical experience have shown us that successful treatment of PND requires a holistic approach, consistent with this model, to equip women with the skills to make positive changes in a *range* of different areas of their lives. Our model of depression also highlights the role of cognitions and behaviours in exacerbating (and maintaining) PND. From this perspective it follows that treatment directed at minimising exacerbating factors will significantly influence the experience of PND. In essence, our interventions are aimed at challenging the exacerbating and maintaining negative cognitive-behavioural triad, while taking into account the vulnerabilities, stressors and cultural factors that exist (see Figure 3). At the same time the presence of an infant and at times a partner means that additional interventions are required if difficulties arise in these relationships.

Exacerbating factors: towards a treatment approach

The next chapter describes how our treatment program has been derived from existing cognitive-behavioural therapy approaches to depression and has been adapted to take into account the other features described in our model.

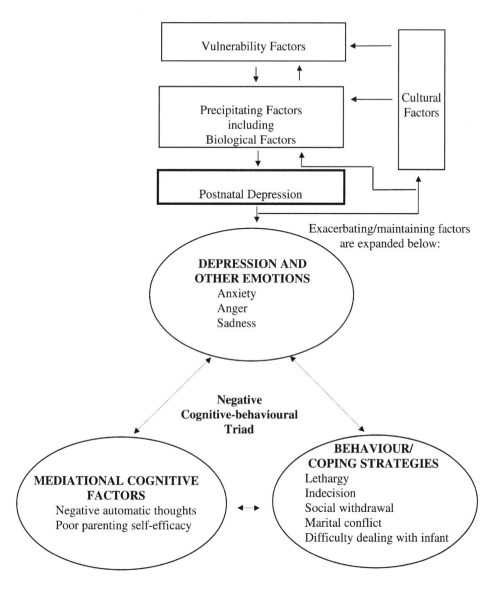

Figure 3   Our model of postnatal depression: intervening with multiple contributory factors

Chapter 2

OVERCOMING DEPRESSION AND POSTNATAL DEPRESSION

In order to understand and develop efficacious treatment approaches for PND, it is important to consider the empirical and theoretical literature that has accumulated with respect to depression in general. This work provides a context for considering the special case of PND. Behavioural, cognitive and biochemical theories of depression have been the most influential in the research and treatment of depression, and will be the focus of this review. Each theoretical orientation encompasses different treatment approaches to depression and this information has been taken into account in the evolution of a combined cognitive-behavioural intervention for PND that will be described subsequently.

TREATMENT OF DEPRESSION BASED ON BEHAVIOURAL THEORY: THE EVIDENCE FROM RESEARCH ON CLINICAL OUTCOME

Behavioural theorists have conceptualised depression as caused by the depressed person having insufficient positive experiences or 'reinforcers'. The level of reinforcement received is dependent upon the frequency of events and activities that are perceived as positive for the individual; the availability of potential reinforcers in the environment; and the individual's personal, social and intellectual skills to elicit such reinforcement (Greenberg & Silverstein, 1983). For example, depression may result from a social skills deficit, if a person has insufficient skills to elicit necessary positive reinforcement, or as a result of either environmental change (e.g., loss of job; break-up of a relationship) or personal inadequacy (Beck & Greenberg, 1974). In general, depression is viewed as due to a loss of, or lack of, response-contingent positive reinforcement, or put more simply, a decrease in pleasant events or an increase in unpleasant events (Lewinsohn, 1974). It is assumed that any environment that involves enduring deprivation of reinforcement or changes in such a way as to eliminate or significantly reduce response-contingent reinforcement will precipitate depressive symptomatology (Lewinsohn & Gotlib, 1995).

It follows from behavioural theories of depression that treatment in the form of increasing positively reinforcing activities that are incompatible with depressed mood, and not reinforcing depressive activities, will lead to a decrease in depressive symptomatology (Lewinsohn & Gotlib, 1995; Lewinsohn, Hoberman, Teri & Hautzinger, 1985). Behavioural therapy procedures such as skills training (contingency management, social skills, problem solving and self-control) and marital/family therapy have also been applied to the treatment of depression (Lewinsohn & Gotlib, 1995). All behavioural interventions include self-monitoring, review and self-reinforcement components. The techniques derived from the general depression literature that we have found most useful in developing a treatment approach for PND are described below.

What works

Increasing pleasant activities and decreasing unpleasant events
As mentioned earlier, depression may, in part, be caused by a decrease in the rate of positive reinforcement and an increase in aversive stimuli. In 1980, Lewinsohn and his colleagues proposed an intervention that aimed to teach depressed individuals to manage their own depression by lowering the rate and intensity of aversive events and to schedule higher rates of engagement in pleasant activities. The program, known as the Coping with Depression course (Lewinsohn, Antonuccio, Steinmetz & Teri, 1984), has been found to be effective in reducing levels of depression, with reports of up to 80% of participants being non-depressed after taking the course (Lewinsohn & Gotlib, 1995; Lewinsohn, Sullivan & Grosscup, 1980).

Social skills training
The importance of social skills training in the treatment of depressed individuals has been emphasised. It has been proposed that many depressed individuals experience a reduction in positive reinforcement because a substantial amount of positive reinforcement is interpersonal in nature (Becker & Heimberg, 1985). Depressed individuals may not utilise adequate interpersonal skills owing to a number of factors, including: having inadequate exposure to role modelling of appropriate social skills; insufficient opportunity to practice interpersonal skills; loss of skill mastery through insufficient use; and failure to recognise environmental cues in social situations (Becker & Heimberg, 1985). Outcome studies on the use of social skills training with depressed individuals have found that social skills training is superior to relaxation training, insight-oriented psychotherapy and amitriptyline. There is a greater improvement in mood, more social activity and personal productivity in both the short and long term, with lower drop-out rates (McLean & Hakstian, 1979, 1990).

Self-control
The self-control model of depression (Rehm, 1977) posits that depressed individuals demonstrate deficits in self-monitoring, self-evaluation and self-reinforcement. Therapy aimed at increasing the depressed individual's skills in these three areas has been found to be effective in the treatment of depression (Lewinsohn & Gotlib, 1995). The self-evaluation component could be classified as cognitive in nature and this intervention is best considered as a cognitive-

behavioural intervention. This is consistent with the finding that the intervention is equally effective in altering cognitive and behavioural aspects of depression (Rehm, 1990).

Problem-solving skills training
Problem-solving skills training has been proposed to have an important role in the treatment of depression. It is thought that problem-solving skills modify the relationship between stress and depression (Nezu, 1987). Problem-solving skills may buffer the individual by allowing him or her to develop solutions to problems that would otherwise be considered to be debilitating life events. If problems remain unresolved, a reduction in response-contingent positive reinforcement is likely to be experienced, contributing to the onset of depressive symptoms (Nezu, 1987). Based on the problem-solving model of depression, the training of problem-solving skills is prescribed. Nezu's structured problem-solving therapy program has been found to be effective in reducing depressive symptomatology, and this is maintained at six-month follow-up (Lewinsohn & Gotlib, 1995).

Relaxation skills
Progressive deep muscle relaxation is a useful adjunctive method for managing generalised anxiety, psychomotor agitation and initial insomnia. Relaxation training has been shown to have a modest additive effect when used along with antidepressant therapy, and is a particularly helpful adjunct to cognitive-behavioural therapy (CBT) when medications are not used (Thase, 1995).

TREATMENT OF DEPRESSION BASED ON COGNITIVE THEORY: THE EVIDENCE FROM RESEARCH ON CLINICAL OUTCOME

Several cognitive models of depression have been proposed. The main theory on which most cognitive models of depression and treatment approaches are based is the cognitive distortion theory of depression developed by Beck (1967). The major assumption of Beck's theory is that affect is determined to a great extent by the person's cognitive constructions of his or her experiences. Beck proposed that depression-prone individuals exhibit distorted cognitive processing through depressive schemata. Schemata are cognitive mediators between stimulus inputs and personality responses. In depression, these schemata comprise a 'depressive cognitive triad' of negative attitudes, beliefs and assumptions about the self, the world and the future. According to Beck, depressive schemata are acquired early in life through learning and they may be reactivated by stressful events that evoke negative cognitions. The irrational nature of these schemata means that the person is more likely to make arbitrary inferences (drawing conclusions in the absence of evidence), selective abstractions (focusing on a detail taken out of context), personalisations (relating external events to oneself) and overgeneralisations of negative events (drawing conclusions on the basis of a single event), and to minimise positive experiences (Becker, 1974; Greenberg & Silverstein, 1983). Beck posited that distorted cognition is central to the aetiology of depression and that variations in symptomatology are due to differing cognitive emphases (Beck, 1967).

The Reformulated Learned Helplessness hypothesis proposed by Abramson et al. (1978) has also been an influential cognitive theory in research into depression. The basis of this hypothesis is that once a person learns that certain outcomes are independent of his or her actions learned helplessness may result. In other words, the person learns that certain traumatic events are out of his or her control, and subsequently generalises this learning to other traumatic events and perceives that they are also out of his or her control, even if this is not the case. Once a person experiences helplessness, it is the causal attribution made that influences: whether the course of the learned helplessness is chronic or acute; the future probability of learned helplessness; and whether or not this helplessness will lower self-esteem. The person may make global attributions (helplessness deficits occur in a broad range of situations), specific attributions (deficits occur in a narrow range of situations), internal attributions (attributing cause to oneself) or external attributions (attributing cause to others or events). The prognosis for the depressive episode is worsened if the person makes internal attributions for the cause of his or her perceived helplessness. The treatment components implicated through this model include: changing the person's expectation from uncontrollability to controllability; and changing unrealistic self-attributions for failure toward external and specific causes.

What works

Cognitive techniques
Cognitive therapy techniques such as challenging cognitive distortions, facilitating cognitive restructuring and self-control procedures (such as teaching the use of coping self-statements) have been applied to the treatment of depression. Cognitive therapy assists the depressed individual to: identify and monitor dysfunctional automatic thoughts; recognise the connection between thoughts, feelings and behaviour; evaluate the evidence for, or reasonableness of, their automatic thoughts; substitute more reasonable interpretations of events for their dysfunctional automatic inferences; and finally, to alter the underlying silent assumptions about the world, self and future that predispose the client toward depressogenic thinking.

While many cognitive techniques rely purely on cognitive theory, more recent approaches incorporate both behavioural and cognitive elements (Clark & Fairburn, 1997). In fact, cognitions and behaviour are so inextricably related that it is difficult to determine a specific effect that is attributable to one theory or the other (Rehm, 1990).

The literature is saturated with outcome evaluations and meta-analyses regarding the efficacy of cognitive therapy for the treatment of depression, and there is overwhelming evidence that this form of treatment is effective in reducing depressive symptomatology faster than would occur without treatment (e.g., Hollon, Shelton & Davis, 1993; Robinson, Berman & Neimeyer, 1990; Scott, 1996). Furthermore, cognitive therapy combined with behavioural techniques has been found to be superior to short-term psychodynamic psychotherapies (Eysenck, 1994; Svartberg & Stiles, 1991). Evidence for the superiority of cognitive-behavioural intervention for depression is accumulating, with reports of lower drop-out rates (Simons, Levine, Lustman & Murphy, 1984) and better maintenance of treatment gains when compared to pharmacotherapy (Kovacs, Rush, Beck & Hollon, 1981; Miller, Norman, Keitner, Bishop & Dow, 1989; Scott, 1996). A treatment response rate of 50–80% success with CBT has generally been reported (Glick, 1995).

TREATMENT OF DEPRESSION BASED ON BIOCHEMICAL THEORIES: THE EVIDENCE FROM RESEARCH ON CLINICAL OUTCOME

Experimental evidence for a biochemical aetiology of depression also exists. Biochemical theories are based on deficits in neurotransmitter levels in the brains of depressed patients (Thase & Howland, 1995). A biogenic amine hypothesis was originally proposed, suggesting that depression is caused by a deficit in monoamines such as noradrenaline (norepinephrine) or dopamine at critical synapses in the central nervous system (Lewinsohn et al., 1985). A more recent model proposes that a deficiency in the monoamine 5-hydroxytryptamine (serotonin), or a problem in its receptors (the specific sites it acts on), causes depression. Serotonin synthesis is believed to be dependent upon the concentration of tryptophan in the blood and deficiencies in this amino acid have been found in patients suffering severe depression (Cutrona, 1982; Handley et al., 1980). There has been concurrent research into the association between mood disturbance and urinary secretion of cyclic 3',5'-adenosine monophosphate (cAMP). It has been reported that urinary secretion of cAMP is lowered in both neurotic and psychotic depression, and increases after treatment (Ballinger et. al., 1979).

Antidepressant pharmacological treatment is effective in the treatment of depression and offers support for the role of monoamines in depression (Thase & Howland, 1995). All known effective antidepressants enhance the efficiency of monoaminergic neurotransmission. Tricyclic antidepressants, such as amitriptyline, were originally the most commonly used antidepressants and were found to be beneficial in the treatment of depression. Common side effects, however, include dry mouth, weight gain and sexual problems, and as different drugs have different profiles some drugs, such as nortriptyline, were more favoured. Other side effects of some tricyclic antidepressants, such as sedation, were found to be useful for depressed patients with insomnia. A potential risk, however, was death following an overdose by arrhythmias. In addition, all antidepressants seem to take at least three weeks to work (De Battista & Schatzberg, 1995). More recently, selective serotonin reuptake inhibitors (SSRIs) have been found to be effective and include drugs such as fluoxetine. These drugs have been more popular, as they have fewer side effects, and are safe even in overdose. However, reported side effects include gastrointestinal upsets and restlessness. SSRIs are as effective as tricyclic antidepressants, with positive response rates in about 70% of patients.

Since all medications have varying degrees of side effects in addition to therapeutic benefits, breastfeeding mothers in particular are concerned about the safety in breast milk. There is a lack of controlled studies in the literature on what level of these medications passes into the breast milk (Buist, 1996). A fuller discussion of the indications for treatment of PND with medication in the context of our knowledge about risks to breastfeeding mothers is given in Chapter 3.

What works

Cognitive, behaviour or pharmacotherapy
The research evidence suggests that initial results for cognitive-behavioural and antidepressant treatments of depression are similar. Clark (1990) reviewed studies comparing the efficacy and relapse prevention outcomes for cognitive therapy versus tricyclic antidepressants. Well-conducted cognitive therapy was found to be superior in the immediate long term (one to two years) compared to pharmacotherapy with six or less months of drug treatment maintenance. Depressed patients administered antidepressant medication that is not maintained have twice the relapse rate (around 50% at one year) of patients treated with cognitive therapy (Kovacs et al., 1981; Rehm & Kaslow, 1984). In addition, greater treatment outcome success has been achieved when cognitive therapy is combined with behavioural techniques (Rehm & Kaslow, 1984). Up to 80% of patients will have a positive response, and at one year the relapse rate is 10–30%. By increasing length of therapy for those patients who show residual symptoms and persistence of dysfunctional attitudes at the time of termination, a further decrease in relapse rate can be achieved (Glick, 1995).

However, cognitive therapy is not superior to pharmacotherapy if drug therapy is maintained for 12 months, either with respect to initial effects or relapse rates (Clark, 1990). Furthermore, while Clark (1990) found no evidence for a higher efficacy of a combined approach, in practice combined treatments are increasingly common. Arguments for a combined approach include the response time to treatments. Most depressed outpatients will respond to CBT in 12–16 weeks of therapy, whereas antidepressants often begin to have an effect within three weeks. This differential response time may be relevant to individuals who may face job losses or other consequences if response time is too long. The current best practice model is of continuing patients on maintenance doses of tricyclic antidepressants for more than four months post-recovery and this results in long-term treatment (Prien & Kupfer, 1986). Glick (1995) concludes that CBT effectiveness is equivalent to other competently administered options, and for many patients this structured, psycho-educational approach is the treatment of choice.

In summary
For depression in general, it seems that well-conducted CBT is as efficacious, in the short and long term, as tricyclic antidepressant therapy with 12 months maintenance. Better maintenance of treatment gains are found for CBT compared to treatment with tricyclic antidepressants, particularly if not maintained for more than six months (Rehm & Kaslow, 1984; Rosenbaum & Merbaum, 1984). The bulk of the evidence is that the combination of both psychological and drug approaches does not seem to improve treatment efficacy or maintenance, although this combination has often been used in clinical practice (Clark, 1990), and others have presented supportive findings (Glick, 1995).

CAVEATS IN THE RESEARCH INTO THE EFFICACY OF TREATMENT APPROACHES TO DEPRESSION

There has been a failure in the research literature to adequately identify subtypes of depression and to systematically evaluate the respective responses of each subtype to different treatments (Conte & Karasu, 1992; Feinberg, 1992). Distinctions between differing forms of minor and major depression have been made inconsistently in the research literature. For example, individuals experiencing an acute major depressive episode may not be distinguished from individuals with a dysthymic disorder (Conte & Karasu, 1992). Frank et al. (1991) reviewed the research literature into the treatment of major depression and noted the inconsistencies between, and sometimes within, studies with regard to the use of terms such as remission, recovery, relapse and recurrence. It seems that such inconsistencies in terminology are severely impeding comparability between studies into the treatment of depression.

Furthermore, the research literature is confounded by the reliance on global terms such as *cognitive therapy* to describe treatment components that may not be comparable between studies. More work needs to be done to delineate core components of therapeutic interventions that are specific (i.e., delineated by theory as active causes of change) and non-specific (i.e., elements that contribute to change but are not explained by the therapeutic theory employed) (Oei & Shuttlewood, 1996). The effect of therapist expertise on treatment outcome also has been largely ignored to date.

Finally, research on the efficacy of CBT with pharmacotherapy has been compromised by the lack of consensus regarding therapeutic and maintenance doses of antidepressant medication (Clark, 1990).

ADAPTATION OF TREATMENT FOR POSTNATAL DEPRESSION: THE EVIDENCE FROM RESEARCH ON CLINICAL OUTCOME

Given the large proportion of women who experience PND and the relative chronic nature of the course of this disorder, it is surprising that there have been few empirical investigations of treatment approaches specifically for PND. Both prospective and retrospective studies of PND have largely concentrated on the identification of maternal risk factors. Although this is commendable, it fails to provide any assistance for those mothers who are currently suffering from PND or have escaped identification by health professionals as being depressed. It is well known from clinical observation that mothers experiencing depression are not likely to seek professional assistance (Cox et al., 1982; Whitten, Warner & Appleby, 1996), and what is needed is the early identification of these women and the provision of early intervention by health professionals. We know very little about how many women independently seek assistance, how many fail to seek assistance, and what type of assistance, if any, is offered to these mothers. Neither are there many systematic attempts to evaluate the responsiveness of PND to the most commonly employed treatment approaches for depression (Brown, 1979), although there are a number of studies that recommend treatment components (e.g., Cutrona, 1982; Gruis, 1977; Jebali, 1991; Nicolson, 1989; Stuart, 1995; Taylor,

1989; Wickberg & Hwang, 1996). More recently, some attempts have been made to redress this problem, resulting in the publication of limited intervention studies for PND conducted within clinical settings and these are reviewed below.

What works

Preventive approaches to treatment
The identification of antenatal psychosocial risk factors has received considerable attention in the research literature (e.g., Wilson et al., 1996). This work paves the way for preventive approaches to be developed. Psycho-education and social support commencing in pregnancy and continuing through six months postpartum have been found to be effective in reducing the prevalence of depression experienced by new mothers (Elliott et al., 1988). This study suggests that to reduce the incidence of PND, mothers at risk need to be identified in the antenatal period or early in the puerperium, and treated appropriately. At present, the identification of women in the postpartum period is only conducted routinely by a small number of clinics around the world, and those mothers who are detected are often treated by a variety of approaches that are not supported by large-scale randomised clinical trials. The final chapter discusses the importance and progress of preventive approaches to PND.

Individual approaches to treatment

Counselling: Counselling by primary health professionals such as maternal and child health nurses has been reported to be an effective intervention (Wickberg & Hwang, 1996). Holden, Sagovsky and Cox (1989) used a Rogerian counselling approach for the management of PND. They trained health visitors to counsel women with PND over an eight-week period, and found that the rate of recovery was greater (69%) than for women in a no-treatment control group (38%). This approach warrants replication on larger numbers of women, and suggests that health visitors or nurses with general counselling training can provide effective treatment for PND. In our current research project, we are comparing the effects of CBT with a *counselling* intervention that has been operationalised in a detailed manual so that it can be reliably implemented and evaluated.

Cognitive-behavioural therapy: Despite findings that CBT is a particularly effective approach to the treatment of depression in general, few studies have compared treatment interventions specifically with reference to PND. In 1991, Olioff strongly advocated a cognitive therapy approach to the treatment of PND. He claimed that this model of intervention '. . . does not ignore the complexity of the phenomenon, allows for flexibility in intervention, and avoids the confusion which may arise from non theoretically based eclecticism'. Olioff (1991) observed three different PND presentations: those women who exhibit depressogenic cognitive content; those that have distorted motherhood-specific schemata; and those who experience recurrent depressive episodes. In addition, he found that a number of cognitive criteria distinguished women with PND from their depressed counterparts at other stages in the life cycle. Perceived parenting self-efficacy, global self-appraisal of parenting ability and perceived vulnerability of the infant were three main cognitive themes. Olioff described a treatment package aimed at reducing the level of depression and improving day-to-day functioning, by addressing these faulty cognitions directly, in addition to the more commonly associated cognitive distortions that are seen in a depression presentation (e.g., overgeneralisation, filtering, self-blame). However, no evaluation of treatment efficacy was given. Two recent studies, however, suggest positive benefits. A recent study, by Cooper and Murray (1997), found evidence of a significant improvement in maternal mood following home-based CBT relative to no treatment. It was equally effective as a counselling or dynamic psychotherapy approach at speeding up remission from depression. In another relevant study, Highet (1998) reported that individually administered cognitive therapy was effective in reducing depression and anxiety when compared to a waiting-list control condition. It was not found to be superior, however, to either non-specific counselling combined with behavioural strategies or to pharmacological treatment. As treatment content was not carefully controlled (it was given by a range of service providers not following a structured manual), this conclusion must be treated cautiously.

Interpersonal psychotherapy: O'Hara, Stuart, Gorman and Kochanska (1998) recently reported the results from a randomised controlled trial comparing 12 sessions of interpersonal psychotherapy with a waiting-list control offered to postpartum women meeting DSM-IV criteria for major depression. Sixty per cent of women treated with interpersonal psychotherapy showed a significant response to treatment, compared to less than 20% of women in the waiting-list condition who experienced a significant reduction in depressive symptomatology. O'Hara et al. (1998) also noted that the general lack of improvement in the waiting-list condition reflected the fact that untreated depression does not remit on its own.

Group therapy
Group therapy for PND offers advantages over individual psychotherapy, in addition to cost-effectiveness. The formation of a group of mothers who can discuss and share similar experiences, fears, unrealistic expectations and so forth can greatly enhance a mother's ability to cope. Mothers meeting in a group report feeling less isolated and more able to be honest with their feelings and to express their thoughts. A group also engages the mother in a social activity, which is valuable as social activities are often curbed with the arrival of a baby. An opportunity to hear others express distorted cognitions can assist a mother to challenge her own beliefs about mothering and the new world she has found herself in. Mothers also have the opportunity to learn creative solutions to problems from one another.

Many group approaches have been reported but most have described only small groups of subjects, and have not been evaluated against a control group (Gordon, Swan & Robertson, 1995; Jones, Watts & Romain, 1995; May, 1995; Pitts, 1995). There have been a few studies, however, that have attempted to be more systematic in their program evaluation. Seale et al. (1988) conducted a group treatment program drawing on theoretical ideas from transactional analysis, rational emotive therapy, existential philosophy, Rogerian theory, communication theory and psychoanalytic theory. They found a significant reduction in women's scores on the Edinburgh Postnatal Depression Scale (EPDS) at the end of treatment compared to controls. Women with both PND and psychosis were included in treatment, and the results were further complicated by the fact that a proportion of the women in the treatment group were undergoing concurrent pharmacological treatment with antidepressants.

In an earlier study, we conducted a pilot group therapy program that combined an educational component with CBT (Milgrom & Meager, 1996). Ten one and a half hour weekly sessions were conducted with a group of mothers identified as having severe PND. Women with postnatal psychosis were excluded from the sample. There was a statistically significant reduction in pre- to post-intervention scores on the Beck Depression Inventory (BDI) and EPDS, in comparison with control subjects. However, the women in the treatment group still exhibited some depressive symptomatology at the end of treatment. As with the trial conducted by Seale, Williams and Reynolds (1988), we did not preclude women who were undergoing concurrent treatment with antidepressant medication, although all had been stabilised for at least three weeks prior to starting treatment. As there was an emphasis on the group process in addition to CBT, it was not possible to analyse the treatment variables that were successful in the treatment of depression. In another pilot study of a cognitive-behavioural approach administered in a group format, we found highly significant reductions in EPDS and BDI scores, and a highly significant increase in quality of life scores, associated with treatment (Martin, 1996). Results from the initial treatment trial (Negri, 1998) and for the current trial using the CBT group treatment package described in this book are elaborated in Chapter 6, and further support the efficacy of group treatment for PND.

Finally, Highet (1998), in her comparison of CBT and supportive counselling offered as community treatments for PND, concluded that individual treatment resulted in more rapid treatment gains than group treatment after six months, but that both were equally effective in the longer term.

Social support
Evidence suggestive of the role that social support can play in the puerperium can be found from an examination of the anthropological literature, where cultures that allow increased social support and rituals around the first six weeks after delivery appear to have lower rates of PND (Cox, 1996; Stern & Kruckman, 1983). Fleming, Klein and Corter (1992) were the first to examine empirically social support conditions and their respective effect in the alleviation of PND. They compared a social support intervention, a group-by-mail intervention and a no-intervention condition. The social support intervention involved a group of mothers (and children) meeting for two hours per week to share common experiences and discuss problems. The group-by-mail intervention consisted of sending mothers a transcript of the social support group meeting. The results suggested that, regardless of the intervention condition, mothers experienced an improvement in mood from two weeks to five months postpartum. Unfortunately, mothers were recruited for this study on the second day after delivery and were asked to complete self-report questionnaires within the first two weeks postpartum. Mothers with postnatal blues and difficulties with adjustment would have

confounded the results as one would expect these mothers to improve considerably by five months postpartum. Furthermore, a major methodological problem with this study was the inclusion of well mothers with depressed mothers in the same treatment groups. It was found that the depressed mothers actually did worse under the social support condition possibly because they were comparing their behaviour and that of their infants with well mothers and their children. Another problem with this research, as with the previous studies discussed, is that there was no attempt to control for pharmacological interventions.

Antidepressant medication
Treatment of PND with antidepressant medication is the most strongly advocated form of treatment (Barnett, 1991). There is a need for more information, however, about the type of antidepressant medication that is most effective for PND with what degree of depression, and with which subgroups of women. Currently, there is little evidence as to whether medication alone or medication in combination with other treatment modalities is most effective. In one of the few published studies, Appelby, Warner, Whitton and Faragher (1997) evaluated the effectiveness of one or six sessions of counselling informed by CBT, with either fluoxetine or placebo. Fluoxetine was found to be superior to placebo, comparable to counselling, and six counselling sessions more effective than one. As with the general depression literature, there was no additive effect of combining fluoxetine with counselling, although the level of severity of depression was mild in this sample. Despite these negative findings, since psychosocial vulnerability factors appear to be extremely important in the development and maintenance of PND, more research into combination treatments for severe depression postnatally is warranted. Medication may not be the most efficient long-term treatment regime; treatment for 12 months or longer is usually advocated to prevent relapse (Barnett, 1991; Millis & Kornblith, 1992). Relapse rates following withdrawal of women from antidepressant medication in the puerperium may be improved by psychological treatment. It may be that brief antidepressant treatment can be followed by psychological treatment dealing with the psychosocial factors that exacerbate the woman's depression, allowing women to be weaned off medication earlier. It is also possible that if women are treated with medication only, subclinical symptoms persist owing to the continuation of psychosocial stressors unmasked by medication.

An important consideration for many mothers is the impact on their baby of antidepressant medication secreted in breast milk. Individual variation in the concentration of antidepressant medication secreted in breast milk has been reported (Buist, Norman & Dennerstein, 1993). It is known that the level to which the infant is exposed is likely to be low; however, more research is required to determine the full impact on the infant (Buist, 1996). Thus, while there are no blanket assurances, antidepressant medications appear to be acceptable as described by Dunnewold (1997) and Jermain (1992). In our clinical experience, many mothers refuse medication, so a CBT approach is appealing.

What mothers say works
In a study conducted by Gilley (1993), 167 mothers with an infant aged between four and seven months were interviewed with regard to their feelings in the initial

postpartum months. Sixty-five per cent of the mothers reported feelings of being low or depressed at some time during this period. When these mothers were asked what helped them with their distressing feelings, they reported the activities listed in Table 1. Talking with someone and being listened to continues to emerge as an important therapeutic activity.

Table 1 What helps mothers cope with distressing feelings?

Activity	Percentage of mothers who reported activity as helpful
Talking to someone	76
Getting out (with baby)	14
Change of attitude/motivation	15
Exercise/relaxation	8
Expressing emotion	7
'Time out' (without baby)	5
Catching up on lost sleep	5
Knowing it would end because had been through it before	3
Stopping or enjoying breastfeeding	3
Painkillers	3
Reading books on depression	3
Interaction from baby (e.g., smiles)	3
Other	7

OUR MODEL OF THERAPEUTIC INTERVENTION

Four main influences have contributed to the treatment package described in this book:

1. Our model, based on the profile of women with PND.
2. The evidence to date: what works.
3. The Coping with Depression course (Lewinsohn et al., 1984), coupled with cognitive concepts derived from Olioff (1991) and Beck (1967).
4. Clinical experience with over 300 women suffering from PND.

Our model

The model described in Chapter 1 combines a biopsychosocial approach to depression with acknowledgement of the risk factors empirically identified as important in PND. As such, the program takes into account vulnerability, sociocultural and precipitating factors to help women understand what has contributed to their depression, and then takes a CBT approach to deal with exacerbating and maintaining factors.

The evidence to date: what works

On the basis of our literature review, we concluded that a combination of cognitive and behavioural techniques provides a powerful approach to the treatment of depression. Furthermore, there is some evidence that group treatment and increased social support have proved useful in the treatment of PND. These ideas have been incorporated into the main group program, with an emphasis on group process, since what mothers say works is 'talking about it' (and being heard!).

In addition, given the coincidence in time of the depression episode with the transition to parenthood, treatment that includes fathers and infants is a critical addition. The extra modules that can be offered draw from other areas of the literature, including marital therapy and developmental psychology, and are described in Chapters 3, 7 and 8.

Adaptation of the Coping with Depression course for postnatal depression

A foundation for our treatment approach was the Coping with Depression course, developed by Lewinsohn et al. (1984) for the treatment of major depression in adults. It is based on a series of hypotheses posed by Zeiss, Lewinsohn and Munoz (1979), regarding the components that are critical for successful short-term CBT for depression:

1. Therapy should begin with an elaborated, well-planned rationale. This rationale should provide the initial structure that guides the patient to the belief that s/he can control his/her own behavior and thereby change his/her depression.
2. Therapy should provide training and skills which the patient can use to feel more effective in handling his/her daily life. The skills must be of some significance to the patient, and must fit with the rationale that has been presented.
3. Therapy should emphasize the independent use of these skills by the patient outside of the therapy context, and must provide enough structure so that the attainment of independent skills is possible for the patient.
4. Therapy should encourage the patient's attribution that improvement in mood was caused by the patient's own increased skill from this, not by the therapist's skilfulness. (Zeiss et al., 1979, pp. 437–438)

The Coping with Depression course (Lewinsohn et al., 1984) was designed to address specific target behaviours (social skills, depressogenic thinking, pleasant activities and relaxation), within the context of general components recognised as important in determining the success of cognitive-behavioural intervention (e.g., self-monitoring, self-change). It consists of 12 two-hour sessions conducted over eight weeks for six to ten participants. Sessions are held twice a week for the first four weeks of the course. Each session involves psycho-education, review of homework exercises, role playing and discussion. The first two sessions are devoted to presenting a social learning view of depression, setting up group rules and teaching self-change skills. The following eight sessions are dedicated to teaching specific skills (relaxation, increasing pleasant activities, gaining control of negative or irrational thinking, and social skills). Lewinsohn and Gotlib (1995) explain that the relaxation skill is taught first, based on the rationale that it is a relatively easy skill to learn and allows participants to experience an initial success experience. The relaxation training is based on the Jacobson (1929) method of progressive muscular relaxation. The cognitive therapy sessions incorporate elements of Beck's (1967) cognitive theories in identifying and challenging irrational and negative thoughts. The social skills sessions focus on assertiveness training, planning and increasing social activity, and techniques for making friends. The final two sessions of the course are devoted to integrating skills already learned and relapse prevention.

The Coping with Depression course (Lewinsohn, et al., 1984) has been evaluated with regard to its efficacy in the treatment of depression. In several outcome studies, this approach proved more effective in the treatment of depression than a waiting-list control condition, and as effective as behaviour therapy conducted on an individual basis (Lewinsohn & Gotlib, 1995).

In our bid to develop a comprehensive treatment program for women suffering from PND, we have attempted to incorporate the elements of successful cognitive-behavioural intervention into a format that is accessible and efficacious in the treatment of women in the postpartum period. Our core program was therefore based on the Coping with Depression course (Lewinsohn et al., 1984), and modified to include the specific cognitive components recommended by Olioff (1991), as well as to take into consideration the model that we have proposed for the aetiology and maintenance of PND in Chapter 1. The major changes to session order and content that were made to adapt the program for women with PND are shown in Table 2.

Our adaptation of the Coping with Depression course occurred in two phases. In the first phase, Lisa Negri, who was studying for her Doctoral degree at La Trobe University, developed a treatment program for women with postnatal depression in collaboration with the Infant Clinic. While maintaining Lewinsohn's session structure (combination of psycho-education, experiential practice and review) and focus on increasing response-contingent positive reinforcement, she also incorporated a number of issues specific to mothers with PND. The core components of cognitive intervention strategies, assertiveness, relaxation, self-control, decision making, problem solving, communication, time management and increasing pleasant activities were also retained. This group program was trialed on 37 mothers. A significant reduction in depressive symptomatology and an increase in perceived family support were found (Negri, 1998). The second phase of adaptation by the Infant Clinic was based on Negri's encouraging findings, and feedback received from participants as well as group leaders (Milgrom, Negri & Martin, 1997). This resulted in a restructuring of the session order, so that all behavioural interventions occurred first. The aim of this was to bring about some positive changes in women's lives (e.g., increase in pleasant activities and reduced anxiety) before attempting cognitive work. Many women felt too overwhelmed initially to take on cognitive challenges. We found we also needed to increase the number of sessions allocated to cognitive work as this was central to many women's problems, but the concepts needed to be introduced slowly. Women's tiredness and the presence of many competing tasks also led us to reduce homework. Finally, repeated administration of the treatment package led us to continually refine the content based on our clinical experience, as described below, simplify instructions and allow more time for the group process to occur at the beginning. The critical role of the infant and partners, and our growing

Table 2 Adaptation of the Coping with Depression course (Lewinsohn et al., 1984) for postnatal depression

Session order	The 'Coping with Depression course'	Session order	'Getting Ahead of Postnatal Depression'
1	*Depression and social learning* Business Pep talk Introduction and ground rules Get aquainted exercise Rationale and overview of the social learning approach to depression Review Session 1 homework Preview Session 2 and assign homework	1	*Understanding and managing PND* Introduction Ground rules Group activity: get aquainted exercise Group discussion: pregnancy, birth and now Psycho-education: ● What is PND? ● Introduction to a cognitive-behavioural approach to the treatment of PND ● Strategies for improving mood Preview Session 2 Assign homework
2	*How to design a self-change plan* Business Pep talk Review Session 1 and related homework Rationale Lecture: self-change skills Review Session 2 homework Preview Session 3 and assign homework		
3	*Learning to relax* Business Pep talk Review Session 2 and related homework Rationale Lecture: progressive relaxation Review Session 3 homework Preview Session 4 and assign homework	3	*Relaxation on the run* Introduction to Session 3 Activity: consolidating pleasant activities Psycho-education: relaxation training Group activity: Jacobson progressive deep muscle relaxation procedure Group discussion Psycho-education: relaxing on the run Group discussion Group activity: relaxation plan for high tension times Preview Session 4 Homework
4	*Relaxation in everyday situations* Business Pep talk Review Session 3 and related homework Rationale Lecture: relaxation in everyday situations Review Session 4 homework Preview Session 5 and assign homework		

Session order	The 'Coping with Depression course'	Session order	'Getting Ahead of Postnatal Depression'

5	*Pleasant activities and depression*
	Business
	Pep talk
	Review Session 4 and related
	  homework
	Rationale
	Lecture: pleasant activities
	Review Session 5 homework
	Preview Session 6 and assign
	  homework
		2	*Pleasant activities—how can I find the time?*
			Introduction to Session 2
			Psycho-education:
			  • The cognitive-behavioural model of depression
			  • Pleasant activities and depression
			Activity: pleasant activities and mood
			Group discussion
			Psycho-education: increasing
			  pleasant activities
			Preview Session 3
			Homework

6	*Formulating a pleasant activities plan*
	Business
	Pep talk
	Review Session 5 and related
	  homework
	Rationale
	Lecture: pleasant activities plan
	Review Session 6 homework
	Preview Session 7 and assign
	  homework		

		5	*Unrealistic expectations of parenting—influences from the past*
			Introduction to Session 5
			Psycho-education: family of origin
			Activity: my family of origin
			Psycho-education: challenging
			  unhelpful thoughts and unrealistic
			  expectations of parenting
			Preview Session 6
			Homework

7	*Two approaches to constructive thinking*
	Business
	Pep talk
	Review Session 6 and related
	  homework
	Rationale
	Lectures: controlling your thoughts;
	  constructive thinking
	Review Session 7 homework
	Preview Session 8 and assign
	  homework
		6	*My internal dialogue—the missing link*
			Introduction to Session 6
			Psycho-education: self-instruction
			  techniques are the missing link
			Group discussion: difficulty
			  following through with tasks
			Group activity: self-instruction
			Psycho-education: using self-
			  instruction
			Small group exercise
			Preparation for termination
			Preview Session 7
			Homework

8	*Formulating a plan for constructive thinking*
	Business
	Pep talk
	Review Session 7 and related
	  homework
	Rationale
		7	*Developing a more helpful thinking style*
			Introduction to Session 7
			Psycho-education: mind games—
			  negative thoughts make me feel
			  worthless and depressed
			Individual activity: tuning into my
			  thoughts

(continued over)

Table 2   *(cont.)*

Session order	The 'Coping with Depression course'	Session order	'Getting Ahead of Postnatal Depression'
8	*Formulating a plan for constructive thinking* Lecture: self-instruction Small group task: positive self-statements Preview Session 9 and assign homework	7	*Developing a more helpful thinking style* Group Discussion Psycho-education: ways to reduce negative thoughts and increase positive thoughts Group discussion Preview Session 8 Homework
		8	*Challenging my internal critic* Introduction to Session 8 Activity: thoughts and feelings Psycho-education: shifting cognitive distortions concerning parenthood Group activity: my expectations of motherhood and parenting Preview Session 9 Homework
9	*Social skills: the ability to be assertive* Business Pep talk Review Session 8 and related homework Rationale and lecture: social skills—the ability to be assertive Review Session 9 homework Preview Session 10 and assign homework	4	*Assertiveness and self-esteem—telling others what I think and how I feel* Introduction to Session 4 Psycho-education: assertiveness skills Group discussion: aggressive/passive/assertive Group activity: assertiveness training Psycho-education: self-esteem Individual activity: love letter Preview Session 5 Homework
10	*Using your social skills* Business Pep talk Review Session 9 and related homework Rationale Lecture: using your social skills Review Session 10 homework Preview Session 11 and assign homework		
11	*Maintaining your gains* Business Pep talk Review Session 10 and related homework Rationale Lecture: maintaining your gains Review Session 11 homework Preview Session 12 and assign homework	9	*Putting it all together—travelling on* Introduction to session 9 Group discussion: what changes in my mood have I noticed? Group discussion: what about another baby? Psycho-education: maintaining your gains Group discussion: social support Individual exercise: my goals Group discussion: termination

Session order	The 'Coping with Depression course'	Session order	'Getting Ahead of Postnatal Depression'
12	*Developing a life plan* Business Pep talk Review Session 11 and related homework Rationale Lecture: making a life plan. Review Session 12 homework Final pep talk, closing remarks		
		10	*Consolidating what I have learned* Introduction to Session 10 Housekeeping issues Review of previous weeks Review 'Getting Ahead of Postnatal Depression' program Review changes in mood Review short to medium term goals Review social supports Preparation for high-risk situations Generalisation training Lifestyle modification
			Partner sessions
		10	Conducted between Sessions 1 and 3, Sessions 4 and 6, and Sessions 7 and 9
		11	Psycho-educational session re: symptoms, aetiology, course and prognosis for PND.
		12	Support From lovers to parents Parenting issues Opportunity for questions and discussion

realisation that difficulties in this area needed to be targeted directly, led us to extend partner involvement into a three-week brief intervention program, and develop an extra module to intervene with parent–infant difficulties.

Clinical experience with postnatal depression: what is needed

To date at the Infant Clinic, we have treated over 300 women with PND in an ongoing research trial assessing comparative interventions. Some of our findings are presented in Chapter 6. From this experience, we have gained knowledge of the needs of these women and developed the Getting Ahead of Postnatal Depression program. Some of the particular needs of women with PND are summarised below:

Firstly, mothers need an opportunity to discuss their pregnancy, birth and early parenting experiences as a means of connecting with the group and feeling safe to participate fully in the group program. This opportunity was provided in the first session, as well as time to discuss and problem solve any issues that might get in the way of attending all sessions (e.g., childcare arrangements). As a result, the psycho-educational material regarding the interconnectedness of thoughts, feelings and behaviour was deferred until Session 2. When presented, this is done very clearly: '*Depression is related to both our past and current problems in living. How we deal with these will influence how we feel. In addition, our feelings are directly connected to the way we behave, and also to the way we think. To change some of our behaviour and thinking we can learn "skills in living" to improve how we feel.*'

Secondly, mothers require assistance with time management (a skill that is taught along with planning pleasant activities) as most mothers find that the task of organising themselves and the baby (and other children, if applicable) to attend sessions, or even to go to the milk bar, is too overwhelming. This issue needs to be resolved before moving on to other skills taught in the program. Thus, room is made for increasing pleasant activities and an emphasis on increasing self-nurturing activities is very helpful early in the program. Including their baby and partner in some pleasant activities is also highlighted.

Thirdly, relaxation skills are adapted for 'relaxing on the run', as one of the issues of early motherhood is having very little time. In addition, as mothers generally believe that their needs are not paramount and the needs of their baby, husband, in-laws and others are more important, issues concerning expectations regarding motherhood and the 'martyr' syndrome are addressed prior to conducting the relaxation sessions. Cognitive techniques are taught later in the program and more time is allowed than in Lewinsohn's program. Women with PND are often particularly overwhelmed by too much information and cognitive restructuring takes considerable time to master. Simplifying cognitive concepts is useful and women are helped to challenge unhelpful thinking patterns in the group and asked to increase positive thoughts with easy-to-use reminders such as fridge magnets. It is important to allow sufficient time for the group process to occur prior to attempting cognitive work, and for some improvement in anxiety and increase in pleasurable tasks to have occurred with behavioural tasks. In addition, material from Olioff (1991) has served to expand the cognitive work.

Fourthly, we have always included the series of three partner evenings described in Chapter 7 when offering women the nine-week treatment program. Most mothers complain of minimal family support (especially from fathers) and about unhelpful comments from family or friends regarding how happy they should be because they have a healthy baby. Psycho-education is provided to fathers and any other family members that the mother chooses to invite to the information and therapy nights which are held between the first and third, fourth and sixth, and seventh and ninth group therapy sessions, respectively. An emphasis on building support networks occurs in this context.

Finally, a social activity is organised after the last session to allow mothers to consolidate and practice the skills that they have learned during the course of the program. The program will be described in detail in Chapters 4–6 and is designed to be conducted on the basis of this manual.

Chapter 3

ASSESSING POSTNATAL DEPRESSION AND TREATMENT OPTIONS

ASSESSING POSTNATAL DEPRESSION

Increasing help seeking

PND often goes unrecognised owing to its slow and insidious onset, and many women tend to hide their depressive symptoms from others. Only a minority of women who suffer from PND seek professional help, and benefit from early intervention to reduce avoidable, prolonged emotional distress and limit consequences on the infant or family. A number of strategies have been advocated to improve this situation:

1. *Normalising* the possibility of PND through discussions and community education, both antenatally and postnatally.
2. *Early identification* through awareness of symptoms by health professionals such as midwives, obstetricians, general practitioners and maternal and child health nurses in the immediate weeks and months following childbirth.
3. Close attention to those women showing evidence of *risk factors* such as unexpected birth events, previous history of depression, stressed marital relationships and social isolation.
4. *Routine screening* shortly after birth, which is emerging as the single most effective and cost-efficient means of identifying mothers at risk of PND, enabling the early treatment of mothers who would otherwise remain undetected.

Screening and diagnosing depression

John Cox and his colleagues (1987) have developed a brief self-rating questionnaire, the Edinburgh Postnatal Depression Scale (EPDS), for screening women in the early postnatal months for symptoms of depression.

The EPDS is a 10-item self-report questionnaire. Women are asked to underline the response that most closely represents how they have felt over the past seven days. For example:

'I have felt sad or miserable'	Score
Yes, most of the time	3
Yes, quite often	2
Not very often	1
No, not at all	0

The scale has been found to be highly acceptable to women, with Murray and Carothers (1990) finding a 97.3% return rate in a mail-out to 702 women six weeks postpartum. Our own use of the EPDS on over 3000 women at 10–14 weeks postpartum has not only been completed willingly by women, but was also found to be extremely helpful to maternal and child health nurses. Women scoring high on the EPDS had sometimes masked their depression and felt relieved that some-one was asking how they felt. Gerrard, Holden and Elliott (1993) similarly found that many health visitors reported being surprised to learn that women who they thought were coping were actually very depressed. For others, it helped confirm their suspicion that something was wrong and made it easier to encourage mothers to talk about what was happening. The scale has now been used world-wide and translated and validated in a number of languages.

Studies using the EPDS for screening PND have been conducted in the UK (Appleby et al., 1994; Areias et al., 1996a; Cooper, Murray, Hooper & West, 1996; Cox et al., 1993), Chile (Jadresic et al., 1995), USA (Reighard & Evans, 1995), New Zealand (Webster et al., 1994), Portugal (Augusto, Kumar, Calheiros, Matos & Figueiredo, 1996) and Australia (Milgrom & Negri, 1999; Robinson & Young, 1982). A threshold of 12.5 is generally used as a cut-off for closer examination of the women.

Since the EPDS has been reported to accurately detect 86–95% of women identi-fied as depressed (O'Hara, 1994), community workers may approach mothers with offers of support or the opportunity to discuss feelings more fully, on the basis of this screening tool. The presence of distress is sufficient to warrant further evaluation and possible intervention. Holden (1994a) describes in great detail how to use and score the EPDS and provides a copy of the scale. She advocates that women who score over 12 should be given the opportunity to discuss her score with a health professional. An explanatory letter during pregnancy, fol-lowed by screening both in the early weeks postpartum, at five to eight weeks, and up to 20–26 weeks, can ensure that most women are identified.

While the EPDS is an invaluable screening tool, it will identify some women who do not have a depressive disorder. It is not a substitute for full psychiatric assessment or clinical judgement (Cox & Holden, 1994). Holden (1994a) suggests that where reliance is placed on the EPDS to measure depression in the absence of a full psychiatric diagnosis, a second EPDS given two weeks later, if still high, is a good indicator of depression. Increasing the reliability of the depressive rating in this way is important as Murray and Carothers (1990) suggest that the sensitivity of the EPDS in a community population may be lower than reported by others, and may be only around 67.7%.

To accurately diagnose depression, particularly for research purposes, stand-ardised psychiatric assessments are used to confirm a diagnosis of depression. The use of these semi-structured interviews results in the ability to classify a woman according to DSM-IV (*Diagnostic and Statistical Manual of Mental Disorders*, American Psychiatric Association, 1994) or ICD-10 (International Classification of Diseases, World Health Organization, 1993b) criteria for various diagnostic categories of depression, with proven cross-cultural reliability and validity. These include:

- The Structured Clinical Interview for the *Diagnostic and Statistical Manual of Mental Disorders* (SCID-P; Spitzer, Williams, Gibbon & First, 1990).
- The Composite International Diagnostic Interview (CIDI; World Health Organization, 1993a), which can be administered by lay interviewers (Wittchen et al., 1991).
- Goldberg's Standardised Psychiatric Interview (Goldberg, Cooper, Eastwood, Kedward & Shepherd, 1970).

The above interviews require training and are generally lengthy to administer. In practice, clinicians often arrive at a psychiatric classification on the basis of a less formal interview, together with the simpler Hamilton Rating Scale for Depression (Hamilton, 1967) or the Beck Depression Inventory (BDI; Beck & Steer, 1987), which also give a severity index.

Distinguishing those mothers suffering from a severe major affective disorder is important both in terms of risk management (e.g., presence of suicidal ideation) and in considering the use of medication. Indications for pharmacological treatment are discussed later in this chapter.

Assessing improvement with treatment is also important. While the EPDS has been used for this purpose in some studies, it is essentially a screening tool. We have used the BDI (Beck, Ward, Mendelson, Mock & Erbaugh, 1961), a well-validated measure of severity of depression, and found it to be useful in postnatally depressed women, as a 'before and after' indicator of the change in depression with treatment. The BDI is a 21-item instrument designed to assess the severity of depression and measures cognitive, affective and physiological components of depression. Scores above nine are considered to be above threshold and requiring further investigation. It is regarded as an excellent measure of depressive symptoms when it is used in clinical samples, and is also widely used in research (Waller, 1993). The BDI has good construct validity and concurrent validity with the Hamilton Rating Scale for Depression and the depression scale of the Minnesota Multiphasic Personality Inventory (Beck & Steer, 1987).

Paradoxically, it was dissatisfaction with self-rating scales such as the BDI that led to the development of the EPDS. There was some concern about the accuracy of this scale in the postpartum period as some items asking about difficulty with sleep, tiredness and weight seemed to tap problems related to night feeding a baby and pregnancy weight gain, rather than depression. Thus, it was felt that disruption in lifestyle and biological changes accompanying a new baby were part of normal psychological processes (Cox & Holden, 1994).

Perusal of this scale reveals, however, that only three items (16, 17, 18) are at high risk of being confounded in the immediate postpartum. Women can be asked to answer questions keeping this in mind. For example, they can be asked to rate how they feel but to focus on sleep difficulties, falling asleep or waking up, unrelated to the demands of their infants. Even without specific instructions, our own results on 143 women screened in the community three to four months postpartum, and diagnosed as depressed, indicate a good correlation between the BDI and high scorers on the EPDS (see Table 1). These women had scored more than 12 on the EPDS and were subsequently diagnosed as suffering from a depressive disorder on psychiatric interview (Milgrom & Negri, 1999). Furthermore, for this group of women with a clear diagnosis of depression, the BDI gives a useful severity index, showing that only 24.4% had Beck scores not in the range for at least borderline clinical depression, a further 17.3% showing a mild mood disorder and the rest distributed along the full range of severity (see Table 2).

Table 1   Correlation between Beck score and Edinburgh score

Mixed depressive diagnoses	$r = 0.76$	$p < 0.01$	$n = 261$
Major depressive disorder	$r = 0.73$	$p < 0.01$	$n = 164$

Table 2   Distribution of Beck scores in women scoring >12 on the EPDS and diagnosed as depressed

n	Beck score	Clinical description
12 (7.1%)	1–10	Normal 'ups' and 'downs'
29 (17.3%)	11–16	Mild mood disturbance
34 (20.2%)	17–20	Borderline clinical depression
55 (32.7%)	21–30	Moderate depression
31 (18.4%)	31–40	Severe depression
7 (4.2%)	over 40	Extreme depression

Boyce (1991), in a study of 98 women at one, three and six months postpartum, also provided evidence of good agreement between the two instruments with respect to identifying 'caseness' of PND (as measured by DSM-III diagnosis) ranging from 91% to 96%, with the highest level of agreement at six months postpartum.

In conclusion, the EPDS is a useful screening tool for identifying women with PND, and is often sufficient to suggest clinical intervention. Accurate diagnosis and severity of depression can be further evaluated using various standardised psychiatric interviews and the BDI.

Encouraging women to engage in treatment

Having identified depressed women, there is some evidence to suggest that new mothers are reticent to accept further assessment or treatment. Few of these women are known to psychiatric services or even their general practitioners (Cox et al., 1982). Robinson and Young (1982) reported that 50% of women refused an offer of a psychiatric interview after being screened with the EPDS. Whitten et al. (1996) asked women, screened with the EPDS and further assessed on psychiatric scales, about their views regarding the diagnosis and the treatment offered. More than half (55%) of the mothers thought that their symptoms were not severe enough to be labelled depression. Primiparous mothers and those in higher social classes were significantly more likely to reject the diagnosis as applying to them and therefore reluctant to accept treatment offers. In an extremely small study conducted by Painter (1995), six out of nine mothers identified as having scores greater than 12 on the EPDS declined referral for further support.

We have found a higher success rate, however, with 70% of women accepting treatment, after being identified on the basis of an EPDS score greater than 12 and a diagnosis of depression. It seems that the way the EPDS score is presented to a new mother, and the normative information given to the mother prior to the screening test, predicts those mothers who will accept help. In our screening programs, mothers are told by their nurses that 'We do this for all women at the 12-week check-up as it is a common problem.' Nurses then need to be available to discuss women's responses to the questionnaires, and to tackle erroneous assumptions about what it means to accept treatment. Very often, challenging beliefs around the following themes can help a woman move from identification to acceptance of treatment:

- Denial.
- Shame.
- Belief that she should cope alone.
- It will quickly go away on its own.
- It is just a bad day.
- Myths about motherhood and social expectations, e.g. 'New mothers should be blissfully happy'; 'If I am depressed it means that I do not care for my baby.'

This approach, we believe, is an effective way of decreasing the claim that women will become more depressed if they are told that they are suffering from PND. It will also help to address the finding that some women scoring high on the EPDS do not agree with naming the experience 'postnatal depression', preferring to explain their feelings in terms of workload or tiredness (Brown, Lumley, Small & Astbury, 1994). Our experience suggests that naming the experience 'postnatal depression' and helping women to understand the contributing factors (such as tiredness in the context of current stressors) is comforting to women. This may also help a woman to understand why getting an extra afternoon's sleep did not help her to feel better. For those women for whom this simple intervention (sleep) was in fact sufficient, it is likely that they were not suffering from a full depressive disorder.

Assessing and managing risk

As part of the depressive experience, some women will express suicidal ideation. It is important that a suicide risk assessment is undertaken in the initial interview prior to intervention.

Suicide risk assessment

- Does the mother score one, two or three on Item 10 of the EPDS?
- Does the mother have a history of suicide attempts?

The EPDS allows for rapid identification of women who are experiencing suicidal ideation. A score of two or more on Item 10 ('thought of harming herself'), according to Holden (1994a), can be regarded as clinically significant and requires further investigation as to whether a woman feels desperate enough to act on her thoughts.

- Does she have a strong conviction that there is nothing worth living for? Mothers of babies have a low suicide rate in comparison to the overall female suicide rate, most probably because they believe they need to stay alive for their baby.
- Does she have a suicide plan? Is the plan feasible (e.g., if the mother states that she could shoot herself, does she have easy access to a firearm?). Is the plan detailed?
- Is the mother often in situations where she is alone and unsupported?
- Has the mother begun to 'tie up loose ends' (e.g., revised will, paid for funeral, written letters, tidied up accounts)?

> *Caution:* Persons expressing suicidal ideation and considered to be at risk can suddenly seem more relaxed, less anxious. This is a warning sign—they may have made a clear decision to suicide. Increase vigilance at this time rather than decrease.

If a mother is considered to be high risk:

1. Consider immediate hospitalisation.
2. Increase support networks so the mother is not alone. Fathers may need to take leave from work as a crisis measure.
3. Refer to a psychiatrist for assessment and possible prescription of antidepressant medication.
4. Engage mother in therapy. Group therapy may still be appropriate if individual support occurs concurrently.
5. Ensure that one particular professional (e.g., maternal and child health nurse, general practitioner) is responsible for case management.
6. Ensure the safety of the baby (and other children). See discussion in Chapter 9 if the infant is at significant risk.
7. Have the mother sign a contract agreeing to keep herself safe (do this on a weekly basis).

Holden (1994a) highlights that it is important to let women know that help is available, and for therapists to have a good referral network for problems outside their professional expertise.

MEASURING OTHER RISK FACTORS

Assessing anxiety

High levels of anxiety are a common feature of women suffering from PND, and in some cases anxiety symptoms begin antenatally. While high anxiety levels during pregnancy have been associated with depressive symptomatology in the postpartum period (Dennerstein et al., 1986; Hayworth et al., 1980; Hopkins et al., 1984), they are not sufficient to predict the likelihood of PND (Atkinson & Rickel, 1984). Nevertheless, since heightened anxiety is often a central feature of women with PND, it is important to assess this, to see if it needs to be specifically addressed in the treatment program for PND. The treatment program described in this book includes strategies for reducing anxiety, such as learning relaxation techniques.

Monitoring change in anxiety can be measured with scales such as the Profile of Mood States and the Beck Anxiety Inventory. The Profile of Mood States (McNair, Lorr & Drappleman, 1992) is simple to use and measures anxiety and five other subscales related to moods: depression–dejection, anger–hostility, vigour–activity, fatigue–inertia and confusion–bewilderment.

The Beck Anxiety Inventory (Beck, Epstein, Brown & Steer, 1988) consists of 21 descriptive statements of anxiety symptoms that are rated on a four-point scale from: 'Not at all' to 'Severely; I could barely stand it'. The items include: 'Numbness or tingling', 'Feeling hot', 'Wobbliness in legs', 'Unable to relax', 'Unsteady', 'Terrified', 'Nervous', 'Feelings of choking', 'Hands trembling', 'Shaky', 'Fear of losing control', 'Difficulty breathing', 'Fear of dying', 'Scared', 'Indigestion or discomfort in abdomen', 'Faint', 'Face flushed', and 'Sweating (not due to heat)'.

Assessing psychosocial issues

In general, other information such as current stressors, level of social support, maternal self-esteem and beliefs about self can be assessed through interview as clinical targets. These issues, typically, become apparent during the early stages of the treatment program. Goal setting can be undertaken within the treatment program to adequately address these psychosocial issues that have been described in Chapter 1 as commonly associated with PND.

For those who wish to use more formal measures of evaluation, the following are two suggested measures.

Coopersmith Self-Esteem Inventory
The Coopersmith Self-Esteem Inventory (SEI) measures attitudes towards the self in personal, social, academic and family areas of experience (Coopersmith, 1987).

Perceived Social Support (Family and Friends) Scales
The Perceived Social Support (PSS) Scales generate separate scores for perceived social support from family (PSS-Fa) and friends (PSS-Fr) (Procidano & Heller, 1983).

MARITAL RELATIONSHIPS AND PARTNER FUNCTIONING

Assessing the marital or partner relationship

Research has consistently demonstrated that women are more at risk of PND if they experience dissatisfaction with their marital/partner relationship. Women suffering from PND often report that their pregnancy created more frequent conflict with their partners which persisted even when their depression remitted (Campbell et al., 1992; Gotlib, Whiffen, Wallace & Mount, 1991; O'Hara et al., 1990). Women suffering from PND view their husbands as less supportive than their well counterparts. Schweitzer et al. (1992) found that women in marriages characterised by high levels of control and low levels of care were at greater risk of experiencing PND.

Structured questionnaires, such as the Dyadic Adjustment Scale (Spanier, 1976), give some indication of whether satisfaction experienced within a partner relationship is an area of concern that should be one of the aims of intervention. The original 32-item scale has a shortened form (eight items) which has a reasonable level of reliability and validity. Both partners can be asked to complete this scale (Sharpley & Rogers, 1984).

Alternatively, an indication of marital difficulties can be obtained by interview and should cover two main areas. Recent research indicates that women differentiate between *practical* and *emotional support* provided by their partners. Practical support includes feeding and bathing the baby, helping with meals, shopping, helping with older children and getting up at night to feed the baby. Financial support is also an important practical factor. Access to finances, particularly when two incomes become one, can raise issues of power and control. Emotional support includes the opportunities for expressing thoughts, concerns and feelings as well as intimacy, and having concerns understood. Women may at times underestimate their partners' awareness of their issues, perhaps because they have not openly discussed problems that they feel helpless to solve (Hunt, 1998).

Assessing partners of women with postnatal depression

Should the partner also be assessed? As described in the previous chapter, there is growing acknowledgement that for women who are depressed, their partners' satisfaction with the marriage, attachment to the infant or their partners' own psychiatric morbidity, anxious mood or depression, needs to be taken into account to maximise the impact of treatment.

Several studies report elevated levels of depression in 13–15% of new fathers (Fawcett & York, 1986; Raskin, Richman & Gaines, 1990). Ballard et al. (1994) studied 200 postnatal couples at two stages. Using the EPDS and a cut-off score of 13 or more, they found that at six weeks postpartum, 27.5% of mothers and 9.0% of fathers were potential 'cases' of depression. At six months postpartum 'caseness' of mothers was 25.7% and that of fathers was 5.4%. They found that fathers were significantly more likely to have depressed mood if their partners were also depressed. Richman, Raskin and Gaines (1991) similarly report that men in general show a slight increase of depressive symptomatology at two months postpartum compared with pre-parenthood. They suggest that men depend primarily on their spouses for social support, and are affected by the reported decrease in spouse support, by both men and women, after childbirth. Zelkowitz and Milet (1996) also speculate that assortative mating may account for some cases where both fathers and mothers experience psychological problems. That is, partners select each other on the basis of personal similarities. Other studies propose that the stress of living with a depressed spouse plays a significant role in the father's mental health, since a depressed spouse may be preoccupied, hostile, lacking in energy and uninterested in having a social life (Coyne et al., 1987; Hinchcliffe, Hooper & Roberts, 1975).

In addition to the presence of depressed mood, general psychiatric morbidity among fathers postnatally has been estimated to range from 3% to 9% (Ballard, Davis, Handy & Mohan, 1993; Ballard et al., 1994). Harvey and McGrath (1988) studied the spouses of 40 women admitted to a psychiatric mother–baby unit. In the index group of women who were admitted to a mother–baby unit, they found that fathers had a high level of psychiatric morbidity (42%), compared with 4% of partners of women who had not required a psychiatric admission. The morbidity mostly consisted of generalised anxiety disorders and major depressive episodes, and was associated with poorer marital and social function. Although this group included spouses of women with psychotic illnesses, when they were excluded the prevalence based on affective disorders remained at 40–50%. Lovestone and Kumar (1993) similarly found that 12 out of 24 spouses of women with postnatal psychiatric illness admitted to a mother–baby unit over a 12-month period were psychiatrically ill themselves, using DSM-IV criteria. This rate was higher than for men whose partners remained well postnatally, and for men whose partners were admitted to a psychiatric unit for non-puerperal illness. They also found associations with psychiatric illness in these men were a history of chronic social problems, previous psychiatric episodes and a poor relationship with their own father.

Not only is there an increase in depressed mood and increased psychiatric morbidity in partners of women with PND, but it has also been found that for both partners marital satisfaction declines after the birth of the first child (Belsky & Rovine, 1990; Wallace & Gotlib, 1990). Men and women may have different concerns during the postpartum period, with women worrying about both intimacy and practical matters (e.g., household division of labour and combining multiple roles), and men more concerned about intimacy and companionship (Broom, 1984; Rubble, Fleming, Hackel & Stangor, 1988). Furthermore, men may be more negative about fatherhood if they perceive more changes in their partners and the spousal relationship (Dragonas, Thorpe & Golding, 1992). Interestingly, depressive symptoms in fathers in the postpartum period have been found to predict maternal depressive symptoms two to three years later (Carro, Grant & Gotlib, 1993).

Berg-Cross and Cohen (1995) found that in marriages with one depressed partner there was a high frequency of depressive behaviours, low cohesion, imbalanced power relationships and high hostility levels. They also found that there were more life stressors, maladaptive coping styles and low levels of social support. They suggested that including partners in therapy may be an effective intervention. In line with studies reported above, Areias, Kumar, Baros and Figueiredo (1996b) found that 'postnatal' depression in 42 fathers was associated with a history of depression in themselves and with the presence of depression in their wives/partners during pregnancy and soon after delivery. They concluded that prevention and early treatment of depression in fathers may benefit not only the fathers but also their spouses and their children.

In our program, we strongly advocate involving the partner, if present, in the additional couples module (see Chapter 7). Contact with partners occurs some weeks after the beginning of group treatment for women, when it is recommended that the additional couples module is included. Until that time, we deal with the woman's perception of her partner and the issues that this raises for her.

We have also found it more useful to conduct assessments on partners once we have engaged them in treatment, usually at the first couples session. If a decision is made to assess partners, similar scales can be used to those already described for women. Since the contact with partners usually occurs in group settings, simple scales such as the Profile of Mood States (POMS) (McNair et al., 1992) have been found to be preferable to longer questionnaires, as they are more 'user friendly'. This gives a quick index of anxiety, depression, confusion or hostility, and may serve as an ice-breaker for men to talk about their feelings. To assess psychiatric morbidity if required, the General Health Questionnaire (Goldberg & William, 1988) is a self-report scale that provides useful information on 'caseness'. The General Health Questionnaire is a 60-item self-administered screening test aimed at detecting psychiatric disorders among respondents in community settings and non-psychiatric clinical settings. The questionnaire has good test–retest reliability, high predictive validity, and correlates well with other interview measures of psychiatric morbidity (Goldberg & William, 1988). It is also available in shortened forms.

Alternatively, group discussion focusing on issues of concern for partners of women with PND can assess issues such as:

- Struggling with work and family demands.
- Confusion about what is happening to their wives and sexual relationships. Women's reduced libido in the immediate puerperium, which is often experienced as a personal rejection by men.
- Lack of understanding of their partners' symptoms and blame.
- Adjusting to responsibilities of parenthood.
- Accepting their partner needs help.
- Knowing what to do to help and when.
- Getting the support they need.
- Family of origin issues.

This assessment can lead fruitfully to ways of managing these difficulties as described in Chapter 7.

MEDICATION

What to advise patients regarding the treatment option of medication

Many mothers have read about or been told by their general practitioners that antidepressant medication is a treatment option. Some knowledge about antidepressants, even for non-psychiatrists, is necessary as some women do very well with combined therapy. There may even be legal implications in not informing clients about the range of treatments available.

In general practice, many women who present to their general practitioners are offered antidepressant medication (Barnett, 1991). There is good evidence that antidepressant medication is helpful in depression, and as effective as cognitive-behavioural therapy (CBT). Whitten, Appleby and Warner (1996), however, found that 81% of 78 women identified by screening on the EPDS and diagnosed as suffering from PND, would not consider taking any pharmacological treatment for depression. This is particularly the case for breastfeeding mothers, as the evidence pertaining to drug levels in breast milk is not clear. The Whitten, Appleby and Warner (1996) finding needs to be considered in view of the suggestion that a proportion of these women would not accept any type of treatment. However, it does support the need to offer alternative non-pharmacological intervention, and for conservative dosing guidelines to be followed, if antidepressants are deemed necessary.

Glick (1995) suggests that treatment is best decided by considering the preferences of the individual. Some mothers prefer to view depression as an 'illness' that can be treated with drugs. For others, a treatment approach such as the one presented in this book not only helps women to feel less depressed but also to solve underlying issues that contributed to their depression and to develop coping skills to prevent relapse.

A number of factors are important to consider (Buist, 1996; Glick, 1995):

- Severity of symptoms: the more severe, the more likely that antidepressants can be beneficial.
- Suicide risk.
- Significant impairment in functioning that may result if the depression is prolonged, e.g. job loss.
- History of recurrent depression is a *good* reason to consider medication.
- Past positive treatment response to antidepressant medication.
- Breastfeeding: limited evidence suggests that some tricyclic antidepressants do not have long-term effects, but little work has been done on the newer antidepressants.
- Presence of anxiety: for depression with a high level of anxiety, a sedative SSRI or a tricyclic antidepressant such as amitryptyline has been recommended, to minimise the need for minor tranquillisers.
- A woman's attitudes and belief system.

The most appropriate referral is to a psychiatrist with broad psychopharmacological expertise who will be willing to consider the advantages and disadvantages for this particular patient, of combining medication and psychological therapies. This requires good contact and communication between health professionals.

Buist (1996) points out that depression postpartum is underdiagnosed and its severity is often not recognised. It is particularly likely that when women do receive antidepressants they do not receive adequate doses. If the woman is breastfeeding, this may influence the treating doctor's decision not to increase dosage. It is crucial, Buist asserts, not to undertreat severe disorders. At the same time, broader issues, other than biological treatments, need to be addressed in all cases. Psychosocial factors, the use of individual, marital and family therapy for long-term effects, as well as parent–infant therapy and maximising support, including that of partners, all need to be considered.

ASSESSING INFANTS

The symptoms of PND, such as withdrawn affect and maternal preoccupation, have an effect directly on the infant's experience. This may have longer-term consequences on child development and may entrench the mother–infant relationship in a negative vicious cycle. The impact on the infant is described more fully in Chapter 8. Thus, it may be relevant when assessing a woman's depression also to assess the *child's development* and the *mother–infant interaction*. In addition, two other areas may warrant assessment: *infant temperament* and *parenting competence*.

Infant temperament, for example, may be a factor that further complicates maternal depression, owing to the stress of dealing with an infant who is more difficult to manage, particularly infants who are difficult to settle or feed. Cutrona and Troutman (1986) suggested that infant temperamental difficulty was related directly to the level of PND as well as playing a mediational role by influencing poor parenting self-efficacy in depression (Campbell et al., 1992; Hopkins et al., 1987). Mothers who have infants who are more difficult to manage, and who receive less positive reinforcement from the mother–child interaction, are more likely to feel a failure as a parent. However, it is unclear whether the temperament of the infant plays a significant role by:

- Introducing a major stress.
- Having a deleterious effect on maternal self-efficacy beliefs. That is, the infant is perceived as extremely unsettled owing to the mother's self-perception that she is not able to comfort her infant and her belief that other babies are much more soothable. As a result, she does not attempt to settle her baby and the baby cries more.
- The mother's inaccurate perception, due to her depression, whereby she sees all her world negatively, including her infant as having a difficult temperament.

When depressed, we have found that mothers describe their infants of three months as more demanding, less adaptive and less reinforcing than their non-depressed counterparts. Their partners view their infants similarly (see example of one subscale, child demandingness, in Table 3). Furthermore, maternal and paternal perceptions of infant difficulty were accompanied by behavioural changes in infants. We found from a record of crying patterns that infants of depressed mothers cried more at three months but not at six months (Milgrom, Westley & McCloud, 1995). Was this due to changes in the mother–infant interaction at three months? Interestingly, utilising a more objective measure, temperamental differences were found to be small at three months and disappeared by six months (see Table 4).

Table 3   Child demandingness, Parenting Stress Index (Abidin, 1986)

Age of infant (months)	Depressed		Non-depressed	
	Mother (*n*)	Father (*n*)	Mother (*n*)	Father (*n*)
3	21.0 (23)	18.5 (15)	15.7 (38)	14.6 (28)
6	19.6 (25)	17.9 (17)	15.7 (30)	15.2 (23)

Table 4 Infants classified according to the Australian Infant Temperament Questionnaire

Age of infant (months)	Type of mother	Easy	Average	Difficult
3	Depressed	8	16	1
	Control	17	28	0
6	Depressed	9	17	0
	Control	21	20	1

This example highlights the complex relationship between maternal depression, infant variables, the mother–infant relationship and parenting competence.

Some indication of functioning in these areas can be obtained by careful clinical observation, or more formal measures may be used, which are described below. Difficulties in any of the areas discussed below would be an indication for the inclusion of the additional treatment module 'Including Infants' as part of the treatment program for the woman's PND (see Chapter 8). We have frequently found that intervention targeting a disturbed mother–infant interaction, and facilitating positive behavioural feedback from the infant, significantly alleviates depressive symptomatology.

Measures of mother–infant interaction

Milgrom–Burn Scale
We have developed an easy-to-administer measure of mother–infant interaction (Milgrom & Burn, 1988). Eighteen behavioural measures were derived from three scales that reported measures of interactions with infants (Brazelton, Koslowski & Main, 1974; Censullo, Lester & Hoffman, 1985; Flick & McSweeney, 1987). Our scale has eight caregiver measures, seven infant measures and three joint caregiver/infant measures. Each measure is rated on a zero to three scale after observing repeated three-minute segments of infant and mother behaviours. Retest reliability, on each measure, can be obtained by observing six three-minute behavioural segments. A shortened version of this scale, showing nine of the most sensitive measures, is included in Box 1.

Measures of child development and child health

Maternal and child heath assessment
Maternal and child health nurses are often well placed to be 'the gatekeepers' of early mother–infant issues. They have an important role to play in the initial identification, referral and ongoing treatment and management of mothers and infants. Maternal and child health nurses' input regarding infant developmental or medical problems is also extremely advantageous. This type of multidisciplinary contribution often ensures the best outcomes for a mother and her infant.

BOX 1
Modified Milgrom–Burn infant/caregiver behavioural measures coding sheet (Milgrom & Burn, 1988)

Definitions

For each of the following behavioural measures, the frequency of the behaviour can be recorded as an estimated amount of time, on a four-point scale, based on repeated observations of interactions.

Score

0	1	2	3
Never observed	Rarely observed	Sometimes observed	Observed most of the time

*Score
(0–4)*

1. Maternal measures

Respond: is determined by the mother's sensitivity in responding to the cues of the infant; i.e., if the infant is distressed the mother will soothe the infant. The higher the score, the more the mother will respond to minimal verbal cues and will be very sensitive to non-verbal messages.

_____

Stimulate/arouse: is based on the amount of time that the mother arouses the attentional state of the infant, using herself or an event or object.

_____

Positive affect: is rated by the amount of time that the mother spends expressing positive emotional feelings to the infant by physical means such as hugging, kissing, smiling, or non-physical means verbalising positive verbal endearments (emotional tone).

_____

Negative affect: is rated by how often the caregiver expresses negative emotional feelings to the infant through anxiety or hostility by frowning, raising of the voice, or other negative behaviours.

_____

2. Infant measures

Infant clarity of cues: is rated by how often the infant clearly gives behavioural cues to indicate his/her needs.

_____

Smile/excite: is determined by how often the infant smiles or displays excitement in some way.

_____

Fuss/cry: is determined by how often the infant whimpers, cries emitting distress vocalisations or shows clear behavioural evidence of discontentment.

_____

Negative affect/avert: is rated by the amount of time that the infant uses physical or verbal angry behaviour towards the mother or avoids interaction (e.g., by gaze aversion).

_____

Alertness: is rated by the amount of time that the infant appears to be groggy or lethargic. High score indicates a very alert infant, 3 = fully alert baby.

_____

3. Mother/infant—joint measures

Reciprocity/synchrony: is rated by the observer if the mother/infant attempts to read each other's behaviour and adjusts his/her stimulation appropriately. It is like a 'dance'.

_____

Adapted from Meitz and Milgrom (1999).

Denver Developmental Screening Test
For those who wish to assess the infant's development themselves, the Denver Developmental Screening Test provides a simple method of screening for delayed development in infants and preschoolers, although it does have some limitations (Meisels, 1989). The test covers five functions: gross motor, language, fine motor, adaptive and personal–social (Frankenburg & Dodds, 1967).

Paediatric assessment
Concerns about infant difficulties may require a full paediatric assessment to eliminate the possibility of a medical or genetic problem.

Measures of infant temperament or infant management difficulty

These infant measures can include:

- The shortened Revised Australian Infant Temperament Questionnaire (RITQ) may be used to assess infant temperament. Scores are summed to obtain five temperament categories: approach, rhythmicity, cooperation/manageability, activity/reactivity and irritability (Sanson, Prior, Garino, Oberklaid & Sewell, 1987).
- The child domain of the Parenting Stress Index (Abidin, 1986). This scale is described in the next section under 'Parenting Stress Index'.
- Behavioural measures of infant difficulty.

Simple ratings on behaviours experienced as problematic by mothers of infants can be completed as shown in Box 2.

BOX 2
Behavioural measures of infant difficulty

My baby has:

None	Mild	Moderate	Severe	
○	○	○	○	Colic/reflux
○	○	○	○	Sleeping problems
○	○	○	○	Excessive crying
○	○	○	○	Eating problems

I have had difficulty:

None	Mild	Moderate	Severe	
○	○	○	○	Separating from my baby
○	○	○	○	Playing with my baby
○	○	○	○	Relating to my baby
○	○	○	○	Baby demanding my attention
○	○	○	○	Other, please specify:_____

Based on material in Seeley, Murray and Cooper (1996) and Sanson, Oberklaid, Pedlow and Prior (1991).

Measures of parenting stress and self-efficacy

Parenting Stress Index

This scale was developed by Richard Abidin (1986) and contains 14 subscales associated with stressors related to parenting. It is in questionnaire format with 120 items. The subscales are grouped under three domains: child, parent and life stress. The *child domain* contains six subscales: (1) adaptability, (2) acceptability, (3) demandingness, (4) mood, (5) distractability/hyperactivity and (6) reinforces parent. High scores are associated with children who display qualities that make it difficult for parents to fulfil their parenting roles. The *parent domain* has seven subscales: (1) depression, (2) attachment, (3) restriction of role, (4) sense of competence, (5) social isolation, (6) relationship with spouse and (7) parent health. High scores in this domain suggest that sources of stress in the parent–child system may be related to dimensions of the parent's functioning. The *life stress* scale provides an index of the amount of stress outside the parent–child relationship that the parent is currently experiencing.

Subscale scores are summed to produce a total mean score for each of the child and parent domains, and a grand total mean score.

Parenting Self-Efficacy

Feelings of effectiveness in the parenting role can be assessed with the eight-item self-efficacy subscale of the Parenting Sense of Competence Scale (PSCS; Gibaud-Wallston, 1977). An additional nine items, which assess comfort and the value placed on the parenting role, are optional. Items are rated on six-point Likert scales (from 'strongly agree' to 'strongly disagree') and include statements such as 'I would make a fine model for a new mother to follow in order to learn what she would need to know to be a good parent', and 'If anyone can find the answer to what is troubling my baby, I am the one.'

At times, in addition to assessing parental perceptions of competence it is important to assess if actual deficits in practical parenting skills exist, such as making up formulas, nappy changing, bathing or settling techniques.

OTHER ASSESSMENT AND TREATMENT ISSUES

Concurrent psychiatric difficulties

When involving women in the 'Getting Ahead of Postnatal Depression' program described in this book, it is important to include women whose major difficulty is depression and associated psychosocial factors. The presence of other concurrent difficulties such as substance abuse, personality disorders, severe eating disorders or other major psychiatric disorders should lead to consideration of alternative treatments that have a dual focus.

Severity of postnatal depression

Some women are so seriously depressed that inpatient admission is necessary. The most appropriate inpatient admission is to the specialised mother–baby units that have evolved in many countries in an attempt to minimise disruption to the developing infant, while enhancing the mother's confidence and skills in her mothering role, and reducing feelings of guilt or inadequacy in the mother. Mother–baby units provide the mother with an opportunity to solve some of the day-to-day difficulties she faces in a context where treatment is available for her psychiatric disorder (Bardon, Glaser, Prothero & Weston, 1968; Brockington & Kumar, 1981).

Factors limiting group participation

Women with limited intellectual capacity or from non-English-speaking backgrounds may find the group dynamics and the heavy didactic input difficult to keep up with. Motivation, psychological insight and concrete thinking are also parameters that may be considered when deciding on suitability for group treatment, as can the presence of major social stressors that need urgent attention (such as no housing). Individual treatment (see Chapter 9) may be indicated in these cases.

Cross-cultural issues

Differences in cross-cultural expressions of PND and rituals around childbirth and early parenting mean that the treatment package may need to be adapted to make it more sensitive to a woman's particular culture. Leff (1990) argues that psychiatric disorders have a social aetiology as a large component, compared to a biological aetiology, and indigenous belief systems need to be considered. Thus, our cognitive-behavioural approach to depression would be flawed without taking this into account.

Medical reasons

It is important to consider the possibility of an organic cause for depression, including thyroid dysfunction or even a cerebral tumour (Cox & Holden, 1994). A dual medical/psychological treatment approach is always necessary. Fatigue may be due to low iron levels following major loss of blood in childbirth.

Adapting the group program for individual treatment

At present, research on matching patient characteristics to treatments has been disappointing (Shapiro, 1995). Clinically, however, assessment of a woman may reveal that group treatment is not suitable. This can occur for a number of reasons. Difficulties in only one area, such as the marital relationship, suggest that greater attention is needed for this issue. Some women may find the thought of a group overwhelming and are best treated individually (see Case 1). Furthermore, practical difficulties may prevent a mother joining the group at its scheduled time.

At other times, it may be that some preparatory therapeutic work needs to be done individually and this can remove obstacles to group treatment (see Case 1).

The 'Getting Ahead of Postnatal Depression' program can be adapted for individual treatment as described in Chapter 9. A one-to-one approach also provides an opportunity for a more comprehensive assessment of issues of concern as described in this chapter. In addition, the individual treatment described combines elements of basic counselling such as reflective listening, exploration of key issues and problem solving, which may suit health practitioners who have had no training in the application of cognitive-behavioural techniques. Since supportive counselling approaches have also been found helpful in PND some professionals may feel their skills are more suited to this treatment modality, which can be combined with selected sections from the main group program, e.g. increasing pleasant activities.

CASE 1
Case study highlighting reasons for individual treatment

Robyn is a 33-year-old woman who had longed for a child and was married to a supportive man who was both helpful and caring. She presented with her four-month-old baby Elisa who was breastfed, and had intermittently not been thriving. There was significant conflict between Robyn and her mother with whom she had a poor relationship. Her mother suggested bottle-feeding Elisa, but because of her anger towards her mother Robyn determined not to follow any of her advice.

On assessment, Robyn had a BDI score of 22, and an EPDS score of 15.

Robyn's difficulties with her mother had come to a crisis nine years previously, when she wanted to move out of home to her boyfriend's house. She was from a religious immigrant family and her mother refused her permission and insisted she no longer speak to her younger sister if she moved out. There was also a history of sexual abuse involving her father, and Robyn felt torn about leaving her sister with no support in the family home. In her efforts to show her independence she refused any offer of help, even when there was a reconciliation and support began to be offered some years later.

Robyn now insists on doing things her way even though she says she has lost all her confidence. At this stage it appears that her mother is offering appropriate help and being very supportive. Robyn wants her mother to help her but is unable to allow her to, as she feels she will have to do exactly what her mother says and lose her autonomy. Robyn has now extended her firmly held views that she must cope alone, by not accepting help from her husband, whom she says works too hard. In addition, Robyn will not leave the house as she breastfeeds all day, and will not feed in public. Elisa is not put down to sleep but will fall asleep on the breast or is settled by her father, which further exacerbates Robyn's guilt at not being a good mother.

On assessment it appeared that a CBT approach would be helpful to Robyn, to assist her in challenging her views on accessing help, increase her confidence and include her partner in therapy. Robyn, however, refused to leave the home because of her breastfeeding and would not come for treatment. The therapist decided first to offer home counselling around baby management issues to increase Robyn's ability to leave the house, by encouraging less frequent breastfeeding in the first instance and increasing her confidence in her decisions around childcare. In this way, Robyn was eventually able to join the group program.

Skills needed to run the 'Getting Ahead of Postnatal Depression' program

This book has been prepared for a wide range of health professionals, including counsellors, psychologists, psychiatrists, nurses, obstetricians, midwives and community health workers. The program, as described, is best suited to those with experience in group work, CBT and general counselling skills. Additional modules such as 'Including Infants' are facilitated by a knowledge of parenting and child development. However, ideas presented in this book can be adapted for a range of skill levels and applications. Basic support and listening, paired with an awareness of maternal, couple and infant issues, can form the basis of a successful front-line intervention approach and are outlined in Chapter 9. This was demonstrated by Holden, Sagovsky and Cox (1989) using a general counselling approach and this book offers further structured targets and techniques for intervention.

In addition, we believe that there are considerable advantages for groups to be led by co-facilitators. This allows one person to deliver the material and the other to be more focused on the group process or what is happening to individuals. At times, couple sessions are usefully run by having both a male and female facilitator. However, we have successfully run many groups with two female leaders. Many facilitators often wonder whether personal characteristics such as gender, being married or having children would make it easier to run this type of program. There are two related types of issue here: are the personal experiences of the therapist relevant to his or her effectiveness as a therapist; and is effectiveness as a therapist affected by the client's perceptions of the personal characteristics of the therapist? Certainly, life experience of what it is like to be a woman, the stresses of having a baby and the conflicts that arise in long-term relationships can be helpful. However, these personal experiences need to be kept separate and not imposed on the group participants, whose issues may be very different. It is our view that, as in any therapeutic relationship, it is not these types of prior experiences that are critical, but the ability to be empathic and 'see the world through the client's eyes', without being judgemental. Feeling that their concerns are understood and not minimised is an important need of postnatally depressed mothers. When a woman tells a facilitator of the agony of childbirth, and her ambivalence on seeing her newborn infant, it is essential that the clinician joins her in her horror of the experience. From this vantage point more skill-based therapy can follow.

With respect to client perceptions, therapists whose personal characteristics do not match their clients (e.g., male, no children, younger) are likely to have to work harder at establishing their credibility than therapists whose personal characteristics come closer to matching those of their clients. As pointed out above, this is not an insurmountable obstacle but, may at times require extra training such as initially sitting in on a group as a co-therapist, or developing knowledge in the areas of women's issues and child development. Suggested readings on PND, which include many case examples and personal accounts, are given at the end of this chapter. Readings on child development can be found in Chapter 8.

In the same way, while self-help groups run by previous sufferers of PND can provide a wonderful sense of being understood by 'someone who knows', this is considered an additional useful support to mothers with PND and separate from therapeutic work on underlying issues contributing to low self-esteem that can be carried out by a skilled professional.

SUMMARY

Major areas to be assessed, prior to inclusion in the group treatment program

1. Assess the risk of depression with a screening tool such as the Edinburgh Postnatal Depression Scale (administer between five and 26 weeks postpartum and use a cut-off of 12). Alternatively, measure severity of depression with the Beck Depression Inventory (see p. 51).
2. Assess the need by interview or formal testing to include infant work (see p. 60).
3. Eliminate suicidal risk and the need for medication (see p. 59).
4. Consider other measures of maternal functioning, such as anxiety (see p. 55).
5. Assess the impact on partners and the couple relationship (see p. 56).
6. Consider exclusion criteria or limiting factors (see p. 65).

SUGGESTED READING

Barnett, B. (1991). *Coping with postnatal depression.* Port Melbourne: Lothian.

Buist, A. (1996). *Psychiatric disorders associated with childbirth: A guide to management.* Sydney: McGraw-Hill.

Green, C. (1988). *Babies.* Brookvale: Simon & Schuster.

James, K. (1998). *The depressed mother: A practical guide to treatment and support.* London: Cassell.

McGrath, E., Keita, G. P., Strickland, B. R., & Russo, N. F. (1990). *Women and depression: Risk factors and treatment issues.* Washington, DC: American Psychological Association.

Pacific Post Partum Support Society (1997). *Postpartum depression and anxiety: A self-help guide for mothers.* Vancouver: Pacific Post Partura Support Society.

Roan, S. L. (1997). *Postpartum depression.* Holbrook: Adams Media Corporation.

Part II

Treating and Managing Postnatal Depression: The Getting Ahead of Postnatal Depression Group Program

INTRODUCTION

This section contains the group treatment program for postnatal depression (PND). The program is described in Chapters 4–6 and is divided into three phases. These have been grouped into:

- Behavioural interventions (Phase I).
- Cognitive interventions (Phase II).
- Relapse prevention and evaluation (Phase III).

The basis for the program has been described in Part I. The treatment framework was derived from the general depression literature, particularly the work of Lewinsohn et al. (1984), and from the cognitive-behavioural treatment for postpartum depression developed and adapted to take into account our model of PND. In summary, our model of PND incorporates vulnerability, precipitating, maintaining and exacerbating factors. The behavioural interventions are designed to target these areas and to be feasible in the context of a young infant and the consequent time demands. Precipitating factors such as a difficult childbirth are discussed. Vulnerability factors such as a difficult relationship with one's mother are dealt with by exploring parenting models learned in early childhood. Maintaining and exacerbating factors such as negative thinking and poor social support are addressed by challenging cognitions and problem solving. Part III offers optional additional modules that include fathers and infants or adapt the group program to individuals.

Selection and order of sessions

Prior to inclusion into the group, assessment of PND can occur as described in Chapter 3.

It is also useful to screen mothers prior to group allocation so that mothers are somewhat matched within the group in terms of age, number of children, level of depression, and socio-economic and marital status. A good rule of thumb is to ensure that there is never one of anything. For example, it is preferable not to include a teenage mother in a group of mothers aged between 30 and 40 years, unless you have at least one other teenage mother. Similarly, a single mother may have difficulty in a group with only partnered women.

These sessions are designed to be conducted in the order and format presented and have been found to be efficacious in the treatment of depression based on the order of material as presented. However, depending on the group process and the number of mothers in the group, some sessions may be expanded across two sessions, or incomplete material from one session may be completed at the beginning of the following session. This program may also be suitable for individual therapy, although the modules are presented for a group format.

In addition, manuals such as this need to be combined with non-specific therapeutic skills, such as responsiveness and listening and the appropriate use of clinical judgement.

Time and length

There are nine weekly sessions of one and a half hours duration in this program, followed by a booster session some weeks later.

Group leaders and group size

Experience in group process, cognitive-behavioural therapy and early parenting issues facilitates use of this material. A co-therapist is usually needed. Groups of six to eight mothers are ideal but, to buffer for drop-outs, you may wish to start with one or two more mothers in the group.

A fuller discussion of these issues and how to manage childcare is included in Chapter 10.

Chapter 4

PHASE I: BEHAVIOURAL INTERVENTIONS

SESSION 1: UNDERSTANDING AND MANAGING POSTNATAL DEPRESSION

NOTES FOR THE THERAPIST

❏   **Group process.**

This is a mother's first contact with a group of other mothers who are experiencing difficulties in the early months of parenting. The mothers in the group will be feeling very vulnerable and will be relying on you to assist them to feel comfortable within the group context. Help the mothers make meaningful links with other mothers, in terms of shared interests as well as difficulties.

In addition to the material you are presenting, it is important to pay attention to the group process and use this session to facilitate 'joining' and feeling part of the group. Mothers who experience alienation within a group context will be unlikely to return to further group sessions. The first session is crucial in ensuring that mothers feel that they are welcome, they are similar to other mothers within the group and they 'fit in'.

KEY

Italics: suggested wording for the clinician

Bold: section headings or overheads

Plain text: core instructions to clinicians

THERAPIST CHECKLIST FOR SESSION 1

Record-keeping suggestions

❏ **Tick off a checklist of the content of this session that you have completed (by the end of the session):**

✓ Group aims	☐
✓ Housekeeping, introducing presenters, ground rules	☐
✓ Activity 1: getting acquainted exercise	☐
✓ Group discussion: pregnancy, birth, now	☐
✓ What is postnatal depression (PND)?	☐
✓ Introduction to our approach to the treatment of PND: the biopsychosocial model of PND	☐
✓ Strategies for improving mood	☐
✓ Preview Session 2	☐
✓ Homework and finish on time	☐

Note: By keeping track of how much material has been covered in the session, decisions can be made about the preferred pace depending on the group composition and process. Extra sessions can then be planned or selected material deleted or incorporated into the next session.

❏ **Keep a summary of issues raised by <u>each</u> mother.**

Session 1 name: _____

Pregnancy	Birth	Experiences now

Notes: _____

_____

_____

INTRODUCTION TO SESSION 1

Group aims

❏   **It is important to recognise the effort mothers have made to get to your session.**

'Congratulations on coming to the group—it is always difficult to get started on something new.'

❑ **Orient the mothers to the aims, procedures and expectations of the group.**

'This group is an opportunity for you to meet other mothers who are experiencing postnatal depression and to share your experiences and your ideas on how to cope with depression.

In the course of the nine weeks we have together in the group, we hope to help you develop some useful skills and to identify some of the factors that influence your mood, to better deal with all the competing demands of motherhood.

As you learn these skills, we hope you will begin to develop a greater sense of control over your depression, and to experience more joy in your life and relationships, particularly your relationship with your baby.

There will be exercises for you to complete at home between sessions and we have tried to make sure that they do not require too much of your time. However, the homework exercises will be what is discussed and worked on in the following session.'

Housekeeping

❑ **Discuss issues such as transport difficulties, parking problems, babysitting problems, situation of tea/coffee facilities, toilets and so forth.**

'Did anyone have difficulties getting here today? How did you manage to organise a babysitter?'

❑ **Keep in mind separation issues.**

Many mothers may be experiencing their first separation from their baby to attend the group. Be aware of their feelings of uncertainty. Mothers may take some time to settle into the group while they are thinking about their baby and whether or not he/she will be all right for the next one and a half hours with a babysitter. Some groups may be able to arrange on-site childcare.

'Was everything okay when you left your baby? You must be feeling anxious if this is the first time that you have let someone else look after your baby for a while?'

Reassure mothers that you will finish on time so that the mothers will be able to return home on time, as they may have planned to return prior to their baby's next feed.

❑ **Mothers' sessions.**

Inform participants that there will be nine sessions of one and a half hours each week, on the same day and at the same time. It is important that the session times do not vary from week to week so that babysitting arrangements and other commitments are not disturbed. Furthermore, mothers will be more likely to remember the time of the session if it remains constant, thereby reducing the possibility of unnecessary absenteeism due to forgetting the appointment time.

❑   **Couple sessions.**

It is recommended that the additional module, including fathers, is offered (see Chapter 7). These three couple sessions are to be held at regular points within the group intervention program (i.e., around the third, sixth and ninth weeks). They are best held in the evenings so that fathers are able to attend and are not required to take time off work. Explain to mothers that their partners will be invited to three additional sessions of one and a half hours duration. If babysitting cannot be organised it is better to allow parents to bring their children along to the partner sessions. Reassure mothers that nappy changing, bottle/food-heating facilities and toys (age-appropriate) are provided at these sessions. Defer discussion about a possible date for the first partner session until the end of Session 1.

The aim of the couple sessions is to provide information about PND and facilitate problem solving about issues commonly struggled with by new parents. Most fathers find these sessions very helpful.

ABOUT THE PRESENTERS

Group leaders should introduce themselves. It is helpful if leaders model self-disclosure and group participation by volunteering information about themselves professionally. Introduce yourselves in your own way, using your own style. For example:

'My name is Louise and I have been facilitating groups for mothers experiencing postnatal depression for the past three years. I have worked extensively with families including those with infants with disabilities. I will be working with you every week in this group.'

GROUND RULES

Set the ground rules for the group.

'So that we all can benefit from these group sessions as much as possible and feel safe to disclose information about ourselves, it is important that we establish some common ground rules that can help us to respect, listen and support each other.'

Generally, these ground rules should include:

❑   **The importance of confidentiality.**

Personal details about others' lives may not be discussed outside of the group. Point out your professional responsibility to take action if the mother, her baby or others are thought to be at risk of harm, although you will discuss this with the mother concerned before taking any action.

❑   **Be supportive of one another.**

Participants should be encouraged to be supportive of one another by listening to each other and not being judgemental in their feedback or suggestions. This includes ensuring that all mothers are afforded the opportunity to talk and contribute to the group.

'It is important that everyone feels that they can talk openly in this group without fear of criticism or interruption. Some of you will feel comfortable talking in the group while others may take longer to feel free to express yourselves. I will be helping everyone to have equal time to speak. So, if you like to talk a lot, please don't be offended if we ask you to wind up so that someone else can be given an opportunity to speak. Alternatively, if you feel uncomfortable speaking up, we will gently encourage you, but you will not be compelled to talk if you do not wish to.'

❑   **Attend every session.**

Attending every session is essential for group cohesion and personal progress. Let mothers know that others miss them in the group if they are absent from a session.

'It is important that you attend every session so that you do not miss out on the discussions and skills taught in each session. The sessions build upon the previous weeks' learning and experiences, so you may feel left behind if you miss a session. Having said that, we are aware that there may be times when you have no alternative but to miss a session (e.g., personal illness) and we will endeavour to keep you up to date with the session you missed. We ask that you let us know if you are unable to attend. Sometimes it may seem like an impossible task to attend this group and we may be able to help you in some way to enable you to get here.'

❑   **Other suggestions.**

It is important that you check out how group members feel about these rules and if they have any misapprehensions or, indeed, any suggestions for further modifications or additions.

'Does anyone have any questions or anything to add? Are you comfortable with these rules?'

ACTIVITY 1: GETTING ACQUAINTED EXERCISE

This activity can be conducted in groups of two or three depending on the size of the group.

'Introduce yourself to the person next to you in a positive light. Tell her your name, the name and age of your baby and where he/she was born. Identify one activity that you love and one activity that you hate doing.'

Allow five minutes for this task. Then, request everyone to form a circle. Request each person to introduce another member to the group, in turn.

'Jane, you have just met Christine. Could you please introduce her to the others in our group?'

Highlight similarities between mothers' experiences and interests.

'That's interesting, Christine really enjoys gardening like Tracey and neither of you has managed to get into the garden recently.'

Finish the activity by summarising the main interests, likes and dislikes expressed by the group.

GROUP DISCUSSION: PREGNANCY, BIRTH, NOW

What women say:

'I hated being pregnant, I was sick all the time.'

'Everything had to be perfect before the baby was born.'

'I hated being out of control.'

'I feel guilty if I'm at home not working and guilty if I'm at the office.'

'Having no routine is hard when I prefer structure.'

'There are so many things to be done, I feel guilty if I have time for myself.'

'My mother had eight children and coped and I want to be that way too.'

'I know I expect too much of myself.'

'If I have an unsettled baby, it means I am a bad mother.'

'Our experiences of pregnancy, birth and early parenting are often nothing like we imagined or expected, even if this is not your first child. Every pregnancy, birth and baby is different and this can influence our early parenting experiences. We are interested in hearing your story. We will ask each of you, in turn, to tell us about your pregnancy, birth and early parenting experiences.'
'Is there anyone who would like to get us started?'

WHITEBOARD 1

Record participant responses under the following headings as they emerge in the discussion.

Pregnancy experiences	e.g.	**Planned/unplanned**
Birth experiences	e.g.	**Complications** **Loss of control around medical staff**
Experiences now	e.g.	**Other family members (siblings) adjusting** **Hard to listen to baby's cries**
Expectations	e.g.	**Baby would sleep more** **My partner would share all the tasks of parenting**

Group leaders should facilitate the discussion and summarise major issues on a whiteboard under the four headings. Begin contrasting participants' current experiences and feelings to their prior expectations of pregnancy, birth and motherhood. Tap into participants' attitudes and beliefs about motherhood,

'I spend so much time getting him settled, that when he is content, I have no opportunity to enjoy him because I'm so tired and there is so much to do.'

for example, myths about what constitutes the 'good' or 'perfect' mother. These examples and themes can be used in later sessions to illustrate main points. The information you provide to mothers will be more salient if you use examples, which they perceive as relevant and reflective of their current circumstances; e.g., women who have a caesarean section often feel disappointed because 'this is not how it was meant to be', and those who have had a traumatic birth may feel cheated out of a happy experience and distressed about how disempowered they felt.

WHAT IS POSTNATAL DEPRESSION?

'It sounds like there have been some difficulties for every one of you in adjusting to your current circumstances. Everyone has a unique set of circumstances although you share the common experience of postnatal depression. So what is postnatal depression? What are some of the signs that a woman might be experiencing postnatal depression?' (Show Overhead 1.)

OVERHEAD 1

Symptoms of postnatal depression

Symptoms of postnatal depression (PND) include:

- **Low mood, sadness**
- **Feelings of worthlessness**
- **Tearfulness**
- **Self-blame or guilt**
- **Anxiety**
- **Irritability or emotional highs and lows**
- **Lack of energy**
- **Lack of interest in activities**
- **Increased or decreased appetite**
- **Reduced concentration and decision-making ability**
- **Sleep disturbance (difficulty getting to sleep or staying asleep unrelated to the baby)**
- **Worries about own health**
- **Confused thought**
- **Slowed or fast speech**
- **Slowed movement or agitation**
- **Feelings of hopelessness**
- **Thoughts about death and suicide**

'Do you identify with any of these symptoms?

There is a lot of controversy among clinicians and researchers about PND and its causes. What are some of the things you have read or been told about PND?'

Briefly elicit some of the participants' own understandings and 'theories' of PND (including what they have read or been told by professionals and friends).

INTRODUCTION TO OUR APPROACH TO TREATMENT: THE BIOPSYCHOSOCIAL MODEL OF POSTNATAL DEPRESSION

'Although some researchers believe that hormonal and endocrine changes in the postnatal period might contribute to depression in women following childbirth, most professionals acknowledge that biological explanations are only part of the story of PND.' (Show Overhead 2.)

'The other part of the story is that the transition to motherhood involves adapting to huge physical, emotional and social changes. While some cultures have structures in place that are supportive of new parents, in our society many mothers are given little preparation for, or support in, their new roles.

It is not at all surprising, then, that many mothers have difficulty adjusting and that they feel, at times, overwhelmed by the demands and expectations of motherhood.

The mythologies in our culture about the "joys" of pregnancy and of "perfect" motherhood also have a powerful influence on us, often creating unrealistic expectations about pregnancy, birth and motherhood. Mothers who hold these expectations and beliefs often feel like "failures" when they experience problems coping, and depression is a common outcome.

Depression after childbirth affects 10–20% of women.'

OVERHEAD 2

The transition to motherhood

- Transition to motherhood involves adapting to physical, emotional and social changes and there is little support in our society for this.

  Therefore:

- Most mothers experience difficulties adjusting to their new role and may feel overwhelmed by the demands.
- Myths about motherhood can create unrealistic expectations.

  Therefore:

- Unrealistic expectations lead to feelings of failure when coping problems occur.

'We believe that depression occurs when there is an imbalance between positive events and negative events in your life. Depression is a signal that the balance has been upset, and the negatives outweigh the positives. It is also why on some days when something good happens you may feel better.

How we feel is one of the hardest things in the world to change. Has anyone had the experience of someone saying "Pull up your socks and get on with it"? Did it help? It didn't help you to feel better because our feelings are so closely linked with what we are doing and how we are thinking about the world. Without changing the way we think and what we are doing, it is very difficult to change how we feel.

The aim of these sessions will be to help you tip the balance in favour of positives. Next week we will be focusing on our behaviour and how it influences our mood. In future weeks we will focus on our thoughts and the huge impact they can have on our feelings.

Some of the strategies we will offer you over the next nine weeks will involve making some changes in the things you do (your behaviour) as well as making some changes to the way you think.' (Show Overhead 3.)

OVERHEAD 3

Postnatal depression: what can I do about it?

Some strategies for improving mood
- **Increasing self-nurturing activities.**
- **Increasing pleasant activities and social interactions, especially with baby and partner.**
- **Learning relaxation skills.**
- **Enhancing assertiveness and communication skills.**
- **Building support networks.**
- **Increasing positive thoughts.**
- **Decreasing negative thoughts.**
- **Challenging unhelpful thinking patterns.**

PREVIEW SESSION 2

In our next session, we will focus on pleasant activities and will explore tipping the balance of what you do in favour of positives. This will, of course, be discussed in the context of the tremendous demands made upon your time as mothers.

HOMEWORK

❑   **Set homework tasks.**

'To help you discover for yourself the extent to which your mood might be affected by what you do in your day, our first homework activity is to:

- *Record your activities for at least one day in the next week.*
  We will provide you with the **Weekly Plan** *(opposite) to record your activities, and be sure to include everything you do. Some things you probably take for granted (e.g., putting the nappies in the bucket to soak) but they are all important tasks which make up your day. Write them all down.*
- *Begin monitoring your daily mood using the* **Daily Mood Rating Form**.*

OVERHEAD 4

Weekly plan: my current activities

Day:	**e.g. Monday**		
Wake up till 8.00 a.m.			
8.00 a.m.–10.00 a.m.			
10.00 a.m.–12.00 p.m.			
12.00 p.m.–2.00 p.m.			
2.00 p.m.–4.00 p.m.			
4.00 p.m.–6.00 p.m.			
6.00 p.m.–8.00 p.m.			
8.00 p.m.–10.00 p.m.			
10.00 p.m. till go to bed			

Give examples of how these forms are to be completed, and suggestions of ways mothers might remember to do these tasks (e.g., put schedule on fridge; keep mood form on bedside table and complete at the end of the day).

Mothers are often not sure what to record as a mood score if they have had a good morning but the day deteriorates into a lousy afternoon and a tearful evening. Instruct mothers to record an average score, i.e., looking back on the whole day, how was it overall? How does it rate compared to other days? The blank column can be used for comments at this stage and later will be used for monitoring thoughts and activities in relation to mood.

❑ **Distribute booklets.**

It is suggested that mothers be given ring binders into which they can keep their handouts. Additional material may be inserted after subsequent sessions. Perhaps devise an attractive front page with the heading: 'Getting ahead of postnatal depression' and include some lighthearted material in recognition of the enormous demands of motherhood. An example is given over the page, and mothers may add and share some of their own favourite humorous material.

Include in the booklet any overheads you think may be helpful and definitely insert the handouts listed at the end of this session.

OVERHEAD 5

Daily mood rating form

Please rate your mood for this day (how good or bad you felt) using the nine-point scale shown. Remember, a low number signifies that you felt bad and a high number means that you felt good.

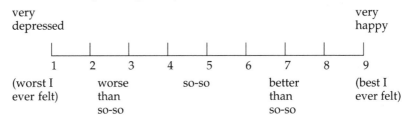

	very depressed							very happy
1	2	3	4	5	6	7	8	9
(worst I ever felt)	worse than so-so		so-so			better than so-so		(best I ever felt)

Mood score (**starting date --/--/--**)

Day	Date	Mood score	
1			
2			
3			
4			
5			
6			
7			
8			
9			
10			

POSITION AVAILABLE

Full time: long days, seven days a week, some time off in the evenings.

We are seeking a kind, considerate person for the challenging position of parent. Qualifications and experience are not necessary, although you will be fulfilling some or all of the tasks of the following trained people: chef, teacher, medical worker, social worker, psychologist, childcare worker, taxi driver, sales representative, manager, entertainer and nutritionist.

This is an honorary position.

Handout 1: (photocopy of Overhead 1) Symptoms of postnatal depression

Handout 2: (photocopy of Overhead 4) Weekly plan

Handout 3: (photocopy of Overhead 5) Daily mood rating form

It is also important that mothers are provided with a contact name and telephone number, so that they can contact the therapist/ alternative support, if need be, before the next session.

❑   **Finish on time.**

Be respectful of mothers' time commitments. ALWAYS start and finish ON TIME. Mothers will become anxious, especially if due home for breastfeeding, if you go overtime. Furthermore, you set the expectation for the following weeks that sessions always <u>start on time</u>.

SESSION 2: PLEASANT ACTIVITIES—HOW CAN I FIND THE TIME?

NOTES FOR THE THERAPIST

It is important to strike a balance between reviewing the past week with mothers and getting through the session content. The introduction and review of the previous week normally take about 15 minutes. While the review is focused on cognitive-behavioural therapy homework, an important aspect is allowing mothers to debrief about their week in general and feeling their issues are 'heard' in such a structured program.

Check that babysitting arrangements, parking, etc. have all gone smoothly. Offer to assist mothers after the session if they are having any difficulties that are best sorted out later. If the difficulty can be sorted out quickly, it is a great opportunity to demonstrate problem-solving skills within the group context.

It is important to review homework that you have set the previous week, otherwise you may find that participants do not complete homework tasks between sessions and thereby restrict the benefits they can achieve through this program. Allow mothers to disclose details about their week, for example events that impacted on the way they felt or made the week an unusual or typical one. Deal with any issues that may have prevented a mother from completing the homework task. At this stage, it is of great benefit if the group can begin to offer suggestions to other mothers for resolution of simple problems but this should be allowed to develop as the group becomes more cohesive.

Allow mothers to freely discuss their feelings and give feedback about the previous session. This is the time when any misapprehension or misconceptions about your program can be cleared up most effectively. It is also an opportunity for mothers to share a common experience and to continue to join with the group.

In this session, the therapist may also need to deal with the guilt a lot of women feel about increasing type B (pleasurable) activities. Typical comments include: 'I shouldn't be taking time for myself in the middle of the day', 'It's not that I don't have time—it's that I feel guilty', 'I need to justify what I've done at the end of the day'. It is also a good opportunity to start challenging 'shoulds' as a precursor to later cognitive work. For example, you might say 'Who says you should?' 'Where is it written?', 'Why should you?', 'Who says that a full-time parenting role should run according to the same routine or clock as a nine-to-five job?'

THERAPIST CHECKLIST FOR SESSION 2

❑ **Tick off a checklist of the content of this session that you have completed (by the end of the session):**

✓ Introduction to Session 2 ☐
✓ Psycho-education: the biopsychosocial model of PND (continued) ☐
✓ Pleasant activities and depression ☐
✓ Activity 2: pleasant activities and mood ☐
✓ Group discussion ☐
✓ Psycho-education: increasing pleasant activities ☐
✓ Preview Session 3 and homework ☐

Record-keeping suggestions

❑ **Keep a summary of issues raised by each mother.**

Session 2 name: _____

Homework issues	Pleasant activities— issues arising	Other

Notes: _____
_____
_____

INTRODUCTION TO SESSION 2

❑   **Housekeeping issues.**

'Did anyone have any difficulties getting here today?'

❑   **Review previous session.**

Briefly review reactions to the material you covered in the previous session.

'How did you feel after last week's session? Are there any feelings or issues that we should discuss briefly now before we move on?'

❑   **Review of homework.**

'What did you find out about your mood from the mood-monitoring task?' OR *'What were your highest and lowest daily mood ratings for the week? What were you doing on those days?'*

PSYCHO-EDUCATION: THE BIOPSYCHOSOCIAL MODEL OF POSTNATAL DEPRESSION (CONTINUED)

'Last week we met one another and began to talk about our pregnancy, birth and early parenting experiences. We also started to look at what postnatal depression is and ideas about what we will do to get on top of it. We learned that people need a favourable balance between interactions with positive outcomes and those with negative or neutral outcomes. Depression is a signal that this balance has been upset. Today we are going to discuss the importance of pleasant activities in our lives, to increase the positives, and an approach to treatment called cognitive-behavioural therapy of depression.'

❑   **Depression is related to how we deal with problems in living.**

It is important to convey the message that mothers can have control over their own mood.

'We take the view that depression is not simply a biological illness, or a heavy cloud that "descends upon us" (although depression is often experienced like this). Rather, we would like to propose to you the idea that depression is related to how we deal with problems in living.'

❑   **Our feelings, behaviour and thoughts are interrelated.**

Our feelings don't just happen. They are a result of our thoughts and/or behaviour. It is not easy to illustrate this point, so you will need to think of some examples prior to facilitating the session. Using examples generated by the group in Session 1 is a good idea.

'Our feelings (our mood or emotional states) are directly connected to the way we behave and also to the way we think. For example, if someone

rushes to get into a car park space that was rightly yours at the super-market, you may think "That selfish person. How dare she push in? That's not fair."

You may feel angry as a result of your thoughts about the unfair nature of the world. However, if the person who gets out of the car is a friend of yours and was having a joke with you, you may think "Oh, typical Irene. She's just trying to be funny and it's actually really nice to see her." As a result of your new thoughts, you may feel calm and happy. You may even laugh.

In the same way, our behaviour can sometimes affect the way we feel. For example, if you stay at home because it's "easier", you may start to resent the fact that you cannot get out of the house and start to feel lonely, isolated and depressed.

Research and clinical experience have shown us that successful treatment of postnatal depression requires a multi-pronged approach that equips women with the skills to make positive changes in a <u>range</u> of different areas of their lives.'

OVERHEAD 6

The relationship between behaviour, thoughts and feelings

Feelings, e.g. low mood

BEHAVIOUR   Thinking

e.g. events associated with   *e.g. negative, self-*
unpleasant outcomes.   *deprecating thoughts.*

Behaviour, thoughts and feelings all influence each other.

Use Overhead 6 to explain how depressive feelings arise from events associated with unpleasant outcomes and also how depressive feelings can result from self-deprecating self-talk and negative evaluations of events. Use appropriate examples, preferably from the mothers' own experiences.

Pleasant activities and depression

❑   **Introduce the focus of this session.**

'This week we will focus on how depressed feelings are directly connected to the way we <u>behave</u>. Specifically, we will look at ways of increasing pleasant activities.'

❑   **Relationship between feelings and behaviour.**

Demonstrate in more detail the functional relationship between be-haviours and mood by introducing the concept of a downward spiral into depression. Explain the depressive spiral to the mothers using Overhead 7. Use examples from the mothers' experiences to illustrate the concept.

'One mother described her depression as like being in a dark hole where the ladder has been taken away. The depressive spiral is a way of explaining how we can end up in that dark hole. The focus of these sessions is to learn skills that will put the ladder back and allow you to reverse the depressive spiral and get out of depression.'

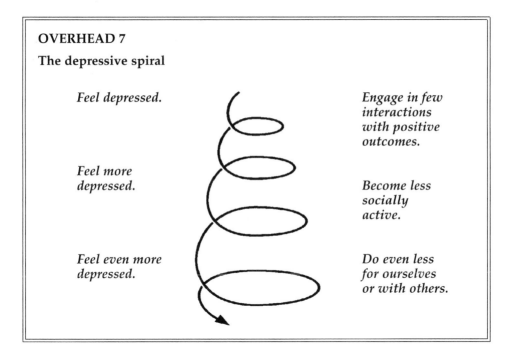

OVERHEAD 7

The depressive spiral

Feel depressed.   *Engage in few interactions with positive outcomes.*

Feel more depressed.   *Become less socially active.*

Feel even more depressed.   *Do even less for ourselves or with others.*

Check if participants recognise that inactivity leads to worsening of depressive thoughts and feelings, and that increasing activity is a powerful starting point for working their way back up the depres-sive spiral.

Elicit other relevant examples from the group to help establish the utility of the model, focusing on mothering activities/experiences/themes.

❑   **Satisfaction and happiness are feelings we experience when we are engaged in pleasant activities with positive outcomes.**

This point is not difficult to introduce. Most mothers will be able to think of a situation in which they experienced happiness and satisfaction. It is helpful if you draw mothers' attention to everyday events that may have had a positive outcome after which they experienced feelings of satisfaction.

'For example, you may experience satisfaction when your baby lies in your arms after a feed and smiles up at you. At the beginning, your baby is hungry and you are there simply to feed, but once your baby is full he/she is able to take the time to interact with you. For some of you, this may be a pleasant experience with a positive outcome.'

As we know that people who suffer from depression filter out positive events (i.e., selectively attend to negative events), it is important that you draw attention to everyday events that have positive outcomes.

❏   **Depression is often experienced when the numbers of pleasant activities we are engaged in each day are outweighed by activities with negative or neutral outcomes. (This is often the experience of mothers.)**

'Pleasant activities play an important role in relation to mood. If the number of pleasant activities falls below a critical level, your mood is likely to become increasingly depressed.'

Illustrate this point with Activity 2.

ACTIVITY 2: PLEASANT ACTIVITIES AND MOOD

Introduce this activity as one that is done alone but will be discussed afterwards in the group. This activity builds on the homework tasks the mothers completed during the week (Weekly Plan).
     Explain the difference between type A and type B activities.

'The activities that occur during a typical day can be conceptualised as two main types. Type A activities are either neutral or unpleasant. They are obligatory activities that we do not enjoy, e.g. washing dirty nappies. Type B activities are the activities that we really enjoy. They are the activities we would choose to do whether obligatory or not, e.g. lying in the warm sunshine talking to a friend. A suggested mnemonic for Type A = "awfuls" and for Type B = "beautifuls". This facilitates ease of discussion in subsequent sessions because it is less wordy.

     *From your **Daily Mood Rating Form** and **Weekly Plan** count the number of activities you did each day that were type A and the number of activities that were type B. Note your corresponding daily mood scores.'*

If some mothers did not complete the homework task, ask them to list all the activities that they did the day before and to record a mood rating for that day.

GROUP DISCUSSION

Group discussion about this activity can be facilitated with the following types of questions:

'What sort of balance do you have between A's and B's?' 'What relationship do you think there is between "awfuls" (type A) and "beautifuls" (type B) activities and your mood?'

'Are there too many type A activities on one day? If so, is it necessary to do all these activities in one day? Could you transfer any of these type A activities to another day?'

'Does there seem to be a critical number of pleasant activities associated with an acceptable mood score for you?' (Quantity.)

'Are there particular activities that seem to have a powerful impact on your mood? (Quality.) For example, for many mothers, social interaction is a potent type B activity and they notice that, when they are at home alone with baby all day, their mood is lower because they feel isolated.'

Discuss quantity versus quality issues. Guide discussion about patterns, especially relationship between activities (number and type) and mood ratings. Note similarities, differences, antecedents and consequences. Deal with any problems experienced with recording.

PSYCHO-EDUCATION: INCREASING PLEASANT ACTIVITIES

❏   **Activities that improve mood.**

'Some pleasant activities are particularly important in your quest to beat depression. As a mother you will benefit from activities that are pleasant for yourself as an individual, as well as between yourself and your baby, and you and your partner.' (Discuss Overhead 8.)

OVERHEAD 8

Activities that help to improve mood

- **Pleasant social interactions**
  e.g. honest and open conversation with a friend, cuddles or a warm bath with baby or partner.

- **Experiences that make us feel competent**
  e.g. successfully learning to do something new; being able to settle our own baby when no one else has been able to.

- **Activities that are incompatible with feeling depressed**
  e.g. sleeping well; laughing; being relaxed.

❏   **Planning to increase pleasant activities.**

Briefly introduce the rationale for this group activity.

'The main goal of this week's session is to start thinking about increasing the number of pleasant activities you engage in each day.

We will start in small steps and together look at a list of possible pleasant activities for you to choose from and integrate into your weekly planner.' (Overhead 9.)

OVERHEAD 9

Pleasant activity ideas

1. Being in the country
2. Meeting someone new of the same sex
3. Planning trips or vacations
4. Reading stories, novels, non-fiction poems, or plays
5. Driving skilfully
6. Breathing clean air
7. Saying something clearly
8. Laughing
9. Being with animals
10. Having a frank and open conversation
11. Going to a party
12. Playing a musical instrument
13. Wearing informal clothes
14. Being with friends
15. Making food or crafts to sell or give away
16. Gardening, landscaping, or doing yard work
17. Wearing new clothes
18. Sitting in the sun
19. Going to a fair, carnival, circus, zoo or amusement park
20. Planning or organising something
21. Having a lively talk
22. Having friends come to visit
23. Getting massages or back rubs
24. Getting letters, cards, or notes
25. Going on outings (to the park, a picnic, a barbecue, etc.)
26. Talking about my children
27. Seeing beautiful scenery
28. Eating good meals
29. Going to a museum or exhibit
30. Doing a job well
31. Having spare time
32. Going to a health club, sauna bath, etc.
33. Learning to do something new
34. Being with my parents
35. Talking on the telephone
36. Kicking leaves, sand, pebbles, etc.
37. Going to the movies
38. Kissing
39. Being praised by people I admire
40. Washing my hair
41. Going to a restaurant
42. Being invited out
43. Reminiscing, talking about old times
44. Writing in a diary
45. Reading the newspaper
46. Doing housework or laundry; cleaning things
47. Listening to music
48. Being with someone I love
49. Shopping
50. Watching people
51. Being with happy people
52. Having people show interest in what I have said
53. Expressing my love to someone
54. Having coffee, tea, a Coke, etc., with friends
55. Being complimented or told I have done well
56. Being told I am loved
57. Seeing old friends
58. Other ideas . . .

Adapted from Lewinsohn, Munoz, Youngren and Zeiss (1992).

'One of the difficulties that you are probably experiencing at the moment is finding enough time to look after yourself. You have all done very well to have managed to find the one and a half hours today and to get here. You

are probably wondering how you are going to fit more pleasant activities into your week.

Some problems with pleasant activities that can happen are due to:

1. *Pressure from activities (type A) that are not pleasant but must be performed (e.g., washing loads of nappies).*
2. *Poor choice of activity (e.g., staying at home rather than going to a friend's house.*
3. *Something happens to remove the availability of a pleasant event (e.g., the demands of a baby may prevent you from going out with friends as often as you did before).*
4. *Anxiety and discomfort interfering with enjoyment (e.g., being anxious about always doing the right thing).'*

Encourage mothers to start right away on planning to increase their rate of pleasant activities. Remind participants of the 'Position Available' advertisement in their booklet and that they are being expected to do an enormous task. Use humour if possible. For example, who says mothering is a 24-hour-a-day job? Our research proves it takes a mere 23 hours and 44 minutes per day. For example, in the first hour upon waking you may find yourself facing the following tasks:

- Hear baby crying and leap out of bed to attend immediately, as recommended by major parenting manuals: two minutes.
- Breastfeed baby, as recommended by Nursing Mothers' Association: 30 minutes.
- Instruct partner to iron own work clothes, as recommended by self-help manual, Intelligent Women, Shocking Choices: one minute.
- Make children's beds, as deemed 'the least you could do' by Nanna: 10 minutes.
- Hang out washing, vacuum, reassure partner about his receding hairline, wash breakfast dishes, and perform morning exercises as recommended by Life Be In It: 40 minutes.

My goal for the next week is to engage in _____
pleasant activities. If I meet this target I will reward myself by

_____

_____

(Choose a reward, such as <u>people</u> you would like to see more of; <u>things</u> or <u>food</u> you would like and can afford; <u>activities</u> you would like to do more of; <u>places</u> you would like to get to.)

Signed: _____

Dated: _____

In view of the many demands, suggest that mothers aim to increase their rate of pleasant activities during the coming week by only a small amount and ask them in the session to complete the contract on the previous page on a piece of paper and sign it.

PREVIEW SESSION 3

'Next week we will be introducing the skill of relaxation as a treatment for anxiety. Having a new baby is usually accompanied by constant demands and may be coupled with other stresses in your lives. Tension will hinder our efforts to overcome depression and interfere with our ability to plan and enjoy pleasant events. So it is important that we look at ways to reduce our tension levels and allow us to continue our battle to beat depression.'

PARTNERS' SESSION

Inform participants that the first partners' session will be held next week. Set the date, time and venue. Allow mothers time to discuss their plans for inviting their partner. Some mothers may, as yet, not have told their partner that they were attending a PND group. Assist mothers to find a way to invite their partner to the partners' session.

HOMEWORK

❑   **Set homework tasks.**

- *'Continue to monitor your daily mood using the **Daily Mood Rating Form'**.*
- *'Starting today, we also want you to keep note of your tension levels. Turn to Handout 3 and insert in the extra column the heading: (0–9) **Relaxation Monitoring**. Each day, give your mood a rating and also your tension/relaxation score. 9 = most relaxed you have ever been; 0 = most tense you have ever been.'*

Give mothers an example of how they would score the **Relaxation Monitoring** section.

'During the next session we will learn to apply relaxation procedures to see if we can lower our average tension level.'

- *Use the **Pleasant Activity Ideas** to help you decide on some pleasant activities. Think of the problems we have discussed that often get in the way of actually carrying out the ideas, and try and pre-empt these.'* (Note to therapist: if you were unable to begin this process in the session, set the contract for increasing pleasant events in a subsequent session.)
- *'You might like to try and use the **Weekly Plan** to help you record and plan your increase in pleasant activities for the week.'*

❑   **Distribute handouts.**

             Handout 2: Weekly Plan (as distributed in Session 1)

             Handout 3: Daily Mood Rating Form (as in Session 1)

             Handout 4: (photocopy of Overhead 9) Pleasant Activity Ideas

❑   **Finish on time.**

SESSION 3: RELAXATION ON THE RUN

NOTES FOR THE THERAPIST

Relaxation training is the focus of this session. Therefore it is useful to set the scene by having subdued lighting, essential oil burners lit as well as mats/cushions available for the relaxation training component. Setting the room up prior to the session ensures that you do not waste time during the session pulling out mats, etc. Mothers often enjoy coming into the room with a soft ambience, and having the first part of the session on mats while they review what they did last week.

It is important to deal specifically with the feelings of guilt some women experience when they allow themselves to do something just for themselves. If this issue is not addressed, mothers may find relaxation practice at home difficult to allow themselves to do.

This is a long session and it is often helpful to allow half an hour each for consolidating pleasant activities from last week, actual relaxation, and discussion of high stress times/homework.

THERAPIST CHECKLIST FOR SESSION 3

Record-keeping suggestions

❑ **Tick off a checklist of the content of this session that you have completed (by the end of the session):**

✓ Introduction to Session 3   ☐
✓ Activity 3: consolidating pleasant activities   ☐
✓ Psycho-education: relaxation training   ☐
✓ Activity 4: Jacobson's progressive deep muscle relaxation
   procedure   ☐
✓ Group discussion   ☐
✓ Psycho-education: relaxing on the run   ☐
✓ Group discussion   ☐
✓ Activity 5: relaxation plan for high tension times   ☐
✓ Preview Session 4   ☐
✓ Homework   ☐

❑ **Keep a summary of issues raised by <u>each</u> mother.**

Session 3 name: _____

Homework issues	High tension situations/*body* cues	Other

Notes: _____

_____

_____

INTRODUCTION TO SESSION 3

❑   **Housekeeping issues.**

'Did anyone have any difficulties getting here today?'

❑   **Review of homework.**

'What did you find out about your mood from the mood-monitoring task? What effect did balancing type A "awfuls" and type B "beautifuls" activities have on your mood? Has anyone had problems with engaging in pleasant activities or recording daily mood?'

Brainstorm creative solutions with the group. Discuss ways that pleasant activities and rewards can be incorporated into daily life with a baby. Encourage mothers to be realistic. A long leisurely bath may not be possible, but a bath with the baby using candlelight or essential oils might be. Discuss ways that partners could be requested to assist with the increase of type B 'beautifuls' activities. Fathers often welcome the suggestion of more pleasant activities and need some guidance from their partners about how this may be made possible (e.g., being ready to take the baby out of the bath and get her dressed while mum soaks for that extra five minutes).

❑   **Review previous session.**

Briefly review the material you covered in the previous session.

'Last week we talked about the relationship between depression and pleasant activities. How did you feel after last week's session? Are there any feelings or issues that we should discuss briefly now before we move on?'

Some mothers may already notice some change in their mood whereas others need to talk about how hard their week was. Allow some time for this, and also reassure them that it may take time to discover which strategies will be best for them to help improve their mood.

ACTIVITY 3: CONSOLIDATING PLEASANT ACTIVITIES IN OUR LIVES

'How did everyone go with the Pleasant Activities Ideas list? Did you get any new ideas that you might like to try or did it remind you of activities that you used to enjoy in the past? What are some of the ideas that are realistic at this point in your life and which you could plan to incorporate into your week?'

WHITEBOARD 2

Pleasant activities with:

Self
Partner
Baby

Encourage the generation of pleasant activity ideas to include spouse and baby. Assist mothers to generate pleasant activities for themselves alone, with their partner and with their baby. Write the ideas generated by the group on the whiteboard using the three columns (self, partner, and baby).

'Why not insert ideas from the whiteboard into your Weekly Plan right now?'

PSYCHO-EDUCATION: RELAXATION TRAINING

'Anxiety and tension get in the way of overcoming our depression because tension interferes with enjoying things. It is an obstacle to getting the most out of the pleasant activities we are building into our lives. Tension causes tiredness (in addition to what we already experience with a baby), irritability and often physical problems like headaches. It is another behaviour that we can try and change, which will impact on our mood.

Of course, a certain level of anxiety, tension and drive is necessary in order to motivate us to carry out our daily tasks and responsibilities. However, it is when this level of anxiety and tension gets too high that it interferes with our ability to cope.

Today we will teach you a technique for learning to relax. People are different with regard to how quickly they can learn to relax. Relaxation is a skill that requires repetition and will improve over time (with practice!).'

ACTIVITY 4: JACOBSON'S PROGRESSIVE DEEP MUSCLE RELAXATION (30 MINUTES)

❑ **Clear the room of chairs and sit in a circle on the floor.**

❑ **Let mothers have a toilet break if required.**

❑ **Ascertain if any mothers have tried relaxation procedures before.**

Ask mothers if they have had experience with relaxation before. If it was not favourable you may need to emphasise the range of available techniques and the need for experimentation to find the right one.

If a mother has participated in the Jacobson relaxation procedure previously, ask her to explain what the procedure involves to the rest of the group. Remember that these mothers have only seen one another twice before and may be anxious about taking the risk of trying something new in the group. If no one has tried relaxation previously, describe the procedure very briefly.

❑ **Ask mothers to make themselves comfortable.**

It is best to provide cushions or mats on the floor and to have some blankets available as some people feel a little cold when they lie still or may feel less vulnerable if they are under a blanket.

❑ **Use relaxation patter provided.**

Do not rush. Take your time and speak in a gentle, soothing voice.

RELAXATION PATTER

Relaxation of arms (time: 4–5 minutes)

Settle back as comfortably as you can. Let yourself relax to the best of your ability . . . Now, as you relax like that, clench your right fist, just clench your fist tighter and tighter, and study the tension as you do so. Keep it clenched and feel the tension in your right fist, hand, and forearm . . . and now relax. Let the fingers of your right hand become loose, and observe the contrast in the way it feels . . . Now, let yourself go and try to become more relaxed all over . . . Now repeat the same procedure with your left fist. Clench your left fist while the rest of your body relaxes; clench that fist tighter and feel the tension . . . and now relax. Again enjoy the contrast . . . Continue relaxing like that for a while . . . Clench both fists tighter and tighter, both fists tense, forearms tense, study the sensation . . . and relax; straighten out your fingers and feel that relaxation. Continue relaxing your hands and forearms more and more . . . Now bend your elbows and tense your biceps, tense them harder and study the tension feelings . . . All right, straighten out your arms, let them relax and feel that difference again. Let the relaxation develop . . . Each time, pay close attention to your feelings when you tense up and when you relax. Now straighten your arms, straighten them so that you feel the most tension in the triceps along the back of your arms; stretch your arms and feel that tension . . . and now relax. Get your arms back into a comfortable position. Let the relaxation proceed on its own. Your arms should feel comfortably heavy as you

Relaxation patter continued

allow them to relax . . . Now let's concentrate on pure relaxation in the arms without any tension. Make your arms comfortable and let them relax further and further. Continue relaxing your arms even further. Even when your arms seem fully relaxed, try to go that extra bit further; try to achieve deeper and deeper levels of relaxation.

Relaxation of facial area with neck, shoulders and upper back (time: 4–5 minutes)

Let all your muscles go loose and heavy. Just settle back quietly and comfortably. Wrinkle up your forehead now; wrinkle it tighter . . . And now stop wrinkling your forehead, relax and smooth it out. Picture your entire forehead and scalp becoming smoother as the relaxation increases . . . Now close your eyes tighter and tighter . . . feel the tension . . . and relax your eyes. Keep your eyes closed, gently, comfortably and notice the relaxation . . . Now clench your jaws, bite your teeth together, study the tension throughout the jaws . . . Relax your jaws now. Let your lips part slightly . . . Appreciate the relaxation . . . Note the contrast between tension and relaxation. Feel the relaxation all over your face, all over your forehead and scalp, eyes, jaws, lips, tongue and throat. The relaxation progresses further and further . . . Now attend to your neck muscles. Press your head back as far as it can go and feel the tension in your neck; roll it to the right and feel the tension shift; now roll it to the left. Straighten your neck and bring your head forward, pressing your chin against your chest. Let your head return to a comfortable position, and study the relaxation. Let the relaxation develop . . . Now shrug your shoulders. Hold the tension . . . Drop your shoulders and feel the relaxation. Your neck and shoulders should feel relaxed . . . Let the relaxation spread deep into your shoulders, right into your back muscles; relax your neck and throat and your jaws and other facial areas as the pure relaxation takes over and grows deeper . . . deeper . . . deeper.

Relaxation of chest, stomach and lower back (time: 4–5 minutes)

Relax your entire body to the best of your ability. Feel that comfortable heaviness that accompanies relaxation. Breathe easily and freely in and out. Notice how the relaxation increases as you exhale . . . as you breathe out just feel that relaxation . . . Now breathe in and fill your lungs; inhale deeply and hold your breath. Study the tension . . . Now exhale, let the walls of your chest grow loose and push the air out automatically. Continue relaxing and breathe freely and gently. Feel the relaxation and enjoy it . . . With the rest of your body as relaxed as possible, fill your lungs again. Breathe in deeply and hold it again . . . That's fine, breathe out and appreciate the relief. Just breathe normally. Continue relaxing your chest and let the relaxation spread to your back, shoulders, neck and arms. Merely let go . . . and enjoy the relaxation. Now let's pay attention to your abdominal muscles, your stomach area. Tighten your stomach muscles, make your abdomen hard. Notice the tension . . . and relax. Let the muscles loosen and notice the contrast . . . Notice the general well-being that comes with relaxing your stomach . . . Continue breathing normally and easily and feel that gently massaging action all over your chest and stomach . . . Let the tension dissolve as the relaxation grows deeper. Each time you breathe out, notice the rhythmic relaxation both in your lungs and in your stomach. Notice how your chest and stomach relax more and more . . . Try and let go of all contractions anywhere in your body . . . Now direct your attention to your lower back. Arch your back, make your lower back quite hollow, and feel the tension along your spine . . . and settle down comfortably again relaxing the lower back . . . Now arch your back and feel the tension as you do so. Try to keep the rest of your

Relaxation patter continued

body as relaxed as possible. Try to localise the tension throughout your lower back area. Relax once more, relaxing further and further. Relax your lower back, relax your upper back, spread the relaxation to your stomach, chest, shoulders, arms and facial area. These parts keep relaxing further and further and further and ever deeper.

Relaxation of hips, thighs and calves followed by complete body relaxation (time 4–5 minutes)

Let go of all the tension and relax . . . Now flex your buttocks and thighs. Flex your thighs by pressing down your heels as hard as you can . . . Relax and note the difference . . . Allow the relaxation to proceed on its own . . . Press your feet and toes downwards, away from your face, so that your calf muscles become tense. Study that tension . . . Relax your feet and calves . . . This time, bend your feet towards your face so that you feel tension along your shins. Bring your toes right up . . . relax again. Keep relaxing for a while . . . Now let yourself relax further all over. Relax your feet, ankles, calves and shins, knees, thighs, buttocks and hips. Feel the heaviness of your lower body as you relax still further . . . Now spread the relaxation to your stomach, waist and lower back. Let go more and more. Feel that relaxation all over. Let it proceed to your upper back, chest, shoulders and arms and right to the tips of your fingers. Keep relaxing more and more deeply. Make sure that there is no tension in your throat; relax your neck and your jaws and all your facial muscles. Keep relaxing your whole body like that for a while. Let yourself relax . . .

Now you can become twice as relaxed as you are by merely taking in a really deep breath and exhaling slowly. With your eyes closed so that you can become less aware of objects and movements around you and thus prevent any surface tensions from developing, breathe in deeply and feel yourself becoming heavier. Take in a long, deep breath and let it out very slowly . . . Feel how heavy and relaxed you have become.

In a state of perfect relaxation you should feel unwilling to move a single muscle in your body. Think about the effort that would be required to raise your right arm. As you think about raising your right arm, see if you can notice any tension that might have crept into your shoulder and arm . . . Now you decide not to lift the arm but to continue relaxing. Observe the relief and the disappearance of the tension.

Just carry on relaxing like that. When you wish to get up, count backwards from four to one. You should then feel refreshed, wide awake and calm.

Adapted from Lewinsohn, Antonuccio, Steinmetz and Teri (1984).

GROUP DISCUSSION

Discuss differences in feelings from the beginning of class and after the relaxation procedure. Discuss ways that the relaxation procedure could be incorporated into the week in order to practice the skill and obtain the full benefit. If a mother did not find it helpful, try not to focus on negatives but how to make it a more worthwhile experience.

PSYCHO-EDUCATION: RELAXING ON THE RUN

'Obviously one cannot always spend half an hour doing a relaxation session, like the one we have just done, every time one feels tense (especially as *a mother). Relaxation skills are particularly useful when they can be used before or during a stressful activity or part of the day. Let us talk about relaxation techniques that we can use quickly in specific problem situations.*

Some examples are:

- *Taking a deep breath and focusing on your breathing for a few minutes.*
- *Repeating your special relaxation word/phrase to yourself, e.g. "calm", "relax" or "you can get through this. It is going to be alright."*
- *Picturing yourself relaxing in your favourite place (mini mental holiday!).*
- *Scanning our bodies for tension and relaxing the muscles that feel the most tense.*
- *Putting a picture of a relaxing place (e.g., beach) on the fridge door, change mat or bathroom mirror.*
- *Write coping statements on cue cards and carry in a purse/put on the fridge door.*

These are just some of the portable relaxation techniques that we could easily incorporate into our daily lives. We are going to expand on these ideas and discuss when the high tension times of the day are and what techniques would be most useful to try at those times to reduce our level of anxiety.'

GROUP DISCUSSION

❑   **Generate ideas for portable relaxation techniques.**

Use the whiteboard to write suggestions. Add other techniques to the list that the group has generated by the end of the discussion.

WHITEBOARD 3

Portable stress busters

- Have a shower, bath
- Deep breathing, focusing attention on breath rather than on thoughts
- Yoga techniques
- Ring a friend, a health nurse, etc.
- Self statements:
    'I'm calm and relaxed'
    'I can do this'
    'this will pass'
- Treat yourself to coffee, wine, chocolate cake (but not in excess!)
- Mini 'mental holiday'—think of favourite holiday destination
- Releasing tension in muscles
- Three deep breaths
- Reminding myself *'I'm not alone'* (as a mum)
- Crying as a release
- Contact with friends
- Comparing self with others in a worse position

❑   **List common high tension times/situations on the white board.**

It is helpful to normalise the experience of tension around dinner time as an extremely common one for families with young children.

'A common time that is difficult for mothers is around dinner time. Just when you need to prepare and serve dinner, the baby launches into crying inconsolably and wants to be held and attended to more than at any other time of the day. This is perfectly normal, although extremely stressful.'

WHITEBOARD 4

High stress times

- 5–7 p.m. dinner time
- Getting ready to go out
- Getting baby to sleep
- New phases of baby's development, e.g. teething, sleeping changes
- Other people interfering with baby's routine
- Tantrums in the supermarket
- Long trips in the car with a screaming baby
- Tensions with partner or an absent partner
- Baby crying
- Other examples . . .

❑   **List the early warning signs of tension.**

Be sure that mothers identify their own cues of anxiety, including bodily sensations. Also, explore thoughts during times of high tension.

WHITEBOARD 5

Recognising early warnings signs of tension

(List mothers' examples on the whiteboard and add any of the following as examples.)

- Shakes
- Back pain
- Slamming doors
- Raised voice, sarcasm
- Rejection of help
- Clenched jaw, palpitations
- Holding breath
- Noises seem louder
- Distressed thoughts, e.g. *'I can't stand this'*, *'I'm not coping'*, *'I should stop this now'*
- Muddled mind
- Lose confidence in own competence
- Indecision
- Overwhelmed

Start to introduce the notion that both our behaviour and thoughts have a powerful impact on our mood. Ensure that the link between thoughts and feelings is clearly illustrated.

This is important preliminary work to the cognitive sessions to follow in Phase II.

ACTIVITY 5: RELAXATION PLAN FOR HIGH TENSION TIMES

❑   **Putting it all together.**

'The main idea is to try to schedule relaxation practice before high tension levels occur or to use portable relaxation techniques ("relaxing on the run") while those situations are actually taking place.'

❑   **Divide group into pairs.**

*'Spend five minutes discussing what the high tension times are for you and how you might develop a plan for dealing with your own tension times/ situations. Jot down your ideas on your **Weekly Plan** in your booklet.'*

Suggest that mothers anticipate how to overcome obstacles to implementing this plan.

'What would stop you from putting your plan into action, and how can you deal with these obstacles?'

Move between the pairs, guiding their discussions and assisting them to problem solve or plan for high tension times of the day.

PREVIEW SESSION 4

'Next week we will be discussing assertiveness skills. When we become parents we are suddenly placed into numerous situations that we have never been in before. Sometimes these situations are difficult to deal with. We will be looking at ways to deal more effectively with conflict, differences in opinion or unsolicited advice regarding parenting.'

PARTNERS' SESSION

Remind mothers that a partners' session will be held during this week. Confirm date, time and venue. Ensure mothers are aware that they may bring their baby and other children with them.

HOMEWORK

❑   **Set homework tasks.**

- *'Practice the **relaxation procedure** one to three times during the week.'*
- *'Continue to monitor your daily mood using the **Daily Mood Rating Form**.'*

- *'Keep a note of your tension levels using the blank column on the **Daily Mood Rating Form**. Note any changes in your tension levels after relaxation practice. You can also make notes of portable stress busters that work for you as a helpful reminder.'*
- *'Continue trying to balance type A and type B activities. Remember to include pleasant activities by yourself as well as with your baby and partner. Review the **Weekly Plan** to look at ideas you jotted down in this session for dealing with tension times and also as a reminder to keep up pleasant activities and relaxation training.'*

❑   **Distribute handouts and tape.**

Handout 2: Weekly Plan

Handout 3: Daily Mood Rating Form

Relaxation tape

Give mothers a relaxation tape with the 'relaxation patter' recorded. It is preferable that you record your own tape with your voice, as a stranger's voice or accent may be distracting when mothers attempt to practice relaxation using the tape.

❑   **Finish on time.**

SESSION 4: ASSERTIVENESS AND SELF-ESTEEM—TELLING OTHERS WHAT I THINK AND HOW I FEEL

NOTES FOR THE THERAPIST

This session involves the use of role-play. Individuals vary with respect to how comfortable they feel with role-plays in front of their peers. Some people actively choose not to attend groups that may involve this type of activity. So, although it is an extremely effective teaching tool, it is important to keep in mind that it is not for everyone. Consequently, the role-play in this session involves volunteers only. This session on assertiveness follows the session on relaxation and relies on greater group cohesion, interaction and risk taking. It is likely that by now mothers will feel comfortable with one another and will be prepared to try something new in the group context.

Assertiveness skills are often confused with aggression. Therapists need to be extremely familiar with the differences between assertiveness, aggression and passivity. The explanations used in this session are a good start, but for those unfamiliar with this concept reading other texts on assertiveness is recommended before taking this session.

This session also begins to explore self-esteem and behavioural interventions for improving difficulties in this area. Further cognitive work on this issue occurs in Phase II.

THERAPIST CHECKLIST FOR SESSION 4

Record-keeping suggestions

❑ **Tick off a checklist of the content of this session that you have completed (by the end of the session):**

✓ Introduction to Session 4   ☐
✓ Psycho-education: assertiveness skills   ☐
✓ Group discussion: Aggressive/passive/assertive styles   ☐
✓ Activity 6: Assertiveness training   ☐
✓ Psycho-education: self-esteem   ☐
✓ Activity 7: love letter   ☐
✓ Preview Session 5   ☐
✓ Homework   ☐

❑ **Keep a summary of issues raised by <u>each</u> mother.**

Session 4 name: _____

Assertiveness issues	Self-esteem	Other

Notes: _____

_____

_____

INTRODUCTION TO SESSION 4

❑   **Housekeeping issues.**

'Did anyone have any difficulties getting here today?'

At this point in the program it is unusual if difficulties arise which have not previously been solved. Therefore, it is an opportunity to reinforce a mother's ability to organise her baby and other children (if applicable) to find time for herself.

'You have all done so well to get everything working smoothly so that you can attend these sessions. You probably thought it would never happen, and it has.'

❏   **Review of homework.**

'What did you find out about your mood from the mood-monitoring task? What effect did the relaxation practice and portable techniques have on your ability to manage high tension times of the day?'

❏   **Review previous session.**

Briefly review the material you covered in the previous session.

'Last week we tried progressive muscular relaxation and discussed relaxation techniques which could be used "on the run" during periods of high tension. How did you feel after last week's session? Are there any feelings or issues that we should discuss briefly now before we move on?'

PSYCHO-EDUCATION: ASSERTIVENESS SKILLS

'Many activities which impact on our mood involve social interactions with other people. Social skilfulness is the ability to interact with other people in such a way that the experience is a positive one. There is no right way. We all have a slightly different style of obtaining positive responses from others. For example, one person may complain about her hairstyle in order to receive positive comments from others that she looks great. Another person, on the other hand, may compliment someone on her hairstyle and receive a positive response in reply. The outcome for both women is positive but they have elicited that positive outcome in different ways.

We have decided to focus specifically on assertiveness skills relevant to motherhood which often places us in situations that we have never been in before. For example, no one has ever told you how to behave on a bus until you have a baby with you. Suddenly, someone tells you that your baby is hungry and that you should feed it. Assertiveness is the ability to express your thoughts and feelings openly (e.g., complaints and affections). We believe assertiveness is particularly relevant to new mothers for a number of reasons.'

❏   **Unsolicited advice.**

'Everyone, it seems, has had some contact with babies at some stage in their life and many are all too willing to give you advice about how you should be doing things, or worse, how you should be feeling. Being able to express your thoughts and feelings openly will mean that you will be better able to request assistance you would like and decline advice/assistance when it is not asked for.'

❏   **Relationships.**

'Assertiveness and open communication can facilitate the development of close, warm relationships. Other people are able to understand your

feelings and needs better if you are able to communicate them in an asser-tive way.'

❑   **Conflict.**

'Assertiveness can help to prevent conflict. Aggression is usually met with aggression, and if a concern is not expressed it is generally ignored. Asser-tiveness allows the thoughts and feelings of everyone involved to be ex-pressed and respected.'

GROUP DISCUSSION: AGGRESSIVE/PASSIVE/ASSERTIVE STYLES

Handout 5 describes communication styles. (See Handout attached at end of this session.)

Guide mothers through the handout. Depending on your thera-peutic style, you may choose to summarise the handout on the whiteboard in a more interactive way or photocopy the figure and guide mothers through it.

WHITEBOARD 6

Various communication styles

	Passive	Assertive	Aggressive
Verbal			
View of self			
Others' view of self			
Non-verbal			

Illustrate communication styles summarised on the whiteboard with examples.

It is important to inform mothers that although assertiveness usu-ally leads to more positive outcomes, there are a number of factors that may prevent us being assertive all the time.

'Tiredness or high anxiety may impact on our ability to be assertive, especially if this does not come naturally. At these times we may slip into our more usual way of interacting with others. It is also true that everyone oscillates between the different forms of communication style depending on the situation at hand. An assertive person will not always be assertive as it is important to consider the cost of being passive or aggressive in a given situation. If you are aggressive in the butcher's shop because your order is not ready on time, you are able to choose whether to go to that particular store again. If you are aggressive with your husband when he is on his way out the door to go to work in the morning, the cost when he returns at night will be high and it is not simple to choose never to speak to him again! The same is true with being passive. It is of relatively little importance if the butcher serves someone before you; however, it is a major problem if your

family continually disregards your views, feelings and rights because you are not assertive. In other words, having the skills to be assertive does not mean you will always choose to use them. It is okay to be passive if that is a conscious choice.'

ACTIVITY 6: ASSERTIVENESS TRAINING

❑ **Ascertain what constitutes an assertive response.**

Expand the assertiveness material on the whiteboard to record the group suggestions about what constitutes an assertive response. Cover all aspects of an assertive response: posture, tone of voice, content, eye contact, and positive regard for self and others.

❑ **Develop an example that will be used for the role-play.**

Ask mothers for examples of situations they have encountered recently that they would like to learn how to handle more assertively. Choose an example that would be easy to role-play and is representative of a common situation that all the mothers may be able to identify with.

Examples:

Your girlfriend rings up to ask if she can stay the weekend. You feel obliged but have already got too much planned for this weekend.

Your mother-in-law insists on putting honey on your baby's dummy.

❑ **Formulate an assertive response.**

Use the group to formulate an assertive response to the nominated situation. Write the content of the response on the whiteboard. Keep the list of elements of an assertive response next to the written response.

❑ **Model an assertive response.**

Role-play the situation that the group has decided to work on. If you are a sole practitioner then request a mother to do the role-play with you. Remember that <u>you</u> need to play the role of the person trying to be assertive because you are modelling how to be assertive.

❑ **Participants role-play an assertive response.**

Ask for two volunteers from the group to participate in the role-play. It is less complicated if the role-plays are for two people only. Mothers role-play exactly the same situation that you have just demonstrated.

❑   **Provide feedback.**

The group can act as coach to the mother who is trying to be assertive (e.g., *'Perhaps you could let her know that you feel worthless when
she walks off without listening to you'*). However, it is important that
other mothers do not interrupt the role-play but offer their suggestions at the end. Encourage mothers to provide feedback using the
three to one rule (three positive comments to one corrective suggestion). For example: *'It was great that you maintained eye contact with
her even when she became aggressive and I also liked the way you kept
sitting calmly in your chair and maintained a reasonable tone of voice. It
may have been helpful to let her know how you were feeling.'*

❑   **Repeat role-play.**

Ask the mothers who have received the feedback to role-play the
same situation again while trying to incorporate the suggestions
they received.

❑   **Provide positive feedback.**

Provide the mothers who have participated in the role-play with
encouragement for their efforts.

PSYCHO-EDUCATION: SELF-ESTEEM

*'Being assertive has a lot to do with how you feel about yourself (your self-
esteem). You are not likely to ask for what you need or to tell others how
you feel if you don't think you're worth it.*

*Self-esteem is the value you attach to your own identity. It is your
prediction of how successful what you do or say is going to be, even before
you have acted. Lowered self-esteem and feelings of worthlessness are part
of the experience of depression. Often, people who suffer from depression do
not act assertively or do few activities that will improve their mood (e.g.,
telephone a friend). Part of the reason is that they are convinced that the
behaviour will not be good enough or they are not worth it (e.g., "I can't
even have dinner cooked on time" or "I'm not worth taking out for
dinner").*

*Self-esteem is developed from our very first social interactions as a baby
through to our current experiences. Although it is very difficult to change
the value that you now place on your self-worth, one way to start to
improve your self-esteem is to notice the skills/talents/attributes that you
do value about yourself. Remind yourself frequently of these.*

*Sometimes self-esteem and feelings of worthlessness are further lowered
by the experience of depression, and women forget the more positive view of
themselves that they had when they were not depressed.'*

ACTIVITY 7: LOVE LETTER

Introduce this self-esteem activity as a homework exercise.

'For homework we would like you to write a love letter to yourself. This is not going to be an easy task because we are not used to saying "I love you" to ourselves. You can write the letter any way you like but make sure you tell yourself about the attributes, etc., that you admire. Put your name and address on the envelope and bring it with you next week. No one will read the letter but it will be sent back to you by mail after the group has ended.'

Allow mothers to discuss their fears and concerns about this exercise. Brainstorm ways that might make the task easier for them. Deal with possible blocks to doing this task. Self-esteem is often a major problem for mothers experiencing PND, so it is crucial that the importance of recognising their own self-worth is made clear. Self-esteem is often one of the factors that predicts early recovery from PND.

Make sure to put a note in your diary to remind you to send all letters received back at the end of the group!

PREVIEW SESSION 5

'Next week we will be focusing on how we were parented. We will discuss our own expectations of motherhood and ourselves as mothers in terms of the kinds of experiences in our families that might have contributed to the development of these. Often conflict between partners arises after the birth of a baby because of differences in opinion regarding child rearing and the respective roles of a mother and father. Conflict with other family members can also occur for this same reason.'

HOMEWORK

❑   **Set homework tasks.**

- *'Continue to monitor your daily mood using the **Daily Mood Rating Form**'.*
- *'Remember to write a **love letter** to yourself and put it in a stamped self-addressed envelope. Bring it to the next session.'*
- *'**Use the Assertion Monitoring Form** to make a list of problem situations you would like to handle in a more assertive way (rate your assertiveness doing this task on a scale of 1–9; where 1 equals not assertive at all, 100% passive or 100% aggressive and 9 equals 100% assertive (task was not at all difficult)).*

*Pick one problem situation that you have recorded on your **Assertion Monitoring Form** and try an assertive response this week. Pick a situation that you will most likely be able to be assertive in. This probably means that you will need to practice being assertive with the butcher (low risk) before you start with your partner (high risk).'*

OVERHEAD 10

Assertion Monitoring Form (9 = 100% assertive)

Situation	Asserting myself 1–9
1.	
2.	
3.	
4.	
5.	

❑   **Distribute handouts.**

            Handout 3: Daily Mood Rating Form

            Handout 5: Communication Styles

            **Handout 6: (photocopy of Overhead 10) Assertion Monitoring
            Form**

❑   **Finish on time.**

HANDOUT 5: COMMUNICATION STYLES

	Passive	Assertive	Indirect	Aggressive
Basic attitude	I'm not okay	I'm okay and you're okay	You're not okay but I'll let you think you are	You're not okay
Philosophy	Take care of others' rights and needs without regard to one's own	Take care of own and others' rights and needs	Take care of own rights and needs while letting others think you care about their rights/needs	Own rights and needs are met at the expense of others
Behaviour	Retreating Giving up Resenting situation	Confrontation Honesty Negotiation	Manipulating Sarcasm	Nasty comments Put-downs Screaming
Response from others	Attention Sympathy	Respect Acceptance Comfort	Suspicion Confusion Feels manipulated	Fear Hurt Humiliation Defensiveness Aggression

Chapter 5

PHASE II: COGNITIVE INTERVENTIONS

NOTES FOR THE THERAPIST

Mothers will find that <u>not every</u> technique that is taught in this program will be useful for them. Each mother will develop her own package of skills that she finds effective in improving her mood. This package of skills will not necessarily be the same for other mothers in the group. It is important to emphasise this point so mothers do not develop unrealistic expectations of themselves. It is normal for mothers to return to the group having found that the new technique that was taught in the previous week's session was unhelpful.

Sessions 5–8 cover the cognitive intervention component of this program. The triad of thoughts, feelings and behaviours provides the underlying structure. Behavioural interventions covered so far may have resulted in some mothers discovering that changing their behaviour improves their mood; but at other times, this is not sufficient to make a difference. The role of cognition is central in depression and this component begins with a description of the critical link between cognition and feeling. Cognitive concepts and techniques are often more complex to teach than behavioural strategies, and it will be useful to advise mothers that they will need to practice the skills taught now and after the program ends to master these new skills.

The focus of this session is on parenting styles and expectations. Emphasise that we view various parenting techniques/styles/preferences as <u>different</u> rather than right or wrong. Major battles are often fought when one parent thinks that his/her partner's opinion is wrong rather than different. Parenting techniques, particularly in the mothercraft area, have changed considerably over the years. For example, given our current knowledge about sudden infant death syndrome, we now consider we are doing our best by placing babies on their backs to sleep, rather than on their stomachs. By contrast, mothers in the past considered that they were doing the best for their babies by placing them on their stomachs. Thus, it is important that the therapist emphasises that parenting practices may be different; the task of this session is to understand how we individually developed these attitudes and to begin to challenge those that are unhelpful to us.

THERAPIST CHECKLIST FOR SESSION 5

Record-keeping suggestions

❑ **Tick off a checklist of the content of this session that you have completed (by the end of the session):**

✓ Introduction to Session 5 ☐
✓ Psycho-education: family of origin ☐
✓ Activity 8: my family of origin ☐
✓ Psycho-education: challenging unhelpful thoughts and
   unrealistic expectations of parenting ☐
✓ Preview Session 6 ☐
✓ Homework ☐

❑ **Keep a summary of issues raised by <u>each</u> mother.**

Session 5 name: _____

Expectations of motherhood	Feelings toward baby	Other

Notes: _____

_____

_____

INTRODUCTION TO SESSION 5

❑   **Housekeeping issues.**

'Did anyone have any difficulties getting here today?'

Deal with any housekeeping issues as quickly as possible.

❑   **Review of homework.**

'What did you find out about your mood from the mood-monitoring task? Did you manage to try out an assertive response? What about the love letter?'

Collect love letters to be sent back when the group ends.

❑   **Review previous session.**

Briefly review the material you covered in the previous session.

'Last week we looked at the difference between aggression, assertiveness and passivity, and we role-played an assertive response. We focused on the impact that expressing our thoughts and feelings openly may have on our lives, relationships and mood. We also explored the impact of our self-esteem on our ability to be assertive. Are there any feelings or issues that we should discuss briefly now before we move on?'

PSYCHO-EDUCATION: FAMILY OF ORIGIN

'Couple relationships change after the birth of a child. Differences in opinions regarding child rearing may begin to cause conflict. You may never have discussed whether or not to use a dummy, for example, prior to having your first child. But, often your partner has strong views about child rearing, just as you have. Unfortunately (or fortunately), you have both experienced different styles of parenting from your own parents. Expectations may come from role models from the past. Often conflict with family members (e.g., your mother-in-law) occurs when there are babies/ children in the family for this very same reason. In addition, the role of each partner is no longer just that of "partner", but, of father or mother.

Thus, our expectations of ourselves as mothers are shaped by our own experiences of being parented and subsequent experiences. Some of these expectations may be unrealistic and unhelpful in our bid to beat depression. We will discuss these issues further as we go along today. However, first we will spend some time looking at your history of being parented.'

ACTIVITY 8: MY FAMILY OF ORIGIN

❑   **Introduction.**

'We will not have enough time to get a family history from each of you today so we will start by drawing one family tree as an example. Would anyone like to offer their family for us to draw a family tree and discuss parenting styles?'

❑   **Draw a genogram on the whiteboard.**

Draw the family genogram from the maternal and paternal grand-parents' generation through to the mother and her partner and their child/ren (see example Whiteboard 7).

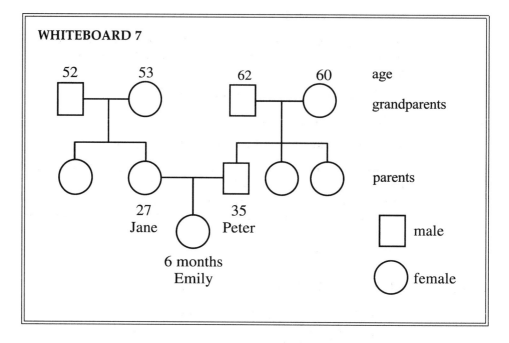

WHITEBOARD 7

You may have time to discuss two to three mothers' genograms. If time permits, other women could draw their own genograms on paper after the demonstration so they feel more included in the activity.

❑   **Discussion.**

Initially, direct the questions to the mother who has offered her family as an example.

'What were your parents like when you were growing up? Do you know what sort of parenting your partner had? What conflicts can you see have arisen between you and your partner as a consequence of your different parenting styles?'

Then open the questioning up to involve the group in a discussion of these questions in relation to their own parenting experience.

'Are your parenting views very different from those of your parents?'
'What do you think has influenced your views?'
'What do you think has influenced your partner's views?'
'Have you ever stated that you will never say something that your mother/ father used to say and then suddenly heard yourself saying the same thing?'
'Do your models of parenting influence your beliefs of yourself as a mother and of how infants should behave?'

Divide the discussion on the whiteboard into belief about self as mother, and your infant, and link these with parenting models.

PSYCHO-EDUCATION: CHALLENGING UNHELPFUL THOUGHTS AND UNREALISTIC EXPECTATIONS OF PARENTING

❑   **Introduction.**

'It is important to consider the expectations of ourselves as mothers that we have developed through our own experience. Our thoughts, like our behaviour, play an important role in the determination of our mood. That is true for you and your partner. If, for example, your expectation is that a mother should be there for her baby 100% of the time and your partner's expectation is that parents should have some time alone without the baby, then you are likely to experience conflict. Neither of these expectations is necessarily right or wrong. However, some expectations are unhelpful or unrealistic.'

Use the Thoughts, Feelings, Behaviour triangle shown in Session 2 (Overhead 6) to illustrate the link.

❑   **Example.**

Request examples from the group about times when they feel most depressed about parenting. Write these situations on the whiteboard as suggested below.

WHITEBOARD 8

Example

Situation	**Colicky baby does not stop crying regardless of what I do.**
Thoughts	*'I'm no good at this. My mother would think I am hopeless. I do not know what to do. This is terrible.'*
Feelings	**Hopeless**
	Helpless
	Depressed
	Worthless
	Angry

This exercise sets the scene for further work on cognition and its role in depression that will be developed in later sessions. Keep it simple, but make the distinctions between thoughts and feelings clear. Mothers will often identify feelings more easily than thoughts so the exercise could be pursued in that order (situation, feelings, thoughts), although it must be pointed out that thoughts and feelings are interrelated.

❑   **Group discussion.**

Assist the group to challenge unrealistic thoughts about parenting or motherhood, going through one example after another.

'Is this thinking helpful? Is it based on facts? Does it allow us to parent more effectively or is it getting in the way? Is this thinking associated with feelings of worthlessness or depression? If so, it is probably an unhelpful or unrealistic thought. How could we challenge this thought and convert it to something more realistic?'

Use Whiteboard 9 to show how the thoughts outlined previously could be converted to something more realistic.

WHITEBOARD 9

Challenging unhelpful thoughts

Situation	Colicky baby crying regardless of mother's actions.
Thoughts	*'I have tried everything that any competent mother would have tried but my baby is still in pain. I will have to rock her until she settles. Perhaps I will make a cup of tea so I can have a drink while I do this.'*
Feeling	**In control**
	Useful
	Hopeful
	Relaxed

Discuss current social support within the context of managing difficult infants. It is not unusual for mothers to restrict their social activity unnecessarily or refuse assistance offered, by holding the belief that *'Mother knows best. No one can care for my baby well enough.'* It is important to begin to challenge these expectations as unhelpful, if the mother is refusing to allow herself to do anything without her baby (e.g., grocery shopping).

❑ **Family of origin and societal influences.**

Explore where some of the reactions to a crying baby might come from. Is it related to parental models or generally held beliefs in our community? For example, a woman might feel that her mother was unable to comfort her and has developed a belief that she too cannot soothe an infant. It may even make her angry, just as her mother was with her, when she was crying. These feelings may then be further compounded by accepting unhelpful cultural myths such as 'mothering is easy and natural'.

❑ **Feelings toward my baby.**

'Our feelings towards our baby are sometimes shaped by our own experience of being mothered. I am wondering, how you are feeling towards your baby at this point in time? Have your feelings towards your baby changed since the birth?'

Guide the discussion towards how mothers feel about their baby. Challenge the belief that 'attachment to the infant should be easy and free of negative feelings'. If it seems appropriate, this could be done using the whiteboard with the same headings as used in the previous discussion.

It is sometimes useful to describe attachment to the infant as the development of a close friendship rather than a love at first sight experience. It can be useful to offer suggestions to mothers regarding age-appropriate mother–infant interaction activities, if mothers are interested in improving their relationship with their infant. For severe difficulties, the optional additional module 'Including Infants' described in Section III can be added to the main group program. Be respectful and ask the group for their own suggestions first.

PREVIEW SESSION 6

'Next week we will be looking more closely at our thoughts and the impact that they have on our mood. Our thoughts play an important role in our battle to beat depression although more often than not our automatic thoughts go unnoticed.'

PARTNERS' SESSION

Remind participants that the next partner session is due next week. Confirm the day, date and time.

HOMEWORK

❑   **Set homework tasks.**

- *'Continue to monitor your daily mood using the **Daily Mood Rating Form**'.*
- *'Talk to your partner about what it was like growing up with his parents.'*
- *'Start to tune into your thinking. What are your thoughts/expectations of yourself as a mother? What are your thoughts/expectations of your partner as a father?'*

❑   **Distribute handouts.**

Handout 3: Daily Mood Rating Form

❑   **Finish on time.**

SESSION 6: MY INTERNAL DIALOGUE: THE MISSING LINK

NOTES FOR THE THERAPIST

This session presents the link between cognition and mood in a more structured way than in the previous session. Mothers will typically find that their recovery from postnatal depression (PND) is a 'rocky road'. There will be times when a mother may feel that she is losing the battle and it is important to validate her concerns but also to accept this experience as normal. This session aims to provide the 'missing link' and to emphasise the power of self-statements (cognitions) as a tool to influence mood.

THERAPIST CHECKLIST FOR SESSION 6

Record-keeping suggestions

❑ **Tick off a checklist of the content of this session that you have completed (by the end of the session):**

✓ Introduction to Session 6 ☐
✓ Psycho-education: self-instruction techniques are the missing link ☐
✓ Group discussion: difficulty following through with tasks ☐
✓ Activity 9: self-instruction ☐
✓ Psycho-education: using self-instruction ☐
✓ Small group exercise ☐
✓ Preparation for termination ☐
✓ Partners' session ☐
✓ Preview Session 7 ☐
✓ Homework ☐

❑ **Keep a summary of issues raised by each mother.**

Session 6 name: _____

Difficulties following through with tasks/ self-instruction	Termination issues	Important cognitions and other issues

Notes: _____

_____

_____

INTRODUCTION TO SESSION 6

❑   **Housekeeping issues.**

'Did anyone have any difficulties getting here today?'

Resolve any issues quickly.

❑   **Review of homework.**

'What did you find out about your mood from the mood-monitoring task? Did you manage to find time to talk to your partner about what his parents were like when he was growing up? Hopefully, you also found time to think about your expectations of yourself as a mother as well as your expectations of your partner as a father. We will be considering this further today.'

❑   **Review previous session.**

Briefly review the material you covered in the previous session.

'Last week we looked at the influence of our own experiences of childhood on the way that we choose to parent. We also considered the impact of unhelpful or unrealistic expectations of ourselves as parents that we may have as a result of our own experiences and perceptions of societal views. We demonstrated the interrelatedness between thoughts and feelings, and began to challenge some of the unhelpful thoughts that we might have about mothering that get in the way of being able to do our task effectively, and threaten our self-esteem. Are there any feelings or issues that remain from last week that we need to address today?'

Family of origin issues are usually very salient for mothers in the immediate puerperium. It is important to recognise the impact that last week's session may have had on a mother's insight into her own situation and possibly on her relationship with her own parents. Address these issues sensitively. However, try not to spend too long on this section unless you are able to add an extra session to have a general discussion of family of origin issues. Some issues can be addressed individually with mothers after the session or by further individual consultation if required.

PSYCHO-EDUCATION: SELF-INSTRUCTION TECHNIQUES ARE THE MISSING LINK

'We have started to look at the impact of our thoughts on our mood. Generally, we are unaware of a great deal of the internal dialogue that occurs inside our heads. Yet, our thoughts have a powerful influence over our feelings. Our thoughts can be our greatest enemy or our greatest ally. Today we are going to consider one way that our thoughts can assist us in our battle to get on top of depression.'

Often people know what they could or need to do, and they know it would be effective if they did it, but somehow they seem unable to actually follow through.

'Self-instruction techniques (i.e., talking to yourself) can be "the missing link" that helps you to actually do the things that you know you need to do to beat depression.'

GROUP DISCUSSION: DIFFICULTY FOLLOWING THROUGH WITH TASKS

The aim of this exercise is to make overt the difficulties that some mothers may be having actually following through with the tasks that are set for them each week between sessions. It is also important that it is demonstrated that thoughts can either hinder or help.

'Have you found problems remembering to increase pleasant activities; be assertive; write that love letter, etc.? Are there some techniques that you have found particularly useful but do not use? What do you think is getting in the way?'

Allow mothers to generate their thoughts and feelings. Write the issues that they raise on the whiteboard in the format suggested below:

WHITEBOARD 10

Situation
Thoughts
Feelings
Consequences

Demonstrate the link between negative or irrational thoughts and consequent feelings and outcomes.

ACTIVITY 9: SELF-INSTRUCTION

Provide Overheads 11 and 12 as handouts **'High-expectations Helen'** and **'Realistic Rachel'**.
    Read the overheads with the group (or convert to handouts) and then facilitate a group discussion about Realistic Rachel and High-expectations Helen.

'Does anyone see themselves in Helen or Rachel? What sort of self-statements are you saying to yourself when you find you are down or having difficulty following through with tasks you know will assist you in your battle against depression? What would be more helpful alternative self-statements?'

OVERHEAD 11

High-expectations Helen

Like many other depressed mothers, Helen felt that she had never accomplished much. Yet, by any objective measure, Helen was clearly a competent person. The trouble was that Helen expected to be one of the best in a number of areas, and because she placed her goals at the highest possible levels she couldn't always reach them. On top of that, she took for granted her accomplishments but was regularly miserable when she failed to do as well as she expected she should do.

Talking to Helen about lowering her expectations was futile. She had an answer to every argument we could bring up. So it was decided to have her work on herself. And, as usual, she did a good job:

'I know that having high goals helps me to do my best and that I don't know if a goal is truly unrealistic until I try, but the fact that I am periodically disappointed enough to feel seriously depressed may indicate that I am setting self-expectations too high. Maybe instead of always comparing my goals to other mothers', I could just notice the things that I have done and the goals I have achieved.'

Adapted from Lewinsohn, Munoz, Youngren and Zeiss (1992).

OVERHEAD 12

Realistic Rachel

After learning strategies for breaking the depressive cycle, Rachel felt that they were unrealistic.

'If things are lousy, why should I do something pleasant, be sociable or think positive thoughts? That wouldn't be honest or realistic. That would be just putting on an act, faking it. I'd just feel more depressed about lying to myself.'

Rachel had difficulty using challenging techniques to control her depression, as she needed to convince herself to use them. She finally latched on to the distinction between helpful and unhelpful alternatives and began to instruct herself to look for the helpful ones.

A helpful alternative is one that helps you 'put yourself together'. Rachel found this distinction useful and 'realistic' when she remembered that a song she liked could make her feel really happy at times and really sad at other times. Because it was the same song, the happiness or sadness must be coming from her, not directly from the song.

Rachel's self-instructions began like this:

'I know I am feeling depressed, and I know that when people feel depressed their reality is distorted in negative directions. Because that's the case with me, I need to balance things by emphasising constructive interpretations of my view of reality. What is the best way I could interpret what is happening right now?'

Adapted from Lewinsohn, Munoz, Youngren and Zeiss (1992).

Write the responses on the whiteboard using the following suggestion:

WHITEBOARD 11

Unhelpful self-talk
Outcome
Helpful self-talk
Possible outcomes

Demonstrate the impact of positive, realistic self-talk, such as 'I'm not the only one'; 'Help is available'.

PSYCHO-EDUCATION: USING SELF-INSTRUCTION

'Self-instruction sounds easy but changing our automatic thoughts takes some practice. Those unhelpful automatic thoughts can sometimes sneak in without us being aware of them and cause havoc with our good intentions to beat depression. It is important to remember that you may lose the occasional battle but you have not "lost the war". It is helpful to think of times when your negative or unhelpful thoughts get in the way as lapses rather than a relapse into depression. In this way you are able to be realistic about your achievements so far and be motivated to continue challenging your unhelpful thoughts.

When you use self-statements it is important to be specific about what you want to achieve (e.g., lower my level of anxiety at dinner time to a score of three or four rather than nine or ten). Decide how you plan to accomplish your goal (e.g., practice relaxation techniques three times per week and use my relaxation on the run strategies from 5.00 p.m. through to the end of dinner time). Then, it is important to write down your self-statements and practice using them (e.g., "I have high levels of anxiety at dinner time which I allow to spill over into the rest of my evening. If I use the techniques that I know are effective for me to lower my level of anxiety, I will be able to enjoy my evening more"). It is useful to imagine yourself using the self-statement you have prepared before you are actually in the problem situation/time of the day. Modify your self-statements if necessary and don't forget to reward yourself for achieving your goal. You have done well to combat your negative automatic thoughts!'

Small group exercise

❑ **Divide the group.**

Divide the large group into small groups of three or four.

❑ **Volunteer a problem.**

Request one person in each group to volunteer a specific difficulty she is having in relation to using the techniques she has so far found useful in combating depression.

❑   **Problem solve.**

Ask each group to:
- Formulate a specific goal in relation to the problem presented;
- Brainstorm different ways that the goal could be accomplished and write down possible self-statements.

❑   **Choose an alternative.**

Request the individual group member who volunteered the problem to choose possible alternatives to solve the problem from those solutions generated by her group, and also to choose possible self-statements from those suggested.

❑   **Write down self-statements.**

The individual mother is asked to write down her possible self-statements on cards to take home.

❑   **Repeat the exercise.**

Repeat the entire exercise again, requesting another group member to volunteer a specific difficulty. Continue until all group members have had a turn.

Throughout this activity it is important for the therapist to move between the groups and assist mothers to complete the task.

PREPARATION FOR TERMINATION

At this stage, mothers will be quite attached to the group and actively involved in the group process. The issue of termination cannot be left to the last session. Begin today by gently raising the mothers' awareness that these group sessions will start drawing to a close. In this way you will facilitate further consideration of support networks, other than the group, that mothers can start to put in place to assist themselves to cope with the end of group therapy.

'Today is our sixth session together. That means that we have only three more sessions together. How are you feeling about this?'

Allow the group to discuss issues of concern regarding termination. Normalise this concern by explaining that most mothers feel apprehensive about the group coming to an end and reconceptualise the experience from one of loss to one of an opportunity to extend support networks.

Ask the group to consider a possible date for the follow-up session after termination as this will include a social aspect (luncheon, afternoon tea etc.). There is no need to set a specific date at this point in time but rather allow mothers the opportunity to consult their diaries and consider possibilities.

PARTNERS' SESSION

Remind participants of the partners' session this week. Reiterate that they are welcome to bring their children and that facilities will be provided for nappy change, feeding, play etc. Supper should also be provided as partners often come straight from work and mothers rarely have had time to have a cup of tea or coffee because they have been busy organising the family for the evening meeting.

PREVIEW SESSION 7

'Next week we will continue to look more closely at our thoughts and the impact that they have on our mood. We will be discussing our "internal critic" and will be discovering other ways to increase positive thoughts and decrease negative thoughts.'

HOMEWORK

❑   **Set homework tasks.**

● *'Continue to monitor your daily mood using the **Daily Mood Rating Form.'***

Handout 3: Daily Mood Rating Form

● *'Practice self-instructional techniques. Put a short positive self-statement on a card and place it where you will frequently see it.'*
● *'Continue to use successful strategies you have learned so far for improving your mood.'*

Fewer new tasks are set for homework for this week as mothers are expected to attend the partners' session, and to continue to consolidate skills learned to date.

❑   **Distribute handouts.**

Handout 3: Daily Mood Rating Form

❑   **Finish on time.**

SESSION 7: DEVELOPING A MORE HELPFUL THINKING STYLE

NOTES FOR THE THERAPIST

This session continues to build on the cognitive work already commenced in previous sessions. The aim is to focus on the techniques of increasing positive thoughts and decreasing negative or self-deprecatory thoughts. The following session (Session 8) will move even further into cognitive work, assisting mothers to challenge irrational beliefs and related automatic thoughts. It is important to be proficient in the application of cognitive theory and the related techniques when you facilitate this session.

THERAPIST CHECKLIST FOR SESSION 7

Record-keeping suggestions

❑ **Tick off a checklist of the content of this session that you have completed (by the end of the session):**

✓ Introduction to Session 7   ☐
✓ Psycho-education: mind games—negative thoughts make me feel
   worthless and depressed   ☐
✓ Activity 10: tuning into my thoughts   ☐
✓ Group discussion   ☐
✓ Psycho-education: ways to reduce negative thoughts and increase
   positive thoughts   ☐
✓ Group discussion   ☐
✓ Preparation for termination   ☐
✓ Preview Session 8   ☐
✓ Homework   ☐

❑ **Keep a summary of issues raised by <u>each</u> mother.**

Session 7 name: _____

Expectations of motherhood and parenting: cognitive distortions	Expectations of relationship with baby: cognitive distortions	Other negative thoughts

Notes: _____

_____

_____

INTRODUCTION TO SESSION 7

❑   **Housekeeping issues.**

                     'Did anyone have any difficulties getting here today?'

                     Resolve any issues quickly.

❑   **Review of homework.**

'What did you find out about your mood from the mood-monitoring task? Did you manage to use self-instruction this week? Are there any thoughts or feelings about the partners' session that we should discuss now before we move on?'

Briefly address any issues that are raised about the homework tasks. In particular, allow some time to obtain feedback about the partners' session as mothers often reveal important information about the dynamics between themselves and their partners as a result of the partners' sessions.

❑   **Review previous session.**

Briefly review the material you covered in the previous session.

'Last week we looked at the impact of our thoughts on our mood. We recognised that our thoughts can be our greatest enemy or our greatest ally. We discussed self-instructional techniques as one way to use our thoughts constructively to assist us in our battle to get on top of depression.'

PSYCHO-EDUCATION: MIND GAMES—NEGATIVE THOUGHTS MAKE ME FEEL WORTHLESS AND DEPRESSED

❑   **Cognitive theory.**

Elaborate on the cognitive theory of depression. So far, the sessions have focused mainly on the link between behaviour and mood and the previous two sessions have begun to introduce the major notion that thoughts and mood are also connected. It is useful to elaborate on the general rationale behind cognitive approaches to the treatment of depression.

'People who suffer from depression are more likely to hold negative attitudes, beliefs and assumptions about themselves, their world and their future. These assumptions or beliefs are acquired early in life through learning and they may be reactivated by stressful events. When a person is suffering from depression, he/she is more likely to draw negative conclusions in the absence of evidence, focus on a detail taken out of context, relate external events to themselves, draw conclusions on the basis of a single event and to minimise positive experiences.'

❑   **Treatment of postnatal depression.**

Review our approach to the treatment of PND that was presented in Session 1.

'When we started to work together, we discussed the following points:

- *The transition to motherhood involves adapting to huge physical, emotional and social changes.*

- *Myths about motherhood can create unrealistic expectations about pregnancy and motherhood, so that we think "we have failed", when we experience problems coping with the mothering role.*
- *Postnatal depression is not just a biological illness, it is connected to both our behaviour and our thoughts.*
- *The best way to deal with postnatal depression is to develop the skills to make positive changes not only in the way you **act in your life**, but also in **the way you think**.'*

❑   **The cognitive-behavioural model.**

Return to the Thoughts, Feelings and Behaviour triad and use it to demonstrate the role that thoughts play in PND (show Overhead 6). Make a simple example by highlighting the negative impact on our feelings that most 'should' thoughts have, e.g. 'I should be less messy.'

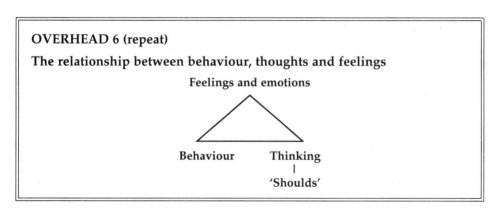

OVERHEAD 6 (repeat)

The relationship between behaviour, thoughts and feelings

Feelings and emotions

Behaviour   Thinking

|

'Shoulds'

Consistently link mothers' experiences to the cognitive-behavioural therapy model. Use examples from the group that you have recorded after each session (e.g., problems with breastfeeding; drugs during labour; difficulties keeping up with housework) to link depressed feelings with negative thoughts. Encourage questions and personal examples from participants.

❑   **Reasons for challenging our thoughts.**

Introduce the notion that although we cannot always control what happens around us (particularly other people's behaviour), we can shift depressive feelings by challenging some of the thoughts we have about the situations that we are in (e.g., unhelpful attitudes and beliefs about how the world 'should' be, or people 'should' act). Changing thinking does not remove negative emotions entirely, but helps to reduce them to manageable levels.

'Thoughts can have a profound effect on mood. Thoughts belong to us and therefore they are under our own control. It is hard to accept this

sometimes, because our thoughts seem automatic and it's easy to take them for granted.

Another problem with our thoughts is that other people cannot observe them, although we easily fall into the mind-reading trap and expect others to know what we are thinking, and expect them to respond appropriately. For example, you may think that your partner can read your mind and will automatically go and put another load of nappies on the line because you have not been able to do it yet. However, he is unable to read your mind and sits down to have a cup of coffee. You automatically evaluate this negatively and feel angry and frustrated as a result of your associated thoughts about your partner not being 'tuned in' to you. If this sort of event happens often enough, you are more likely to experience feelings of depression.

Today, we will be discussing one approach to changing negative thoughts and thereby changing the way you feel. In this session we will learn ways to increase positive thoughts and decrease negative thoughts.'

ACTIVITY 10: TUNING INTO MY THOUGHTS

Example

'I can never get up on time'

'I'm always running late.'

'I'm so disorganised.'

Ask each participant to think back to the start of today and to write down all the thoughts that they can remember having. Encourage mothers to write everything down, including neutral thoughts such as 'I must remember to buy another litre of milk on my way home today.'

Allow approximately 10 minutes for this task, as most people find tuning into their thoughts quite difficult and will need time to reflect on their experiences and associated thoughts for the day.

Once mothers complete their lists ask them to review their list of thoughts and count all the positive thoughts they have had, all the negative thoughts they have had, and any neutral thoughts.

GROUP DISCUSSION

As a group, discuss the results of the Individual Activity. Ask for examples and point out how negative thoughts seem to outweigh positive thoughts. Generate discussion about how these negative and positive thoughts seem to influence mood. Ask each participant to review their list and mark which thoughts seem to be the most influential in determining their mood.

PSYCHO-EDUCATION: WAYS TO REDUCE NEGATIVE THOUGHTS AND INCREASE POSITIVE THOUGHTS

'Once you become more aware of your thoughts and the role that your internal critic plays in determining your mood, you can start to challenge those thoughts. To start with, it is helpful to focus on decreasing the rate of negative thoughts and increasing the rate of positive thoughts. Let us look at ways we may be able to do this.'

❑   **Ways to decrease negative thoughts.**

Provide a range of examples of effective techniques. Your suggestions may include:

- Thought interruption (e.g., 'STOP! I'm not going to think that now.')
- Worrying time schedule. If you need to think about certain negative thoughts, then schedule a time to do so (no more than 30 minutes per day). Limit your negative thoughts to that time period.
- Blow-up technique. Take your negative thought to a ridiculous extreme. What is the worst that you can imagine?
- 0–100 scale. Determine what would be the 100% terrible event that may happen in your life. Then, determine what would be 50% terrible and 25% terrible. Now, place your current concern in context. You will probably find that it is not 100% terrible.
- *'If I can't change it, I can learn to accept it.'* As previously discussed, point out the importance of developing acceptance of events, habits etc. that one cannot change.

❑   **Ways to increase positive thoughts.**

Provide a range of examples of effective techniques. Your suggestions may include the following:

- Carry cards with positive self-statements written on them. Review them frequently throughout the day.
- Notice what you accomplish rather than what you do not accomplish, by making a list of daily successes.
- Reward yourself with positive thoughts (e.g., *'I did well to get three loads of washing done today'*).
- Review positives in your life.
- Make a list of your achievements.
- Compliment yourself.
- Review nice postcards and letters.

Provide examples of each technique to illustrate their implementation.

GROUP DISCUSSION

Ask mothers to think of other ways to reduce negative thoughts or to increase positive thoughts. Brainstorm ideas with the mothers.

Generate a list on the whiteboard. Ask mothers to write down the ideas from the whiteboard for reference during the week.

PREPARATION FOR TERMINATION

'We have only two more sessions together and one more partners' session before this group comes to an end. Are there any thoughts about this that you would like to discuss?'

Allow mothers to discuss their concerns as well as their hopes for the future. Again, raise the issue about the farewell lunch/morning tea/afternoon tea and begin setting possible dates for consideration over the next couple of weeks.

PREVIEW SESSION 8

'Next week we will continue to look more closely at our thoughts and the impact that they have on our mood. We will be examining our irrational automatic thoughts in relation to our expectations of motherhood and ourselves as mothers. We will learn more ways to challenge our unhelpful thinking and replace our negative thoughts with more constructive ones.'

HOMEWORK

❑   **Set homework tasks.**

- 'Continue to monitor your daily mood using the ***Daily Mood Rating Form.***'
- *'Tune into your thoughts and try to stop the negative automatic thoughts whenever you catch them. I would also like you to start increasing positive thoughts about yourself, your world and your experiences by using some of the techniques we have discussed today.'*
- *'Continue to use successful strategies that you have learned so far for improving your mood.'*
- Optional: Read Chapter 5 entitled 'Cognitive distortions' from McKay, M. and Fanning, P. (1993). *Self-esteem.* Oakland, CA: New Harbinger.

❑   **Distribute handouts.**

Handout 3: Daily Mood Rating Form

❑   **Finish on time.**

SESSION 8: CHALLENGING MY INTERNAL CRITIC

NOTES FOR THE THERAPIST

The aim of this session is to assist mothers to challenge irrational beliefs and related automatic thoughts. For best results, proficiency in the application of cognitive theory and the related techniques are required to facilitate this session (e.g., Clark & Fairburn, 1997).

It is also important to remember that some mothers will struggle more than others with the concepts presented in this session. Although the therapist may be clear about the link between thoughts and feelings, some people find this link difficult to clarify or to apply to their own experience. Try to be aware of terminology used and explain concepts in simplified rather than psychological terms.

THERAPIST CHECKLIST FOR SESSION 8

Record-keeping suggestions

❑ **Tick off a checklist of the content of this session that you have completed (by the end of the session):**

✓ Introduction to Session 8 ☐
✓ Activity: starting to challenge thoughts and changing feelings ☐
✓ Psycho-education and activity: disputing and shifting cognitive
  distortions ☐
✓ Preview Session 9 ☐
✓ Partners' session ☐
✓ Homework ☐

❑ **Keep a summary of issues raised by <u>each</u> mother.**

Session 7 name: _____

Thinking style. Common cognitive distortions expressed by mother	Is mother clear about the link between thoughts, feelings and behaviour?	Other

Notes: _____

_____

_____

INTRODUCTION TO SESSION 8

❑   **Housekeeping issues.**

'Did anyone have any difficulties getting here today?'

Resolve any issues quickly. At this stage it is rare that major difficulties arise; however, it is important to allow mothers the opportunity to raise an issue if it occurs. If this opportunity is not provided, you may find a mother dropping out of your group at this late stage because she has experienced difficulties with the organisational aspects of attending the sessions.

❑   **Review of homework.**

'What did you find out about your mood from the mood-monitoring task? Did your attempts to increase positive thoughts and decrease negative thoughts have a positive effect on your mood? Did you manage to read the chapter that we suggested during the week? We will be discussing aspects of the reading during this session.'

Briefly address any issues that are raised about the homework tasks.

❑   **Review previous session.**

Briefly review the material you covered in the previous session.

'Last week we looked at the impact of our thoughts on our mood. We started to tune into our thoughts and discussed ways to increase positive thoughts and decrease negative thoughts. This week we will be looking more closely at our beliefs and expectations about motherhood and ourselves as mothers, and we will start to challenge the more unhelpful beliefs or expectations that we hold.'

ACTIVITY: STARTING TO CHALLENGE THOUGHTS AND CHANGING FEELINGS

Once again, demonstrate the link between a situation, the associated thoughts, consequent feelings and outcomes using an example relevant to the mothers' experience. Write the example on the whiteboard.

Continuing with the same example, request the group to brainstorm a number of possible alternative thoughts and consequent emotional responses to that particular situation. Relate the differences in feeling responses back to differences in the content of thoughts. Thus, you are demonstrating that feelings do not arise independently of thoughts, but are a consequence of them.

Continue to elicit other examples from the participants' experiences, perhaps drawing on themes that arose from the group discussion on pregnancy experiences, birth experiences, and experiences now, recorded from Session 1.

WHITEBOARD 12

	Examples
Situation	Watching partner settle baby effectively.
Thoughts	'I can't stand it. That just proves that I am no good as a mother.'
Feelings	Defeated Depressed Hurt
What I say or do	'All right then, if you're so good at it, I'll go to work and you can stay home.'
Outcomes	Partner mistakenly believes you are ungrateful for his help.

WHITEBOARD 13

	Examples
Situation	Watching partner settle baby effectively.
Alternative thoughts	'Thank goodness someone has finally managed to settle him.'
New feelings	Relieved Less anxious
What I say or do	'That's great. Thanks.'
Outcomes	Partner helps to settle baby more often.

For example

'Getting up in the morning is too hard, there is an impossible amount to be done.'

Apart from emphasising the connection between thoughts and corresponding emotional reactions, help participants to learn to identify their negative thoughts about aspects of mothering.

PSYCHO-EDUCATION AND ACTIVITY: DISPUTING AND SHIFTING COGNITIVE DISTORTIONS

❑   **Disputing non-constructive self-talk.**

'Many of the thoughts that we have about the events we are involved in are non-constructive and automatic. They get in the way of beating depression and developing more positive relationships with others, as well as damaging our self-esteem. Many of the errors that we make in thinking were discussed in the chapter we suggested you read for homework, entitled

"Cognitive distortions". The most common non-constructive thinking styles are:

- *Using evaluative words such as "should" or "must";*
- *Using catastrophising words such as "it's awful" or "it's devastating".*
- *Overgeneralising by using words such as "never" or "always".*

In order to develop more constructive ways of thinking, it is important to evaluate your thoughts and question if there is evidence that the thought is 100% accurate and 100% true.'

Some examples of disputing include:

For example

'I should be neater and more organised.'

For 'shoulds' and 'oughts': 'Why should I or the other person behave in this particular way?'

'Why must an event occur just the way I wanted it?'

For example

'It's awful the way my mother-in-law drops in all the time.'

For 'terribles' and 'awfuls': 'I would have liked this person to do or say this, but is there any good reason why he (or she) must do or say what I'd like?'
'I would have liked for this to have happened in a different way, but is it really awful (or horrible or terrible) that it didn't?'
'It would have been nice if that person had done or said this, but is it really terrible that he (or she) didn't?'

For example

'No one ever takes any notice of me.'

For 'overgeneralisations': 'Just because this didn't work out the way I wanted, is there any good evidence that it can't work out better another time?'

'Just because that person said something about me that I didn't like, does that really mean that everyone is going to feel that way?'

❑   **Activity.**

Ask participants to recall thoughts generated from the first activity in this session (starting to challenge thoughts and feelings) and begin to test the accuracy of their negative thoughts, disputing the 'shoulds', 'awfuls' and 'overgeneralisations'.

With each example, continue the exercise until there is a reduction in the certainty of the negative thoughts, and recognition of the resulting modification/improvement in mood.

Using the overhead 'Challenging my thoughts', work with participants in assisting them to understand the concept of challenging dysfunctional cognitions that lead to feelings of failure and depression.

Emphasise that although we can allow ourselves to be tricked into believing them, automatic thoughts arise from beliefs and attitudes that can be challenged and changed, they are not truths.

OVERHEAD 13

Challenging my thoughts

Expectation/belief	Related automatic thoughts	Refutation of related automatic thoughts
1. The biological transition to parenthood should be smooth.	'I should not require use of anaesthesia, forceps, or episiotomy.'	
2. Attachment to the infant should be easy and free of negative feelings.	'I should always feel love for my baby.' 'Negative feelings toward my baby are wrong.'	
3. Being a parent should be manageable, and any problems easily solved . . .	'I should know what my baby needs/wants automatically.' 'It should be easier with the second child.'	

Adapted from Olioff (1991).

Extend the examples of negative thoughts to include unrealistic expectations concerning pregnancy and parenthood (see Overhead 13). In talking to women who experience PND, one common theme that comes through is that many of these mothers hold very high (often unrealistic) expectations about what pregnancy and parenthood 'should' be like.

And as we have emphasised before, it is hardly surprising that so many women adhere to these beliefs, given that our culture bombards us with such messages (as do our family, friends, neighbours and strangers, at times).

Try to elicit examples that relate to common cognitive themes in PND (Olioff, 1991):

- Perceived poor parenting self-efficacy.
- Global negative appraisals of self as an 'inadequate mother'.
- Perceptions of the infant as vulnerable to catastrophic events.

You may wish to use items from the Parenting Self-efficacy Scale to start discussion, e.g. 'Being a parent should be manageable, and any problems easily solved' (Gibaud-Wallston, 1977).

❑   **Cognitive distortions.**

Refer to Overhead 14 for unhelpful thinking styles.

OVERHEAD 14

Definitions of Cognitive Distortions

1. ALL-OR-NOTHING THINKING: You see things in black-and-white categories. If your performance falls short of perfect, you see yourself as a total failure.

2. OVERGENERALISATION: You see a single negative event as a never-ending pattern of defeat.

3. MENTAL FILTER: You pick out a single negative detail and dwell on it exclusively so that your vision of all reality becomes darkened, like the drop of ink that discolours the entire beaker of water.

4. DISQUALIFYING THE POSITIVE: You reject positive experiences by insisting they 'don't count' for some reason or other. In this way you can maintain a negative belief that is contradicted by your everyday experiences.

5. JUMPING TO CONCLUSIONS: You make a negative interpretation even though there are no definite facts that convincingly support your conclusion.

   (a) *Mind reading*. You arbitrarily conclude that someone is reacting negatively to you, and you don't bother to check this out.
   (b) *The fortune teller error*. You anticipate that things will turn out badly, and you feel convinced that your prediction is an already established fact.

6. MAGNIFICATION (CATASTROPHISING) OR MINIMISATION: You exaggerate the importance of things (such as your goof-up or someone else's achievement), or you inappropriately shrink things until they appear tiny (your own desirable qualities or the other fellow's imperfections). This is also called the 'binocular trick'.

7. EMOTIONAL REASONING: You assume that your negative emotions necessarily reflect the way things really are: 'I feel it, therefore it must be true'.

8. 'SHOULD' STATEMENTS: You try to motivate yourself with shoulds and shouldn'ts, as if you had to be whipped and punished before you could be expected to do anything. 'Musts' and 'oughts' are also offenders. The emotional consequence is guilt. When you direct 'should' statements toward others, you feel anger, frustration, and resentment.

Overhead 14 continued

---

9. **LABELLING AND MISLABELLING: This is an extreme form of overgeneralisation. Instead of describing your error, you attach a negative label to yourself: 'I'm a *loser*.' When someone else's behaviour rubs you the wrong way, you attach a negative label to him: 'He's a goddamn louse.' Mislabelling involves describing an event with language that is highly coloured and emotionally loaded.**

10. **PERSONALISATION: You see yourself as the cause of some negative external event which in fact you were not primarily responsible for.**

Adapted from Burns (1980).

For example, identify:

- **Magnification.**
- **Generalisation.**
- **Internal negative attributions.**

And so forth, in the thoughts generated by the group. Name the various cognitive distortions and assist the group to identify which thoughts outlined on the whiteboard previously showed these errors. Ask them to consider more helpful and accurate thoughts/evaluations of events based on challenging these types of distortions.

PREVIEW SESSION 9

'Next week is our last session together. We will be focusing on support networks, reviewing what we found most helpful during this program, and planning for the future. We will be having a follow-up session in a few weeks' time and we will be setting a date for this to occur, so please bring your diaries.'

Allow discussion of issues regarding termination of these sessions.

Partners' session

Remind participants that the last partner session is to be held next week. Confirm the day, date and time.

HOMEWORK

❑   **Set homework tasks.**

- *'Continue to monitor your daily mood using the **Daily Mood Rating Form**'.*
- *'Use your **Daily Mood Rating Form** handout and insert the following subheadings into the blank columns:*

OVERHEAD 15

Daily monitoring form

Event (A)	Beliefs or self-talk (B)	Dispute of self-talk
• (Briefly describe the situation or event that seemed to lead to your emotional upset.)	• (Things that you say to yourself about A.) THEN • (Go back and place a checkmark beside each statement that is non-constructive or 'irrational'.)	• (For each checked statement in Section B, describe what you would ask or say to dispute your non-constructive self-talk.)

Attempt to identify activities and thoughts linked with mood ratings that are low. Develop alternative, more constructive thoughts about yourself and parenting that you have identified through our exercises today, using the "Dispute of self-talk" heading.'

• *'Review the skills that we have covered in this program and decide which ones seem to have been most effective in improving your mood.'*

❑   **Distribute handouts.**

Handout 3: Daily Mood Rating Form

Handout 7: (photocopy of Overhead 15) Daily Monitoring Form

❑   **Finish on time.**

Sometimes participants like to stay a little longer on the penultimate session to talk informally about the sessions coming to an end. Allow an opportunity for this to occur as it is an important preparation for termination.

Chapter 6

PHASE III: RELAPSE PREVENTION AND EVALUATION

INTRODUCTION

An important and often disregarded part of any cognitive-behavioural therapy (CBT) intervention is the termination sessions and what happens after therapy. Studies that have examined relapse rates following CBT or antidepressant medication for depression suggest that CBT is as effective as imipramine at preventing relapse when medication is continued at a maintenance dose for a period of at least 12 months. CBT has been found to be superior to antidepressant medication if the medication is not maintained for at least 12 months (see Chapter 2). These results suggest that training clients with a CBT approach to critically examine their cognitions and to challenge unhelpful belief systems, as well as training them in more adaptive behaviour that is incongruent with depressed mood, significantly contributes to the maintenance of therapeutic gains. Although many individuals suffering from depression have achieved complete remission of depressive symptomatology following cognitive-behavioural treatment, it is estimated in the general depression literature that approximately 20–40% of clients will relapse within two years post-treatment, so strategies to increase the chances of maintenance of therapeutic gains are essential. Once a structured, manualised treatment for postnatal depression (PND) has been administered, it is imperative to draw together everything that has taken place over the course of nine weeks of therapy. Putting it all together is often the most powerful point in the intervention process, providing clear goals of termination, consolidation of previously learned skills and planning for maintenance of therapeutic gains. These chapters describe an approach to the final session aimed at terminating therapy in a constructive manner to optimise the benefit gained from the manualised program. A structured booster session (Session 10) ensures that therapeutic gains are more likely to be maintained. There are also numerous ways that maintenance of therapeutic gains and prevention of relapse can be built into each session of the Getting Ahead of Postnatal Depression program presented in the preceding chapters. Each and every session should introduce ideas and collate information that will assist participants to anticipate expected and unexpected stressful life events, identify their own body cues and signs of depression, and to have a plan to mobilise in the event of a lapse.

In this section, the final Session (9) is called 'Putting it all Together—Travelling On'. It describes strategies to optimise the maintenance and generalisability of therapeutic gains for mothers who have participated in the Getting Ahead of Postnatal Depression program. Session 10, 'Consolidating What I Have Learned: Relapse Prevention', is presented separately, as it is intended to be conducted as a follow-up session rather than immediately after Session 9.

Finally, some research findings are provided. The 1990s have heralded a strong movement towards evidence-based therapy and the cognitive-behavioural, scientist–practitioner model is consistent with this trend. Following Session 10, this chapter will provide information both on the efficacy of this treatment program and encouragement to any clinician implementing the Getting Ahead of Postnatal Depression program to evaluate therapeutic outcomes.

SESSION 9: PUTTING IT ALL TOGETHER: TRAVELLING ON

NOTES FOR THE THERAPIST

This session is the final regular session that you will be having with these mothers as a group. It will be as difficult for mothers to say goodbye as it will be for you to do so. Group process models sometimes refer to this stage of group process as a 'mourning' stage. Mothers will express disappointment at the group coming to an end and will attempt to keep the group going (as a social one) by exchanging telephone numbers, and this should be encouraged. In our experience, mothers from these groups rarely stay in contact with one another, more often than not becoming absorbed in the many tasks of motherhood and not finding time for social contacts that they developed through the group. However, it is an important aspect of this session that social supports be encouraged, built-up and utilised.

Some mothers may be concerned that they do not feel that they can keep up their gains alone. It is crucial that the therapist ensure that the mother is encouraged to utilise her family and friends as resources, and not to evaluate her efforts to beat depression as 'failed' if she requires further professional input.

Most mothers will have experienced a significant improvement in mood as a result of this program (consistent with evaluation data available to date). However, some mothers may still require further intensive exploration of their specific issues in relation to their experience of depression, and it is important that, if needed, follow-on therapy is organised to begin as soon as possible, preferably in the week following the end of group therapy.

THERAPIST CHECKLIST FOR SESSION 9

Record-keeping suggestions

❑ **Tick off a checklist of the content of this session that you have completed (by the end of the session):**

✓ Introduction to Session 9 ☐
✓ Group discussion: what changes in my mood have I noticed ☐
✓ Group Discussion: what about another baby? ☐
✓ Psycho-education: maintaining your gains ☐
✓ Group discussion: social support ☐
✓ Individual exercise: my goals ☐
✓ Group discussion: termination ☐

❑ **Keep a summary of issues raised by each mother.**

Session 9 name: _____

Mood changes	Most useful skills/ program components	Other (referrals, social supports, follow-up, outstanding issues)

Notes: _____

_____

_____

INTRODUCTION TO SESSION 9

❑   **Housekeeping issues.**

It is a good idea for the therapist to 'mark' the final session as different from previous sessions and one of a celebratory/ congratulatory nature by providing a special cake/morning tea. Group members sometimes like to reminisce about the difficulties they had organising themselves to come to the group, and recognise the ease of making time for themselves that they now habitually enjoy each week. Therapists should encourage the continuation of this time slot to engage in pleasant activities, now that babysitters and so forth are organised and reliable.

❑   **Review of homework.**

'What did you find out about your mood from the mood-monitoring task? Did you manage to develop an effective challenge to your beliefs or expectations about parenting or your relationship with your baby?'

Briefly address any issues that are raised about the homework tasks. In particular, allow some time to obtain feedback about the partners' session, as mothers often reveal important information about the dynamics between themselves and their partners as a result of the partners' sessions.

❑   **Review previous sessions.**

Briefly review the material you covered in the previous sessions.

'In the course of the nine weeks we have had together in this group, we hope we have helped you to develop some useful skills to get on top of depression.

As you learned these skills, we hoped you would begin to develop a greater sense of control over your depression, and to experience more joy in your life and relationships, particularly your relationship with your baby.

We haved looked at our model of understanding postnatal depression and the relationship between our thoughts, our feelings and our behaviour. We reflected upon the depressive spiral and we learned a range of skills which would allow us to turn that depressive spiral into a positive one. We learned relaxation on the run techniques, assertiveness skills, techniques for increasing positive and decreasing negative thoughts and challenging unhelpful thinking styles. We also learned about the impact of our families of origin and started to build our self-esteem.

Each one of you will have gained something unique from this experience. What one of you discovered was ineffective in controlling your mood, another may have found invaluable. You will all have a set of new skills that you have discovered work best for you.'

GROUP DISCUSSION: WHAT CHANGES IN MY MOOD HAVE I NOTICED?

'Let us spend some time reviewing the changes in your mood that you have experienced over the last nine weeks. Looking back over your daily record of mood over the last nine weeks, what worked best? What didn't work so well?'

'What are you doing differently now compared to before the group?' (To facilitate internal attributions for improved mood.)

Allow mothers to respond individually to this question. It is important that everyone is given a turn to express her opinion. By asking *'What didn't work so well?'* you have given mothers permission to talk about aspects of the program that they did not find useful or did not enjoy. Be sure to accept this feedback and not inadvertently give the message that all you wish to hear about are positives. By the same token, be sure to have mothers selectively attend to the positive outcomes, as individuals prone to depression are more likely to attend selectively to the negatives, and attribute self-blame or failure.

GROUP DISCUSSION: WHAT ABOUT ANOTHER BABY?

Mothers who have stated that they would never have another baby have often softened by the end of the group once their mood has lifted significantly. They appreciate the opportunity to discuss the possibility of having another baby and what the chances are of experiencing depression next time round.

'I wonder how many of you have considered the possibility of having another baby? It is not uncommon for mothers to call us a few months after the group finishes to tell us the exciting news. Perhaps you have fears or concerns about this possibility that we should discuss now.'

Allow mothers to discuss their hopes, fears and concerns. List these on the white board.

WHITEBOARD 14

Another baby?
Fears and hopes
Strategies

'Research on postnatal depression suggests that mothers who have experienced an episode of postnatal depression are more likely to experience another episode after a subsequent delivery than women who have not had an episode previously. It is most likely that mothers who have learned to recognise their own signs of depressed mood and strategies to beat depression through their behaviour and thinking will have a reduced risk of postnatal depression after the next baby.'

Generate a list of strategies on the whiteboard to plan for and cope better next time. Emphasis should be made on social supports.

PSYCHO-EDUCATION: MAINTAINING YOUR GAINS

'It is important to maintain the gains that you have made in this program and to continue to practice the skills that you have learned. There are a few important things to remember. Firstly, take time to integrate what you have learned. A lot of the skills we have covered take time and practice to master.

Secondly, monitor your mood on a regular basis. The best way to stay on top of depression is to catch it early rather than wait until you feel overwhelmed by your depressed mood. Think about your own warning signs of depression. You will remember that we have discussed the many symptoms of depression. Keep that list handy, to refer to, if needed. Finally, remember that life events do not have to be negative to cause distress and/or depression. Other events in your life, or the life of someone close to you, may trigger depressive feelings. Go back and use the techniques that worked best for you. Now let us review what we learned.' (Overhead.)

OVERHEAD 16

What have we learned?

- Pleasant activities: introducing them for me and baby
- Relaxation
- Assertiveness: telling others how I feel
- My parenting models
- My internal critic
- Couples sessions

Allow the group to elaborate on the skills they have learned and add to the overhead.

GROUP DISCUSSION: SOCIAL SUPPORT

Discuss social supports (family and friends) and agencies that can be of assistance to mothers and families. Generate a list of options and contact numbers that mothers can write down for future reference if required. Ensure 24-hour emergency contact numbers are provided or are available to every mother (e.g., Parents Anonymous).

INDIVIDUAL EXERCISE: MY GOALS

(Poster paper and felt-tip pens need to be provided.)

Ask mothers to develop a poster depicting short- to medium-term goals for the future. Allow sufficient time for mothers to do this, and give permission for mothers to keep their poster private if they wish to.

The posters are presented to the large group on a volunteer basis. Discuss possible skills mothers could use to achieve these goals and to prevent depression.

Individual participants take their poster home with them.

GROUP DISCUSSION: TERMINATION

Discuss how group members feel about termination. Normalise feelings of anxiety and deal appropriately with issues of fear, perceived lack of support and so forth. Make sure mothers have written down the ideas for social support generated on the whiteboard earlier.

BUSINESS

Set date for booster session and follow-up in approximately three to four weeks.

'Love letters' that mothers wrote to themselves some weeks ago are sent to mothers two weeks after this session.

FINISH

Liaise privately with mothers who require further specialist intervention, preferably setting up an interview time.

SESSION 10: CONSOLIDATING WHAT I HAVE LEARNED

NOTES FOR THE THERAPIST

This session is a maintenance session. It should be conducted no longer than three to four weeks after Session 9. Although mothers were in a regular routine that facilitated their attendance at the Getting Ahead of Postnatal Depression program, do not assume that mothers will be able to attend the maintenance session easily. Mothers are very quickly consumed with commitments, obligations and child rearing. As such, it is probably realistic to consider that the organisation of this maintenance session will be as time consuming as it was to set up the Getting Ahead of Postnatal Depression program initially. However, it is a crucial aspect of the program that cannot be discarded in favour of pragmatism.

Allow sufficient time to contact each mother and ensure that she is able to attend the maintenance session. It is wise to book the session on the same day and at the same time as you ran the Getting Ahead of Postnatal Depression program, and to advise mothers in advance (preferably at the end of Session 9). The group, once parted after Session 9, will lose its cohesion and it is often difficult to get all mothers back for the maintenance session. It is important that mothers are aware that they will be missed by the group if they do not attend the maintenance session, as some mothers may detach themselves so completely after the end of the last session that they believe that no one will notice if they do not attend.

Assure mothers who have required further professional input that they will not be seen to have 'failed' by other group members. Help the mother reframe her experience as one of great courage, strength and motivation to continue the battle against depression. On the other hand, some mothers will feel so well that they feel that they do not need to attend another session. Emphasise the social aspect of the maintenance session as well as the importance of consolidating what they have learned. The maintenance session is a great opportunity for mothers to clarify any questions they may have about the skills they have learned through the Getting Ahead of Postnatal Depression program now they have had the opportunity to practice further. It is an important phase in the treatment, and allows mothers to develop a plan to deal effectively with expected and unexpected stressful life events as well as lapses in the future.

We suggest that mothers be invited to bring their baby with them to this session. It is important, however, that mothers are given the choice. Some women may feel uncomfortable parenting in the context of the group, particularly if they perceive that they have a 'difficult' baby. When mothers bring their babies to a session, the therapist must be vigilant that the session does not deteriorate into 'comparison making' between babies, and the offering of un-solicited advice. Mothers who experience PND are often discouraged from attending new mothers' groups because they feel that they and their baby are being scrutinised and compared with others. It is essential that the group remain non-judgemental and supportive.

This session is conducted within a social context. Allow mothers to decide whether they wish to bring a plate or put in a small sum of money to buy lunch (e.g., pizzas). This is an opportunity to challenge the unrealistic expectations that mothers sometimes have that they 'must always prepare food from home and are not good enough if they have to buy take-away'. Encourage mothers to individually decide whether they would like to bring a plate, but always suggest the option of contributing to the cost of a lunch that you will order.

❑   **Housekeeping issues.**

Set up the room with age-appropriate toys and activities for the babies. Set up a table for lunch. Make sure that the lunch is practical for mothers with babies. A sit-down lunch at a table is inappropriate. A buffet-style lunch is suggested. Mothers who arrive early often like to help with the preparation, and it gives them an opportunity to practice those 'relaxation on the run' techniques while they attend to their baby at the same time.

Allow sufficient time for mothers to settle in with their baby. Ensure that nappy-changing facilities and food/bottle-heating facilities are available. Mothers will need to move in and out of the room during this session so it is preferable that a room close to the kitchen and nappy-changing facilities is used.

It is crucial that the therapist pays adequate attention to safety issues. This is an opportunity to demonstrate safe play. For example, power points should be covered with approved safety plugs; power cords or small objects should be removed from the floor; kitchen and steps should be inaccessible to crawling babies; sharp corners should be covered or furniture shifted to remove danger. Make sure the toys you provide are clean. Mothers will not feel comfortable allowing their babies to explore their new environment if it is not safe to do so.

❑ **Review of previous weeks.**

Allow mothers to discuss how they have been since the completion of the Getting Ahead of Postnatal Depression program. Although other mothers may be distracted by their babies, the therapist must remain attentive to the mother who is telling her story. Ensure that the group is supportive.

❑ **Review previous sessions.**

Briefly review the major topics covered in the Getting Ahead of Postnatal Depression program: relaxation, social supports, pleasant activities, self-esteem, family of origin, self-instruction, positive thinking, and challenging unrealistic expectations/beliefs. Ask mothers if they are still using the techniques that they found most useful. Reinforce successful use of the strategies taught in the Getting Ahead of Postnatal Depression program. Clarify any misuse of the strategies. Assist the group to brainstorm creative solutions to 'forgetting' to use the strategies found to be the most successful, and falling into 'old habits'.

❑ **Review changes in mood.**

Administer the Beck Depression Inventory (BDI) to individual mothers. Provide pens and clipboards and allow mothers the time and space to complete the form privately. This may mean that you will need to interact and play with her baby for a while. Reassure mothers that the results will not be discussed within the group but there will be an opportunity after the session to discuss the results by telephone (or an individual appointment if desired). Once the forms are completed, ask mothers to reflect on the changes that they have noted in their mood and other symptoms of depression.

'What did you notice about the way you were answering the questions this time compared to before you started the Getting Ahead of Postnatal Depression program? What changes have you noticed in the symptoms of depression that you were experiencing? Has anyone else in your family noticed the changes?'

Discuss individual mothers' body cues/early signs of depression.

'What are the early warning signs of depression for you? How does your body tell you that you are beginning to feel depressed? What symptoms seem to set in before others?'

Scribe their responses on individualised 'maintenance plans' that will be developed throughout this session and given to mothers to take home for future reference. It is usually a good idea to partially complete these forms prior to Session 10 using the information you noted on mothers at the end of each session in the Getting Ahead of Postnatal Depression program.

❑   **Review short- to medium-term goals.**

'Thinking back to the picture you drew in the last session of the Getting Ahead of Postnatal Depression program about your future plans, are you closer to achieving your goals? Is there anything that you would draw differently now?'

Allow mothers to discuss their plans for the future. Some mothers may have some news to reveal. Reinforce all attempts to achieve the short- to medium-term goals they have set for themselves. Normalise the need to constantly review and perhaps change goals that we set for ourselves.

'When we set goals for ourselves, it is important to go back and review them from time to time. Are they realistic? Do I still value this goal I have set for myself or would I like to set myself a new goal? How far am I towards reaching my goal? Do I need to break my goal down into achievable steps?'

Pull the discussion together and relate achievements to the use of successful techniques learned through the Getting Ahead of Postnatal Depression program.

❑   **Review social supports.**

Inadequate social support is a risk factor for PND. As such, it is also a risk factor for relapse. Social support from partners, family, friends and professionals should be discussed.

'Now that you have had a few weeks without the group as a weekly support, what other supports have you used? Have you discovered some supports that you haven't used before? Are some supports more reliable and useful than others? How have you procured the support from others?'

Scribe the social supports found most helpful on the 'maintenance plan' for each mother.

❑   **Preparation for high-risk situations.**

An important element of maintenance of therapeutic gains is to recognise and have a plan to utilise in high-risk situations. Discuss what constitutes a high-risk situation for each individual mother. Remember that you are gradually developing individualised maintenance plans for each mother so focus on each mother in turn.

'For you, what are high-risk times of the day, month or year that may contribute to depressive feelings or a tendency towards depressive thinking or behaviour? What is a high-risk situation for you? Are you anticipating any stressful life events (e.g., weddings, job changes of a family member, long-awaited holiday)?'

Scribe mothers' responses on the individualised 'maintenance plans'. Then, move on to discuss skills mothers have learned that they could utilise in high-risk situations.

'What could you do in the future at high-risk times of the day/month/year or prior to an expected stressful life event to prevent or deal with depressive thoughts, feelings or behaviour?'

Encourage mothers to draw upon the skills taught in the Getting Ahead of Postnatal Depression program that they found useful. Referring to your notes from Sessions 1–9 on each mother is a useful aid, as mothers sometimes have difficulty recalling all the skills that they have previously found helpful.
     Write these down on the 'maintenance plan'.

❑   **Generalisation training.**

Some mothers may have difficulty generalising from the situations that have been discussed throughout the Getting Ahead of Postnatal Depression program to other novel situations. As a result, they are able to use the skills taught only in situations that closely resemble those discussed in the Getting Ahead of Postnatal Depression program. Generalisation training can help to overcome this problem and increase the likelihood of maintenance of therapeutic gains.
     Present a couple of novel situations that are similar to those previously discussed (e.g., car breaks down rather than babysitter doesn't turn up when expected). As a group, assist mothers to brainstorm ways to deal with this situation more effectively, drawing on skills training and cognitive restructuring techniques taught through the Getting Ahead of Postnatal Depression program. Encourage the recognition that these situations, although different, contain some elements (e.g., emotional responses) that can be dealt with effectively through the use of the skills taught in the Getting Ahead of Postnatal Depression program.

❑ **Lifestyle modification.**

Mothers who have attended the Getting Ahead of Postnatal Depression program will have made some lifestyle changes during the course of the program. Some mothers may have already made significant changes to their lifestyle in an attempt to create an environment in which they can function and interact more effectively. Other mothers may still be struggling with difficult lifestyle issues such as an unwanted boarder in the family home, a partner who has a gambling problem, or being uncertain whether or not to return to work. At this stage in the group process, it is not appropriate to ask mothers to attempt further self-disclosure of issues previously undisclosed. However, it is important that the therapist pre-empts the fact that sometimes these lifestyle issues can get in the way of mothers' attempts to get ahead of PND and that individual mothers may require further assistance to resolve these problems on an individual basis. Offer to be available to discuss these issues with mothers in the future (or immediately after this session, if appropriate) and to arrange individual therapy or referral if necessary.

❑ **End session.**

Give mothers a copy of the individualised 'maintenance plan'. The session should end on an informal basis as mothers may still be eating their lunch and attending to their babies. It is sometimes useful for the therapist to allow mothers to socialise without the therapist present. After allowing sufficient time for individual mothers to approach you if they need to speak to you privately, it is usually a good idea to leave mothers to unwind and enjoy themselves.

EVALUATING TREATMENT EFFICACY

HAS MY INTERVENTION BEEN EFFECTIVE?

There are numerous measures that can be utilised to formally evaluate the efficacy of treatment through the use of this manualised treatment program. It is recommended that both quantitative and qualitative means of evaluation are pursued. Chapter 3 outlined quantitative measures that could be used which are relatively easy to administer and not too time consuming for mothers. These measures included the BDI, the Beck Anxiety Inventory, the Coopersmith Self-Esteem Inventory and the Perceived Social Support Scale. As a minimum, it is recommended that depression is evaluated before and after treatment to determine if further intervention is necessary.

QUALITATIVE METHODS

Assessing the efficacy of an intervention program through validated self-report measures does not always capture the impact that the intervention has had on the participants' lives. Sometimes the group process and social support it provides are as important to the quality of participants' lives as changes in depression, and therefore to the efficacy of the treatment program. This letter, received from one mother who participated in the Getting Ahead of Postnatal Depression program, demonstrates the context that needs to be taken into account when interpreting questionnaire results.

> Dear Lisa,
>
> Sorry I couldn't make it to our class's break-up party, as Thomas (her baby) and I had the flu. I didn't get a chance to thank you and Carol for helping me feel better. I have been managing things a lot better, but I have been a lot stressed out at the moment though, because Thomas isn't sleeping and Alex [her ex-partner] is still hassling me. So the surveys came at a bad time, because they'll probably show that I've still got postnatal depression, but I don't think I have. Anyway, thanks again . . .' [Names have been changed to protect the mother's identity.]

Interviewing mothers individually about the perceived personal benefits of the program, even by telephone, provides a means of evaluating treatment outcomes that may not have been expected and would have been missed if evaluation relied solely on quantitative techniques.

Often, clinical information obtained during the group identifies areas of gain. Case 1 describes the presenting difficulties of a woman suffering from PND in terms of our model, and the gains she made using a cognitive-behavioural approach.

CASE 1

Case study of a participant in the Getting Ahead of Postnatal Depression program

Zara is a married first-time mother in her late twenties, tertiary educated and employed in a professional role. Factors predisposing her to depression in the postpartum include a past history of depressive illness, the fact that the pregnancy was unexpected, difficulties in her family of origin including parental mental health issues, and conflictual relationships with both parents. Additional vulnerability factors were fatigue and diminished resilience to stress owing to having worked in a stressful role right up to delivery. This may also have inhibited psychological preparation for childbirth, thereby increasing the likelihood of adjustment difficulties postpartum. A perfectionistic attitudinal style was also apparent, particularly toward parenting. The pregnancy itself had been marked by a series of stressful medical problems. The events precipitating depression were a difficult delivery, followed by medical complications.

Factors perpetuating Zara's depression were a 'difficult' baby, marital conflict, lack of support from her husband, financial stressors, her personality style characterised by perfectionism, passivity, and tendencies toward control and role conflict (mothering versus work). All these factors generated a high degree of psychological distress and distorted negative thinking that were accentuated by undeveloped assertiveness skills. Zara was offered the opportunity of participating in the Getting Ahead of Postnatal Depression program. Factors that facilitated Zara's engagement in the program included her well-developed problem-solving

Case 1 continued

skills, psychological mindedness and cognitive flexibility, as well as an ability to relate to other group members.

Throughout the treatment, Zara was able to implement behavioural strategies such as scheduling pleasant events to lift her mood, reappraise rigid unrealistic expectations with regard to parenting and work, and to challenge feelings of guilt.

Initially, Zara identified cognitions and associated feelings such as 'I feel guilty if I'm at home all day doing nothing', 'I feel guilty because I'm failing my baby', 'I feel guilty if I go out to work because I should be home with my baby'. Through the program, Zara was able to shift her feelings of guilt by putting more value on the social and emotional tasks of parenting, for which there are fewer tangible rewards at the end of the day. She also developed a greater sense of competency in her mothering, by focusing on the positive experiences she provided her baby with, and on his healthy development. She was able to challenge rigid ideas about being available to her baby 100% of the time, which reduced her sense of guilt about her professional activities.

Thus, via the process of cognitive restructuring, she was able to resolve the role conflict of mother versus professional woman by adopting a more realistic and flexible outlook, with a resultant reduction in distress. Zara was also able to develop assertiveness skills and apply these to set limits in various situations in her life, such as intrusiveness from her mother-in-law, with a resultant increased sense of efficacy and reduced resentment and fatigue.

In terms of her relationship with her partner, Zara began to see her need for support as legitimate, and not indicative of a sense of failure. From this basis, she was better able to negotiate with her partner about their differing views of parenting. Her partner held a more traditional view that parenting was primarily her responsibility, whereas she preferred a shared care arrangement. Couple therapy helped her with these issues and also her partner to recognise Zara's need to be valued and renegotiate the spending of family finances. At the same time, Zara began to appreciate that her husband's way of helping was to ensure financial stability. In terms of her relationship with her baby, initially it seemed difficult for Zara to enjoy her baby because of the conflict she felt in the role of mother. By the end of the group, however, her increased confidence around her baby resulted in a much more comfortable interaction and she found immense joy in the relationship.

RESEARCH RESULTS ON THE GETTING AHEAD OF POSTNATAL DEPRESSION PROGRAM

Given the large proportion of women who experience PND and the relatively chronic nature of the course of this disorder, it is surprising that there have been few empirical investigations of treatment approaches. The manualised treatment program described in this book is the result of an ongoing evaluation of the efficacy of this program. In the first phase, a pilot study tested the application of cognitive-behavioural therapy to women suffering from PND. We were encouraged by the responsiveness of women with severe and persistent PND to this approach. Depressive symptoms decreased significantly within a 10-week treatment period. In this clinical sample, mean scores on the BDI at inclusion were 29.7 and on retest immediately after treatment had dropped to 16.8. Given the chronicity of symptoms in this group (average six to eight months), the substantial improvement was highly significant (Meager & Milgrom, 1996).

The second phase in the development of this program involved an extensive refining and extension of the treatment content. The application to a community sample was evaluated by screening women attending their infant health centres for symptoms of depression (Negri, 1998). Participants were recruited using the procedure described in Chapter 2 for screening. Mothers who scored at, or above, a cut-off of 12 points on the Edinburgh Postnatal Depression Scale (EPDS) were asked to participate in a further assessment, in their homes. Clinical interviews were conducted to determine if they met DSM-IV criteria for depression, and the EPDS was readministered together with the BDI. Each mother was given an opportunity to discuss the issues that she believed were contributing to the way she was feeling, and invited to take part in the intervention study if she scored 12 or above on the EPDS, 10 or above on the BDI, and was assessed as experiencing a major depressive episode. Exclusion criteria included: experiencing any psychosis or prodromal symptomatology; taking illicit substances; having a physical condition that would better explain symptomatology; being at high risk of harming self or baby; already receiving psychotherapy for PND and having started antidepressant medication in the previous three weeks.

A total of 59 mothers were included in the study, and a CBT group intervention was compared to routine primary care (RPC) on a series of measures (see Table 1). Overall, 37 mothers participated in the CBT program, completed at least five sessions, and returned both pre- and post-intervention questionnaires. Twenty-two mothers received RPC and returned the pre- and post-intervention questionnaires. Participants in the RPC condition were case managed by their maternal and child health nurses as they would normally be, if a specific PND program was not available.

The study utilised Version 1 of the Getting Ahead of Postnatal Depression program (Negri, 1998). This version has been edited and refined and also differs from the version described in this book mainly by the inclusion of only one partner's session (compared to three in the book version), the order of sessions and a reduced amount of cognitive compared to behavioural therapy. No 'including infant' sessions were administered in Version 1.

Table 1   Questionnaire administration schedule at 0 weeks and 10 weeks

Measures
Demographics Questionnaire
Edinburgh Postnatal Depression Scale
Beck Depression Inventory
General Health Questionnaire-60
Parenting Stress Index
Spielberger State–Trait Anxiety Inventory
Coopersmith Self-Esteem Inventory
Perceived Social Support (Family and Friends) Scales

PARTICIPANT CHARACTERISTICS AT PRETREATMENT

The mean age of women included in the study was 30.2 years, with multiparous mothers having between two and five children. The average age of infants was 5.3

months. Other characteristics, such as history of depression, antidepressant medication use, and inpatient or outpatient treatment for PND prior to referral to the present study, are shown in Table 2. There were no significant differences between the two groups at pretreatment with respect to these demographic variables.

Table 2 Characteristics of control (RPC) and CBT mothers at pretreatment ($N = 59$)

Historical variable	Control group (%)		CBT group (%)	
	Yes	No	Yes	No
Previous history of depression	59.1	40.9	73	27
Antenatal onset of depressive episode	45.5	54.5	51.4	48.6
Antidepressant medication	9.1	90.9	29.7	70.3
Previous inpatient treatment for PND	0	100	16.2	83.8
Previous inpatient treatment for mothering skills	22.7	77.3	32.4	67.6
Previous outpatient treatment for PND	13.6	86.4	29.7	70.3
Previous outpatient treatment for mothering skills	13.6	86.4	16.2	83.8

Note: 'Antenatal onset' of depressive episode was denoted if the mother reported depressive symptoms that began in pregnancy and persisted in the puerperium.

EVALUATION OF COGNITIVE-BEHAVIOURAL THERAPY FOR THE TREATMENT OF POSTNATAL DEPRESSION

The results evaluating the efficacy of the CBT program (Version 1) for the treatment of PND are summarised below. The mean and standard deviation for the BDI for depressed women at entry into the trial was 22.5 (SD 7.1) and for the EPDS was 16.7 (SD 3.9). Women were then randomly allocated in blocks of six to a CBT group or the RPC condition.

CBT resulted in a greater reduction in depression than RPC. A mean change of almost 12 points on the BDI for mothers in the CBT group was found to be significantly greater than that observed in the RPC group, $F (1, 58) = 6.04, p < 0.05$, as determined by a one-way analysis of variance. Unfortunately, it was found that the CBT mothers had significantly higher scores on the EPDS, $F (1, 57) = 4.91, p < 0.05$, and BDI, $F (1, 57) = 6.28, p < 0.05$, than the RPC mothers at pretreatment. Therefore, any change in depression level must be interpreted with caution.

However, in order to correct for regression to the mean, the law of initial values technique was used. Thus, a new variable was created by dividing the difference between the mothers' scores on the BDI at pretreatment and post-treatment by the mothers' initial scores on the BDI at pretreatment. A two-way analysis of variance was then conducted on the mean adjusted scores for the RPC group and the CBT group. The results revealed that there was a significant improvement in depression scores for the CBT group in comparison to the RPC group when regression to the mean was controlled for, $F (1, 58) = 6.71$, $p < 0.01$ (see Table 3).

Results from a standard multiple regression analysis also revealed that the more depressed mothers were at pretreatment, the more likely they were to experience greater improvement in their level of depression through participation in the CBT group (Negri, 1998).

In conclusion, it appears that Version 1 of the Getting Ahead of Postnatal Depression program was successful in the treatment of depression (Negri, 1998). Women experienced significantly greater improvements in depressive symptomatology than their counterparts who received RPC. It is important to consider that the comparison made, CBT versus RPC, compared two groups of women who were receiving some support. Thus the improvement in the RPC condition is likely to mean that support from maternal and child health nurses is beneficial and CBT treatment adds value. Other aspects, such as parenting stress, self-esteem and anxiety, did not differentiate the CBT group and the RPC group at pre- or post-treatment. The CBT group, however, experienced a significant improvement in level of perceived social support from their families at post-treatment, which may have been due to the fact that fathers were included in an information night, and that the ability to request assistance from family and friends, as well as assertiveness, was addressed in the CBT program.

Table 3 Means and standard deviations of improvement in EPDS and BDI scores from pre- to post-treatment for the CBT and RPC groups ($N = 59$)

Treatment group	Measures			
	EPDS2 – EPDS1	SD	BDI2 – BDI1	SD
RPC n = 22	–6.32	4.27	–5.91	7.53
CBT n = 37	–8.00	6.69	–11.62	9.21

Note: EPDS2 – EPDS1 = difference between the Edinburgh Postnatal Depression scores at pre- and post-treatment; BDI2 – BDI1 = difference between the Beck Depression Inventory scores at pre- and post-treatment. A negative score denotes improvement in depression score.

CHANGES IN THE PARENT–INFANT RELATIONSHIP

In our pilot study, we found that as the mothers' depression levels decreased with group treatment, so too did their perception of parenting stress; however, their perception of child temperament difficulty remained unaltered (Milgrom & Meager, 1996). We had also demonstrated in another sample of depressed women treated in an inpatient unit that parenting stress both in the parent and child domain continued to differentiate women with PND from controls over a one-year period (Milgrom & McCloud, 1996).

In the community sample of women who received our Version 1 package, we again confirmed that women with PND experience very high levels of parenting stress. Examination of the mean scores on Abidin's Parenting Stress Index (PSI) for the child domain and parent domain for the RPC and CBT groups revealed a similar pattern to that reported by Milgrom and Meager (1996). For all mothers, the full-scale PSI scores at pretreatment fell within the critical range, between the 90th and 95th percentile for parents with infants less than one year of age. High scores on the parent domain are reflective of clinically significant problems in the parent–child system indicative of stress or potential dysfunction (Abidin, 1986).

Mothers suffering from PND continued to experience an unacceptably high level of parenting stress at post-treatment. Parenting stress did not appear to respond differentially to CBT or to RPC, even though the CBT intervention was effective in reducing depressive symptoms and increasing perceived social support from family. Nor did parenting stress spontaneously remit without intervention. These findings led us to develop the additional treatment module found in Chapter 8, for dealing with mother–infant relationship difficulties.

THE GETTING AHEAD OF POSTNATAL DEPRESSION PROGRAM

The final phase of evaluation of the refined CBT program (see Chapter 2), the Getting Ahead of Postnatal Depression program described in this book, is ongoing. Initial findings again confirm the efficacy of this treatment program in reducing PND. Following treatment, a group of mothers with an initial mean Beck Depression Score of 25, experienced a significant 36% decrease in their depression rating. Furthermore, similar results were obtained for mothers with major depressive disorders compared to those with a range of diagnoses for depression (minor depression, adjustment disorder with depressed mood, mixed anxiety–depressive disorders), and treatment was again superior to RPC. While numbers are still small ($n = 23$), encouraging preliminary results also show that the revised version of our program results in a decrease in other variables such as anxiety. We found a significant decrease in anxiety ($t = 3.5$ $p < 0.01$), with a 54% improvement from an initial score of 25.3 on the Beck Anxiety Inventory following CBT. By contrast RPC resulted in no change in anxiety. The data on both Version 1 and the final Getting Ahead of Postnatal Depression program, therefore, both confirm that this type of CBT intervention is effective at reducing symptomatology in depressed women.

We are continuing to evaluate this program as part of a large randomised control trial that will provide further information about the effectiveness of the CBT group program relative to the individual approach described in this book, and the inclusion of the extra modules to intervene in the parent–infant relationship. Long-term data will also emerge, as will the benefits of self-help groups in maintaining treatment gains (see Box 1).

CONCLUSION

The above findings suggest that CBT applied to the treatment of PND as described in this book is effective in reducing depressive symptomatology. Our results are particularly encouraging as they showed an improvement compared to RPC, which was a condition where women were already engaged with a primary health care professional. Thus, CBT seems to offer an additional benefit to baseline support. O'Hara *et al.* (1998), by contrast, found that only 20% of women who

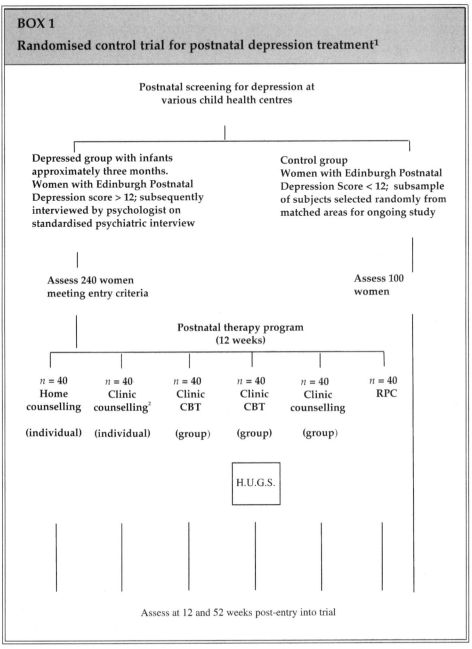

BOX 1

Randomised control trial for postnatal depression treatment[1]

Postnatal screening for depression at
various child health centres

Depressed group with infants
approximately three months.
Women with Edinburgh Postnatal
Depression score > 12; subsequently
interviewed by psychologist on
standardised psychiatric interview

Control group
Women with Edinburgh Postnatal
Depression Score < 12; subsample
of subjects selected randomly from
matched areas for ongoing study

Assess 240 women
meeting entry criteria

Assess 100
women

Postnatal therapy program
(12 weeks)

$n = 40$	$n = 40$	$n = 40$	$n = 40$	$n = 40$	$n = 40$
Home counselling	Clinic counselling[2]	Clinic CBT	Clinic CBT	Clinic counselling	RPC
(individual)	(individual)	(group)	(group)	(group)	

H.U.G.S.

Assess at 12 and 52 weeks post-entry into trial

[1] Austin & Repatriation Medical Centre, Melbourne, Australia with support from RADGAC.
[2] Also separately trialed with additional support from a self-help organisation for PND.

received no support over 12 weeks but were in a waiting-list condition experience
significant reduction in depressive symptomatology.

The results of our studies are consistent with a recently published report of
three brief home-based psychological interventions: non-directive counselling,

CBT and dynamic psychotherapy. Cooper and Murray (1997) found that all three treatments significantly increased the rate of recovery in comparison to a routine primary care group.

Long-term maintenance of gains

Only one follow-up study has been published with respect to the maintenance of treatment gains in the treatment of PND (Cooper & Murray, 1997). Maintenance of treatment gains over the nine- and twelve-month follow-ups were reportedly best for the CBT. Lower attrition rates were also noted for the CBT group, in comparison to the other psychological interventions studied. This clearly requires replication. A confounding problem in follow-up studies in the area of PND is the subsequent delivery of another baby. It is known that there is an increased risk of developing a major depressive episode in the puerperium if one has experienced a previous postpartum episode, but not an increased chance of developing a non-postpartum episode (Cooper & Murray, 1995; Philipps & O'Hara, 1991). Keeping this in mind, another test of the efficacy of an intervention program for PND is whether or not the treatment outcomes can be maintained subsequent to the birth of another child. Data on this issue has not been reported in the research litera-ture. It is of major clinical importance, however, to be able to tell mothers who have experienced an episode of PND what their chances are of experiencing another episode with a successive delivery and if treatment for one episode may help them with a second. Mothers who have experienced a previous episode of depression postpartum experience heightened levels of anxiety and hyper-vigilance following a subsequent childbirth, which may in turn actually impair parenting performance (Olioff, 1991). Mothers in this situation may appraise the fact that they have previously experienced PND as evidence that they are poor mothers, contributing to the development of depressive symptomatology.

Are mothers who have received cognitive-behavioural intervention for PND less likely to develop a depressive episode following a subsequent delivery? Our program empowers the mother to identify and monitor her own signals (cognitive, be-havioural and emotive), to identify when she is experiencing a depressive episode, and to differentiate this experience from day-to-day feelings which may at times include dysphoria. Mothers are assisted to reframe the experience of PND as a learning one in which they are learning important skills to improve their mood and day-to-day functioning. They are also encouraged to develop their own individual 'kit' of techniques that they find useful in altering their mood, and which they can draw upon in the future. The depressive episode experienced is thus redefined as a learning curve through which one can gain skills to be applied, if necessary. As such, mothers who have received this intervention may be less likely to develop PND consequent to another delivery. Whether CBT reduces the risk of another episode of PND remains an empirical question, which requires further investigation.

This program, however, also provides additional modules to deal with relation-ship issues that some women have, with both their partners and their infants. These areas of difficulty seem resistant to change without specific intervention and future research will determine the effectiveness of targeting not just maternal difficulties but also infants and partners.

Part III

Clinical Management Options

INTRODUCTION

The group program presented in Part II can be supplemented as indicated with couple sessions. Wherever possible, this provides an important additional module, since the impact of postnatal depression (PND) on the couple has been described. In addition, for many women who suffer from PND, there are long-term consequences on child development. Early intervention that targets difficulties in the parent–infant relationship is also provided as an optional module. Finally, there are situations that require an individual approach to PND, and this approach is elaborated using a combination of counselling skills and cognitive-behavioural therapy techniques.

Part III ends with clinical issues that may arise for the therapist during the group program and in its implementation.

Chapter 7:   Describes a three-session program for couples.

Chapter 8:   Describes a three-session program for parent–infant difficulties.

Chapter 9:   Describes how the Getting Ahead of Postnatal Depression group program can be adapted for individual treatment.

Chapter 10:   Provides some concluding comments on clinical issues as well as discussing the important role of prevention and future research directions.

Chapter 7

INCLUDING FATHERS

With contributions from Jennifer Ericksen

NOTES FOR THE THERAPIST

Attitudes

Fathers may wonder why you want to see them as well as their partner, particularly if they perceive that the mother is the only person with a problem to resolve. They may have preconceived ideas about why they are being included in the treatment process (e.g., 'so you can gang up on me'), how the session may be conducted (e.g., 'discussing feelings is a waste of time') and about psychological treatment in general (e.g., 'it's a load of rubbish'). The belief that they will somehow be blamed is not uncommon. Many men need help to see why they should be included when it is their partners' problem.

Attendance

In order for the father to attend, he not only has had to deal with his own feelings about it, but he has also had to make arrangements to leave work, which can be difficult. It is important to recognise the efforts he needs to make in order to attend, by commenting and acknowledging this in the invitation.

An invitation sent directly to fathers has been found to be effective in recruiting them for the group, as mothers may have preconceived ideas about their partners' likelihood of being involved (e.g., 'he would never come', 'he's too busy'). Sending an invitation takes the onus off the mother to encourage her partner to attend, and places it onto the father. Sometimes a follow-up call is necessary to facilitate the attendance. The invitation should be sent to him with his name and his partner's name on it. It needs information about where to come, and when and what will be discussed, such as information on postnatal depression (PND). It is also important to explain what the aims of the father's sessions are and the expectations you have of him.

Box 1 depicts the information that is useful to include in an 'invitation brochure' to fathers. Additional information that can be included is attached at the end of the session.

BOX 1: INVITATION BROCHURE

Postnatal depression
Couples support group invitation

Where: _____   When: _____   Why: _____   What: _____

Topics and issues that will be covered

- What is postnatal depression?
- Treatment of postnatal depression
- Effects on partners
- Strategies for support
- Relationship issues
- Change and communication
- Role of extended family
- Looking to the future

Partner's support

Fathers have a valuable role in supporting their partners suffering from postnatal depression. Through their commitment and support, fathers can have a direct impact on their partner's recovery.

Confidentiality

Fathers will come to their sessions somewhat at a disadvantage. They have not been privy to the discussions that you have had with their partner. Often you may know more about their relationship and the partner's thoughts and feelings than he may know himself. It is important that you do not breach confidentiality with the information from the mother's sessions. Instead, the aim is to raise areas of concern to all parents of infants and allow the couple to divulge and discuss issues that they feel comfortable about revealing in the session. Other issues that may be important for the couple to resolve do not have to be raised during the session. However, once communication lines are put in place the couple can then deal with their issues in their own time. 'Pick the right time' is a useful theme.

Women without partners

It may be the case that not all the mothers in the group have partners whom they wish to, or can, invite. Even estranged couples should be encouraged to attempt at least the first session. It has been found that Session 1 is useful for anyone who is involved in supporting the mother, if the baby's father is not attending, e.g. friends, parents. Their involvement is encouraged and is very beneficial. Sessions 2 and 3 are not relevant to anyone other than live-in partners.

The benefits

Although fathers often get off to a reluctant start, we have become increasingly aware of the benefits of their involvement, not only for their partners but also for themselves. In many cases, there is a sense of relief that the concern they have for their partner and family is now spread to others and that help is at hand. There is also an opportunity to unburden and to get some coping strategies in place. The sessions give fathers the opportunity to express their own fears and feelings of helplessness. This can help the mother understand that her partner has been feeling burdened and afraid. In general, fathers are positive about their involvement and frequently would like to be more involved. Some have suggested an opportunity to talk candidly with other fathers without the partners being present. Fathers have commented that they have felt left out of things up until the couples' sessions, and may either feel pleased to be in-cluded or ambivalent (*'Why should I participate now?'*).

This couples' program has been devised from the literature and our clinical practice (Dix, 1986; Berg-Cross & Cohen, 1995). It can be administered as part of the group program and is also useful with individual couples in therapy (see Chapter 10).

Aims of couple sessions

- To provide information about the symptoms, causes, course and treatment of PND.
- To give fathers an opportunity to talk about their feelings, to provide support to fathers and to help them to understand their feelings.
- To involve fathers in the problem-solving aspect of the counsell-ing process so that they can assist their partner in recovery.
- To normalise parenting stress and to highlight the impact on both parents.
- To encourage open and effective communication between the parents.
- To provide survival tips for partners, to help them to use the support available and to learn to ask for help so they may be able to look after themselves and their partner.

SESSION 1: PARTNERS AND POSTNATAL DEPRESSION

NOTES FOR THE THERAPIST

This session aims: to build rapport with the couples; to explore couples' feelings about parenthood; to give information about PND; and to begin to encourage partners to discuss how they have been managing and feeling over recent weeks.

INTRODUCTION TO SESSION 1: PARTNERS' SESSION

❑   **Welcome.**

'Thank you everyone for making the effort to get here. We know that for many of you it has taken quite a bit of organisation. We appreciate your efforts and hope that you find this session informative and a worthwhile experience.

  Your attendance is a sign of support for your partner and is a very great step forward toward recovery.

  'I am _____ I have worked here at _____ (organisation) for _____. This agency sees _____ .

Some details about the clinic they have come to, a brochure about the service and explanation about how the couples have come to be in treatment is useful. It is our experience that a good approach when fathers are present is to provide context and factual information.

❑   **Ground rules.**

Some ground rules should be set prior to the main part of the session.

Confidentiality

- Personal details about others should not be discussed outside of the group.
- Trust other members.

Contribution

- Be supportive of each other, not judgemental.
- You are encouraged to contribute, but not compelled to if you would rather not.

Attendance

- Attend every session.
- Start and finish on time.

Concerns about safety

At times, depression can be severe and risk of suicide may be real.

- If anyone in the group, including the therapist, is concerned about someone's safety, then action must be taken. If a partner is concerned, he may call emergency services in his area. Local emergency contact numbers should be provided to the group at this point.

❑   **Organisational or housekeeping issues.**

- Eating.
- Tea and coffee arrangements.
- Toilets.
- Parking, etc.

AIMS OF THE TREATMENT SESSIONS

Orient couples to the following six aims:

1. To learn about postnatal depression

'This series of three couples' sessions will allow participants to become familiar with the range of symptoms women with postnatal depression may be experiencing and to learn more about depression.'

- Not all of the women will have the same symptoms and this can be confusing and will need discussion.

2. To gain understanding about the effects of depression

Through discussion, it is hoped that an understanding is reached between each couple about the specific areas of difficulty that they are experiencing; and that through the group some strategies for dealing with depression, and the day-to-day aspects of parenthood, can be explored.

'We know that hearing others talk about their thoughts and feelings, and contributing to the discussion yourself, will lead to a greater understanding of your own situation and difficulties.'

3. To encourage effective communication

Many partners are acutely aware that aspects of their relationship have not been quite right since their baby arrived. Our experience has been that they are only too happy to take on extra roles around the house, with the baby, or running errands. Mothers are not good at asking them for help. *'Why do I need to ask him? It's obvious it needs to be done.'* In addition, the feedback when fathers do carry out these activities is rarely positive, which then makes the fathers less inclined to try again, e.g. *'I might as well have done it myself.'* A comment often made by fathers is that they are *'damned if they do and damned if they don't'*. This dilemma confronts them constantly and they often flee to the workplace where life is more 'normal' and 'predictable'. They must then deal with the concern and guilt that this generates. This is reinforced by frequent comments from their partners: *'It's okay for you, you go to work each day, you don't know what I have to put up with.'* *'Your life hasn't changed the way mine has.'*

Communication between mothers and fathers is an essential part of the treatment process.

'Being able to talk to your partner and express your feelings and needs is very important. Asking for help and being able to accept it without being critical or feeling guilty is a major aim for treatment.'

4. To explore fathers' feelings and how life has changed since the baby

'Many of you expected that the decision to have a baby would affect your life in a variety of ways, for example, less leisure time. Do other things come to mind?'

Fathers can feel very pushed aside. Well-meaning friends and relatives focus on the baby and the mother, and few include the father. His partner too can become consumed by the needs of the baby to the exclusion of her partner. His life changes dramatically also. You can ask for other suggestions from the group. *'I would be surprised if any of you anticipated just how much would have changed.'*

5. To provide some survival tips for partners

'We have some survival tips for partners that have been suggested by fathers who have had to deal with a partner with postnatal depression. We will talk more about these in later sessions.'

We know that, while it is tough on the depressed person, it can also be very tough on the other family members dealing with the situation.

6. Aims for today

'We are now going to become more familiar with postnatal depression, its symptoms, what contributes to it, possible causes and what treatment helps. We will then spend some time discussing how your partner's depression and the arrival of your baby have affected you.'

WHAT IS POSTNATAL DEPRESSION?

This section is similar to the one given to mothers in Session 1 of the group program. This serves as an opportunity for the mothers to revise this information, as we know that one of the symptoms of depression is reduced ability to think and concentrate.

❑ **Symptoms of postnatal depression.**

'Symptoms of postnatal depression have typically been reported to include':

OVERHEAD 1

Symptoms of postnatal depression

- Lowered mood, sadness
- Feeling worthless
- Tearfulness
- Self-blame or guilt
- Anxiety
- Lack of energy
- Lack of interest
- Appetite disturbance
- Reduced concentration

- Sleep disturbance
- Worries about health
- Confused thought
- Slowed speech
- Slow movement
- Thoughts about death
- Trouble deciding
- Agitation
- Suicidal thoughts

This overhead will be familiar to mothers as it was presented in Session 1.

Lead a discussion about the symptoms partners have noticed.

- *'When did you first start noticing a change?'*
- *'What were the first things you noticed?'*
- *'What things are you aware of at the moment that cause your partner difficulty?'*
- *'What did you think was going on?'*
- *'Do you think she is depressed?'*
- *'Had you heard of postnatal depression before?'*
- *'What did you think postnatal depression was?'*
- *'Have you known of other people with postnatal depression?'*

Explain postnatal depression is not just experienced by women, and that men also can suffer from depression after their child's birth.

- *'Some of you also may be experiencing these symptoms.'*

❑   **Contributing factors.**

'Some researchers believe that hormonal and biochemical changes contribute to depression in women following childbirth. Most professionals acknowledge that the biological explanation for depression is only part of the answer.'

Discuss with the couples the four points on the overhead below.

'It is not surprising that many mothers have difficulty adjusting and that the demands can be overwhelming. Quite often it can be our own expectations of ourselves that are the hardest to overcome.'

'Postnatal depression is not different from depression at any other time in one's life.'

'It generally results when positive experiences, feelings of being competent, having adequate positive self-concept and positive feedback from others are outweighed by negative experiences (e.g. colicky baby), feelings of being inadequate as a mother (e.g., unable to settle an overtired baby), negative self-concept (e.g., I'm a hopeless mum) and negative or no

---

OVERHEAD 2

Issues associated with postnatal depression

- The transition to motherhood involves adapting to huge physical, emotional and social changes
- Most mothers experience difficulties adjusting to their new role
- Myths about motherhood can create unrealistic expectations
- Unrealistic expectations lead to feelings of failure when coping problems occur

---

feedback from others (e.g., I'm a mother, I'm expected to manage all these things. No one says: Wow, you managed to do all the washing today. Good work. People are more inclined to offer advice).

We believe that depression occurs when there is an imbalance between the positive events and negative events in your life. When the negatives outweigh the positives, depression can result. Mood can change in response to changes in the balance during a day, or a week. When something good happens you may feel better for a while.'

Other causes of depression—life events:

OVERHEAD 3

Life events that may cause depression

A. Social separations:
   — Death of spouse, close family member or close friend
   — Divorce
   — Marital separation
   — Son or daughter leaving home
   — Change in residence

B. Health-related events:
   — Major change in health of self or close family member
   — Personal injury or illness

C. New responsibilities and adjustments:
   — Marriage
   — Addition of new family member

D. Work-related events:
   — Change to different jobs
   — Promotion and/or major change in work
   — Being fired
   — Trouble with boss
   — Retirement from work
   — Spouse starts or stops work
   — Change to new school
   — End of formal schooling

E. Financial and material events:
   — Burdensome debts
   — Financial setbacks
   — Loss of personal property through fire, theft, etc.
   — Legal problems

From Lewinsohn, Munoz, Youngren and Zeiss (1992).

❑   **Father's expectations of parenthood.**

'Fathers too will have had hopes and expectations about their ability to move into fatherhood. Are any of you able to remember what you expected it would be like?'

Many couples expect the physical demands but are surprised by the emotional demands of parenthood. Try to encourage discussion from fathers about their expectations. Fathers typically feel helpless and afraid as things are going wrong and they do not know how to fix it.

❑   **How common is postnatal depression?**

OVERHEAD 4

Feelings after birth

Baby blues:
- 80–90% of women feel tearful
- 3–4 days after birth for a short time

Postnatal depression:
- 10–20% of women feel depressed
- Onset in the first year after birth

Psychosis:
- 0.001% of women feel out of touch with reality
- Onset in first six weeks

'Postnatal depression affects 10–20% of women. It has its onset during pregnancy or within the first six months after the baby's birth. Women can experience the symptoms of depression to a greater or lesser degree.

Postnatal depression should not be confused with the baby blues that 80–90% of women feel three to four days after having their babies. This is a short period of tearfulness that is commonly experienced by women.

Postpartum psychosis is another condition with its onset in the first six weeks after a baby's birth. This affects a very small percentage of women (0.001%) and results in women feeling out of touch with reality, frequently unable to care for themselves or their baby and needing hospitalisation and medication. This is a more severe condition.'

Treatment: what helps?

'There are a range of treatments available for postnatal depression. Just as there are different degrees and symptoms of postnatal depression, there are different approaches to treating it. The cognitive-behavioural therapy you are involved in is one effective approach. Some women may need anti-depressant medication as well as ongoing therapy. Medication can help to alleviate the symptoms of depression, which can give individuals relief while they continue to work through the group sessions. Similarly, mobilising support and finding time-out can be helpful.

Women whose partners are supportive and participate in the couples' sessions often benefit more from the treatment given.'

Fathers' feelings and experience of parenthood

In this session fathers will be exploring what it has been like living with someone who is depressed, and a new baby; and what feelings the father has been experiencing.

'This is probably something you have not discussed together. It may be a sensitive subject for many of you, but we wonder whether we could discuss what it has been like living with someone who is depressed. We know it can't have been easy.'

There are a range of common issues that include:

- Lack of sleep.
- Not knowing how to help.
- Being criticised.
- Work commitments.
- Managing child care.
- Managing home duties.
- Enquiries from family, friends and work colleagues.
- Being left out.
- Job and money issues.
- If applicable—hospitalisation, separation, care of other children.

'In summing up, each of you have had to deal with quite a range of things. How have you managed? Who has been looking after you? It's not always easy to hang in there.'

❑   **Summary.**

- Summarise the main issues discussed in this first session.
- Encourage couples to take home and read a handout (photocopy Box 2) which covers and expands the ideas raised in the session.

BOX 2

Postnatal depression: yes—it exists!

The birth of a child is supposed to be one of the happiest times in a woman's life.

Sadly, for many women, nothing could be further from the truth. In fact, in the year or so after childbirth, a woman's chances of developing a depressive illness are significantly increased.

Many women, believing that mothering should always be blissful, feel too ashamed to tell anyone that they are not coping. Often, even their own mothers will make comments like 'Well, I coped. So should you' or 'Just get on with it all.'

About 14% of women will develop a depressive illness in the first year after childbirth, with a further 40% feeling significantly distressed and not coping. It is vital for women to recognise the signs and symptoms of PND and know where to seek appropriate help.

Box 2 continued

Symptoms

- Depressed and/or irritable mood most of the time
- Bouts of crying
- Sleep disturbance: unable to get to sleep, waking during the night or too early in the morning
- Loss of appetite (occasionally increased)
- Anxiety
- Tiredness
- Feelings of guilt
- Loss of self-esteem
- Loss of sexual interest
- Confusion
- Memory problems
- Poor concentration
- Not wanting to go out
- Negative feelings about motherhood
- Negative feelings towards the baby
- If severe, suicidal thoughts or suicide attempts

What causes PND?

There are usually many factors that lead to the development of PND.

There are significant hormonal changes that occur immediately after childbirth. Rather than there being any definite hormone deficiencies or excesses, it seems that some women are more sensitive than others to these changes. These women are also more likely to suffer with premenstrual syndrome.

Other physical causal factors include traumatic or difficult birth or illness in the postpartum period. Also important is a past or family history of depression.

Psychological and social factors, for most women, probably play a great role. Such factors include:

- Adjustment to new role as mother
- Career change from working woman to mother at home
- Increased workload
- Loss of identity and social isolation
- Poor experience of mothering from one's own mother
- Expectations of herself as a mother
- Certain personality types that find the demands of mothering hard to tolerate
- History of physical or sexual abuse
- Lack of family, marital and community support
- Coping with a 'difficult' baby
- Marital problems

What helps?

- **Mobilising support, allowing 'time-out' from mothering and alleviation of the 'super-woman syndrome'**
- **Involvement of partner for emotional and practical support**
- **Working with negative thoughts**
- **Looking at adapting to role change**
- **Group support**
- **Dealing with past problems, e.g. relationship with family of origin**
- **Improving feelings of competency**

Box 2 continued

Medication

Because the illness has biological, psychological and social causes, the treatment should be approached from the same perspective. In most cases, women have tried to 'snap themselves out of it' but find they cannot. This is because there are usually significant chemical changes that take place in the brain's chemistry, that cause the symptoms previously mentioned. Antidepressant medications which correct these imbalances may be an important cornerstone in treatment. They are non-addictive and usually require a course of approximately six months. Because there are many community misconceptions about these drugs, some women who could benefit are missing out by refusing this medication because of fear or lack of knowledge.

Depending on severity of illness, this can be accomplished as an outpatient or inpatient.

Adapted from Phillips (1995).

Read through the handout.

- Organise the next session.

Suggested additional information to go with the father's invitation.

Postnatal depression

Postnatal depression occurs in approximately 20% of women following the birth of their baby. This illness can occur antenatally in some women.

Postnatal depression varies in its severity and duration. Social, physical and psychological factors contribute to recovery.

Symptoms of postnatal depression

All of these symptoms may be present and may affect women in the following ways:

- Tearfulness
- Mood swings
- Loss of confidence
- Poor self-image
- Difficulty with concentration and remembering
- Sleep deprivation
- Stress on relationship
- Loss of interest in sex

Effect on partners

Although women suffer the primary symptoms of postnatal depression, their partners can also be affected and sometimes become depressed.

Demands placed on partners can include:

- Sleep deprivation
- Work commitments
- Managing child care

Continued

- Separation from spouse
- Home duties
- Visits to health professionals
- Enquiries from family, friends and work colleagues

These stressors lead to partners experiencing feelings of powerlessness, anger and guilt. Uncertainty, self-doubt and insecurity about the future can also arise.

SESSION 2: THE COUPLE RELATIONSHIP

NOTES FOR THE THERAPIST

The focus of this session is on the changes in the couple's relationship after the birth of their baby. The communication between the mother and father is encouraged as each explores their feelings. The issues of time-out for the couple and their sexual relationship are focused on. Discussion about these topics is usually easy to elicit as it is an area of contention between most couples.

INTRODUCTION AND SESSION CONTENT

❑ **Welcome back.**

'It's good to see so many of you back again for our second couples' session. We are going to continue on from where we left off last time. As you will remember, we were discussing the strains put onto couples when they have a baby and, in particular, the additional strains when the mother is depressed.'

❑ **Feedback from last session.**

'Have any of you got any comments about how you found the last couples' session?'

Spend a few minutes eliciting feedback. It is often the case that couples discuss the sessions and that, in between sessions, issues are dealt with and resolved.

Many husbands feel supported by the sessions and may express this or a sense of relief or optimism. Lead the discussion into the topics for this session. Ascertain if either partner has noticed any changes in the other. It can be reinforcing to hear that changes and improvements are occurring.

❑ **Lovers to parents.**

'Last session we talked about how your life had changed since the birth of your baby. Today we will focus on how your relationship has changed as you go from being lovers to parents.'

Many couples feel a loss of intimacy in their relationship together— there are changes. Enormous amounts of energy go into the baby, often leaving the partner feeling left out. The focus changes from the couple to the baby. Fatigue plays a large part. The old life is lost. The time to just be together, to eat, to sleep, to talk or make love together is gone. Couples need to be encouraged to make time for these things again, now their baby has arrived. Priorities change. *'What have you noticed about your relationship?'* Changes may have occurred between the couple in terms of equality, and sharing of things, and more traditional roles may be taken. This change occurs insidiously rather than through planning. The wife can feel left out as she no longer earns an income and the loss of independence can be very dramatic. Husbands also change how they relate to wives and do not ask about things they used to ask about previously.

❑   **Time for us.**

Allow the couples to raise, discuss and attempt to problem solve any issues about the availability of time for them as a couple (or individuals). Encourage them to brainstorm about things they used to do and miss, e.g. discussing politics of the day.
    Normalise their feelings.

'In the first year after the birth of your baby it is normal for couples to have less time available to do the things they normally used to do. This period of life is characterised by enormous changes.'

Go through the topics on the overhead below and try to problem solve some of the issues raised. Couples may be encouraged to continue to discuss these issues and to come up with their own solutions between sessions. Time spent encouraging couples to do some things together is important. It is useful to get some undertaking that they will try something between sessions.

OVERHEAD 5

Time for us

- **Lovers to parents**
- **Communication: does it still exist?**
- **Making time to talk**
- **Organising time-out together**
  - **— sleep time**
  - **— walking with pram**
  - **— offers of babysitting**
- **Time saving options**

❑   **Communication.**

'The ability to communicate is essential for the recovery process. Depression often makes communication more difficult. Lack of motivation, feelings of worthlessness and low self-esteem make women less inclined to try to tell

their partner how they feel. Confused thoughts and lack of concentration make it hard to really communicate to someone else how you are feeling.

Communication can disappear in the relationship. The mother is confused and thinks that she is asking for help. Many women do not know what to say or how things might be made better. The partner is not able to understand her ways of asking, or need for help. Anger, fear and confusion are common feelings expressed by partners when the one they care about is distressed, helpless and not managing.

It may be hard to start to share these feelings alone, and that is the purpose of the couple sessions. Some common feelings are presented in Overhead 6.'

OVERHEAD 6

What happens to us?

For many couples, the prospect of parenting brings with it a multitude of expectations and emotions: the dream of being a family. Each partner has their own expectations of being a parent and what their baby will be like. For some, these expectations are very high and lead to couples feeling disillusioned when their dreams to not match reality. Often the more difficult aspects of parenting are not anticipated and a consequent painful period of readjustment may ensue.

The birth of the baby can shift the power balance in the relationship. Financial, social, sexual, emotional and domestic issues all need to be discussed and negotiated by the couple. Unaddressed difficulties in the relationship can lead to resentment and anger, and an inability to deal with these feelings. Some partners may cope by throwing themselves into their work, consuming alcohol or drugs, or coming home late rather than facing the situation at home. One partner's withdrawal may leave the other partner feeling isolated, abandoned, and overwhelmed by the chaos of early parenting.

When your relationship begins to be consumed by frustration and resentment, it is time to acknowledge that something is wrong and you need to do something.

The demands of a new baby are constant. Very often there is little time or energy left for the couple's relationship. Spending some time together can allow feelings to be shared and a loving relationship to be revived. It is important to encourage communication about feelings so relationships can be rebuilt, maintained and strengthened. A useful start is to:

- Accept each other's feelings
- Share your experiences
- Listen without interruption or judgement (there is no need to have all the answers)
- Understand that it will take time to adjust
- Ask what sort of help your partner needs most from you
- Be prepared to help in practical ways and to accept help when it is offered
- Do not hesitate to seek professional help if you need further support and particularly if you are concerned about your own safety, your partner's or your infant's (most areas have 24-hour crisis telephone services).[†]

Continue to communicate. You can get through this together.

[†]Material for Overheads 6 and 8, and supporting text, drawn from the following resources: *Postnatal Distress* (1993) (pamphlet published by Adelaide Women's Community Health Centre, Adelaide, Australia), and *Postpartum Depression and Anxiety: A self-help guide for mothers* (4th edn), (Vancouver: Pacific Post Partum Support Society, 1997).

Discuss the overhead, which may be photocopied as a handout.

'What are some of the ways you can start to communicate better? One idea, if verbal communication is difficult, is to leave a note when you think of something.' Brainstorm other ideas.

❑   **Time for me.**

Both individuals in the couple relationship need a bit of space, some time-out. Partners need to understand that mothers need time-out from the home and the baby. Partners may need to review their out-of-home activities, to provide support, even if this is only in the short term. Support offered at this crucial time will help to get things back on track. Lack of support often results in resentment and a more protracted recovery.

❑   **Survival tips.**

'Here is some advice from a father who has been in your situation' (Paul, 1996). (See Overhead 7.)

1. Don't be too embarrassed to tell friends and family. It is an illness. Life became much easier for us once we told more people of the real situation.
2. Accept help from everyone. This can include home help, food in the freezer, childcare and gardening.
3. Stay in close contact with friends and family. Make sure you have someone to talk to about your problems both at home and at work.
4. Stay active—play sport or undertake a hobby. It is preferable to play high-energy sports, e.g. basketball, squash, than time-consuming sports such as golf or cricket. It gets you out! One father told us, 'I gave up cricket four months after Marcus was born, but did not replace it with any sport until Cindy was virtually off the medication . . . a mistake, I can assure you!'
5. Make sure you and your wife go out (with or without the children—it's more fun without them) on a regular basis. Get out of the house.
6. If you can, get away for the weekend—just the two of you.
7. At times, take the anger should it fly your way.
8. Be prepared that some people close to you and your wife will not understand the severity of your problems.
9. Make time to go out with your mates/work colleagues. This is another way of making time for yourself. Of course, this should be done in moderation.
10. Always stay positive in front of your wife even if your confidence in what the future holds is wavering. Encourage her that she will get better, as she needs all the positive reinforcement she can get.

OVERHEAD 7

Survival tips for husbands

- Don't keep it a secret
- Accept help from others
- Talk to family and friends
- Make time for yourself, play sport, see mates and work colleagues, in moderation
- Find time together regularly
- Accept that some people will not understand
- Stay positive in front of your partner

'Who do you find supportive?'

Encourage each person to use whatever supports are there for them and, if any individuals don't feel adequately supported, problem solve in the group ways of improving their support network.

❏   **Sex after birth.**

Many couples experience problems making love after the birth of their baby.' We find that this section always generates lots of discussion.

OVERHEAD 8

Is there sex after birth?

- Total exhaustion
- Pain from stitches, haemorrhoids or coccyx
- Hormonal state—vaginal dryness—reduced sexual urge—reduced arousal
- Contraception—fear of pregnancy
- Lack of time and opportunity
- Changed body image—weight—slack muscles
- Need for a little privacy and space

Discuss the reasons why it usually takes some time for the couple's sexual relationship to return to normal following childbirth, using Overhead 8 and the questions raised by the text below.

'Most couples with new babies have very little sexual contact. Can you think of any reasons? Overhead 8 describes some of the most significant factors in reducing sexual contact in couples, particularly exhaustion, lack of time and opportunity. Women also commonly experience negative feelings about their bodies after childbirth. A woman's body changes dramatically during pregnancy, childbirth and postnatally. Some women may experience vaginal pain or discomfort following a difficult labour. Physical pain or feeling uncomfortable with one's body interferes with enjoyment of the sexual relationship. In addition, women often find the physical

intimacy and cuddling with a baby, particularly during breastfeeding, very fulfilling, and partners may feel jealous. Losing sexual feeling is also common when a woman is depressed. She often feels tired, uninterested in most things, tense and ugly.

During the period of readjustment to these many changes the sexual relationship between partners will also need to change. Difficulties may be experienced by couples when this is overlooked and not discussed. If, for example, a partner reacts to the other partner's loss of sexual interest by feelings of rejection, this may result in a vicious cycle of withdrawal, resentment and further loss of intimacy.

These are all normal experiences of early parenting that can, with understanding and planning, be overcome. Partners, nevertheless, may still find enormous benefit from physical expressions of affection even if they do not want to make love.'

OVERHEAD 9

Sex after birth: common myths

- **Sex equals intercourse**
- **Couples must have sex regularly**
- **After six weeks, the mother's body is sexually back to normal**
- **Sex after the baby will be how it was pre-pregnancy**
- **It is a woman's duty to provide sex for her partner**

Discuss some of the common myths or misconceptions about sex and childbirth.

'Some women tell me that they don't even want to kiss or cuddle as they fear what it might lead to.'
'Men have said that they feel a sense of rejection.'

❏ **Summary.**

Briefly summarise the group proceedings from the evenings. Encourage couples to continue to consider the issues raised and to try to problem-solve issues as they arise between sessions.
Set the time for the next session.

SESSION 3: DOING IT OURSELVES

NOTES FOR THE THERAPIST

This session aims to be more a discussion about previous material presented than covering very much new ground. The content of the first two sessions is high and this final session should focus on how the couples are using the previously presented material, and encouraging them to do so. Problem solving is also useful. Some couples reporting success will serve to encourage others. It is also aimed at discussing the likely path recovery might take as well as the issues that planning another child will raise. Many couples are fearful that they will suffer depression again.

INTRODUCTION AND SESSION CONTENT

❑   **Welcome back.**

'Welcome to all of you again.' If a couple has been unable to attend, it is good to mention this and the reason. *'Tonight Liz and John cannot be here as their child is too sick to bring out'.*

'This session we are going to spend time discussing the previous sessions and how they have changed things for you as a couple. This is our last session together and we are keen to have some feedback about how you have found them.'

'We will also discuss the future and any questions you might have about recovery from depression and possible future episodes of depression.'

❑   **Symptoms.**

In the first session, we looked mainly at the symptoms of postnatal depression.

'Have you noticed any changes in your partner's symptoms, or any changes in general?'

'As you will remember, this is our list of symptoms.' (Refer back to Overhead 1.)

It can be reinforcing for the mother to hear from her partner how she has changed. Reinforce the couple for the gains that have been made through the treatment program.

❑   **Support.**

Congratulate couples for attending and supporting each other. Discuss who else has been a support to the father.

'We hope that these sessions have helped you to use the supports available to you. It is important for you to continue to do this in the future.'

'Have people got some examples of accepting help or finding support from family or friends? Very often, people find support in unexpected places.'

❑   **Relationship.**

'Last session, we talked about how your relationship as a couple changes when you have a child. We touched on the need for remembering to have time again as a couple and individually.'

'How have you been going with this? Have you noticed any changes since we talked about this?'

The therapist is trying to get couples to remember the last session and to encourage discussion about changes couples have made, difficulties couples came up against and solutions others have found. Lead a general discussion, explore the issues and reinforce those couples who have made an effort. Try to explore with couples who have not had such success what the barriers are for them. The group may have some valuable suggestions.

❑   **Communication.**

'We also discussed the need for communication between partners as a way of dealing with issues. Have you been able to find the time to talk?'
    'Have you been finding talking to each other easier? Do you feel that you have been able to be really understood?'

The therapist needs to focus on the efforts that couples have made. This also gives another opportunity to stress the importance of each partner making the effort to understand what the other one is trying to say or is feeling.

❑   **Sexual relationship.**

As a flow-on from communication, sex can also be discussed. This is often one of the areas that improves quickly when couples are able to communicate their needs more clearly.

❑   **Where to from now?**

OVERHEAD 10

Where to from now?

- Rocky road to recovery
- Lapse, not relapse
- Picking up cues as needs change:
  — increased risk of postnatal depression
  — previous treatment reduces risk
  — early detection of signs
  — early treatment
  — planning

'Recovery often consists of highs and lows rather than a steady or sudden improvement in mood. Occasional lapses are expected and should not be seen as relapses. The time between low days gets longer. The lows are less debilitating and are more easily overcome.'

Mothers become better at detecting their own cues of depressed mood and are able to take action to avert it.

'Mothers', fathers' and babies' needs change with time.'

It is important that this is understood and that the couples are going to have to continue to communicate and problem solve as they confront each new challenge of parenthood.

Couples planning to have another baby should also be discussed.

'Having had depression once is a predisposing factor for having it again. However, having treatment such as this reduces the risks. You have all learned lots of things about your own depression and have learned strategies for coping.

If you consider another pregnancy, you have the advantages of being able to plan, of being prepared, and of being able to recognise the early signs. You know about what is available to help you and how to access it. Friends and family are also already prepared.'

'There are some practical things you can do to reduce the risk of another episode of postnatal depression.'

OVERHEAD 11

Things you can do to reduce the risk of another episode of postnatal depression

- Get help with cleaning
- Childcare
- Use help offered
- Be realistic about what you can do
- Pace yourself

- Leave time for yourself
- Exercise
- Relaxation
- Practice positive thinking
- Communicate how you feel to others

❏ **Summary.**

Lead a general discussion about what couples have found useful or not. Canvas any suggestions for other couples who are in this situation. Focus on the father's views.

'What have you found the most useful thing that we have talked about? What advice would you have for other fathers?'

Thank the couples for their participation, enthusiasm and commitment to one another and their baby. Their willingness to confront these issues makes it more likely that they will continue to see improvement in their relationship and family functioning.

It is now time to close the session and to give couples time to socialise together. It is a good idea to set a limit to this, otherwise these sessions become very long.

'We now have 30 minutes to talk together over supper.'

Chapter 8

INCLUDING INFANTS: BABY H.U.G.S.

A BRIEF REVIEW OF THE LITERATURE

The importance of the early mother–infant relationship on subsequent child development is supported strongly by research evidence. Parental depression interferes with behavioural and emotional interchanges that are now recognised as necessary for a successful mother–infant interaction. The long-term consequences are detrimental not only for the infant's cognitive, social and emotional adjustment but also because a damaged relationship between mother and infant does not always recover. Interactional difficulties may persist even when circumstances improve. The secondary effect of ongoing parenting difficulties on maternal depression may in turn result in continuing symptomatology in women as a result of their sense of failure as parents (Milgrom & McCloud, 1996).

In this chapter we will present an additional treatment module that intervenes directly with difficulties in the mother–infant dyad. In addition, a brief review of the literature on relevant key concepts in infancy theory and research, the impact of maternal depression on infants and the growing evidence that we can intervene with early relationship difficulties, precedes the treatment program.

KEY CONCEPTS IN INFANCY

Early mother–infant interaction

We used to believe that the newborn infant was like a lump of clay, ready to be moulded by the world around, passively taking in what was being offered. It is now recognised that the infant plays an active role in social exchanges. He or she arrives equipped with a particular temperament and a range of skills, including an ability to imitate the facial expressions of the first person he* sees (Meltzoff & Moore, 1983). By 10 days, crying can signal different types of distress and by three to four weeks the infant smiles preferentially to his mother's voice (Rutter & Durkin, 1987). From the moment of birth, a mother and her infant begin an interchange that gradually increases in complexity and settles into a rhythmic pattern.

---

* The term 'he' is used for convenience and is intended to be interchangeable with 'she'.

Research on what constitutes 'normal' interactions between mothers and infants in the first year of life provides a basis with which we can compare what happens to depressed mothers and infants. Already in the first eight hours, the infant and mother can be seen to be making sounds back and forth, and from the first feed the sensitive mother will touch her baby mainly during pauses in sucking, so as to least interfere with the infant's preoccupation (Pridham, Berger Knight & Stephenson, 1989). By three days, the infant anticipates a feed by reaching to the mother, turning his head, and opening the mouth. From then on, the interaction between mother and child becomes more and more elaborated (Lier, 1988).

Brazelton, Tronick and others have described characteristics of a successful parent–child interaction in the first months of an infant's life. In the normal course of a day, mothers and infants engage in this type of face-to-face interaction sufficiently frequently to lay the foundation for social development. Structurally, the interactions are rhythmic, with escalating cycles of engagement and disengagement (Cohn & Tronick, 1988; Penman, Meares, Baker & Milgrom-Friedman, 1983). A number of maternal behaviours enhance the success of the interaction (Brazelton et al., 1974; Milgrom, 1991) and are summarised in Box 1.

BOX 1

Maternal behaviours that enhance mother–infant interaction

- Eye contact
- Sensitivity with immediate and appropriate responses to infant cues
- Empathy
- The mother's response being paced by her infant's cues
- The ability to produce an environment that creates an expectancy for interaction
- Reduction in interfering activities and balancing quieting with stimulation
- Emotional and physical interplay.

Most importantly, the 'good enough' interaction involves sensitive responsiveness to infant cues and allows for 'pauses' initiated by infants so that the mother's response is paced by her infant's cues. In this way, an interaction achieves a mutuality and a reciprocity. Physical stimulation and joyful emotional interplay are also features, as is maternal awareness of developmental stage (Lier, 1988).

Psychodynamic theorists postulate that the baby develops a sense of self through the environment of the 'ordinary devoted' mother's dependability and adaptation to her baby's needs (Winnicott, 1974; Davis & Wallbridge, 1981). Thus, the 'good enough' mother provides a space for playing and communicating creatively. She provides a secure and continuous 'holding environment' that adapts to provide just what the baby is looking for. It is this illusion that the baby can create his world that gives him a sense of self. The mother's ability to respond sensitively to her infant's cues, and respect his pauses, also contributes to the infant's development of a sense of mastery and control over events. Without this, he develops a sense of hopelessness and helplessness, and a sense that he cannot 'affect' the world. Gradually, the mother makes the baby wait and he becomes aware that she is separate and that he is his own independent self.

Lack of contingent responsiveness may also have a negative effect on the infant's ability to experience order in his world. This adversely affects the infant's ability to pay attention to and learn about objects and understanding of interactive rules and conventions.

In addition, this 'holding environment' allows the infant to learn to regulate his emotions, without overwhelming anxiety. Constant exposure to negative affect results in deregulated affect in the infant and interferes with the ability to process information (Tronick & Weinberg, 1997). Boys seem to have more difficulty with emotional regulation than girls and are particularly vulnerable to a lack of responsiveness. Stern (1985) has further developed theories about the sense of self of the infant that emanates from the parent–infant relationship.

There is also empirical evidence to support these theories and disturbed mother–infant interactions have been found to result in poorer development of cognitive and social ability in preschoolers, especially boys. A number of longitudinal studies have linked developmental status in childhood with the pattern of parent–infant interaction in early months, as detailed later in this chapter. Preterm infants who experience less mutual gazing at one month and less contingent responsiveness at three and eight months perform more poorly on sensorimotor assessments at nine months (Beckwith, Cohen, Kopp, Parmelee & Marcy, 1976) and at two years (Sigman, Cohen, Beckwith & Parmelee, 1981). Similarly, shorter attention spans and language production delays at three years correlate with gaze aversion and fussiness at three months (Field, Dempsey & Shuman, 1981; Pawlby & Hall, 1980). Teacher ratings at three years have also been correlated with early mother–infant interactions (Bakeman & Brown, 1981). More recently, Cairns, Cairns, Xie, Leung and Hearne (1998) found significant continuities between parenting practices observed in infancy and multiple aspects of the children's early school performance and aggressive behaviour.

It can be argued that inappropriate responses to infant cues and needs, in their extreme form, can be experienced as neglect. In our early research on the nature of mother–infant interactions, we tried to develop a control situation for an active mother–infant interaction. Mothers were instructed to look at their babies keeping their face blank. Babies reliably became distressed (Milgrom-Friedman, Penman & Meares, 1980). We did not understand the significance of this finding until Tronick, Als, Adamson, Wise and Brazelton (1978) published their observations about the aversive effect of a non-interactional face on infants: they will protest, cry and eventually withdraw. They called it 'the still-faced exposure' and described this situation as a paradigm of neglect: 'when infants' attempts fail to repair the interaction they lose postural control, withdraw and self-comfort. The disengagement is profound, reminiscent of Harlow's isolated monkeys, and the still-faced mother is a short-lived experimentally produced form of neglect . . .' (Tronick & Weinberg, 1997, p. 66). This demonstrates what can happen when there is a break in the mutual regulatory process and intersubjective experiences'.

The still-faced situation is an example of psychological unavailability of the caregiver, which can result in unintentional emotional deprivation. It is therefore critical to consider compensatory experiences for infants (e.g., with fathers) in instances of severe PND when a woman may be too ill to interact with her infant over a significant period of time. Furthermore, the long-term consequences of even minor disturbances in interaction with infants that accompany depression are discussed in a later section of this chapter.

Parenting style and attachment

Attachment
Infants develop not only a sense of self, but also a secure attachment relationship from experiencing appropriate maternal responsiveness (Ainsworth, 1979; Brazelton et al., 1974; Stern, 1985; Winnicott, 1965). Attachment theory has its roots in the work of the analyst Bowlby, who in 1953 warned against separating children from their mothers 'even if they were untidy and neglectful'. He showed evidence that maternal deprivation or separation from a maternal figure to whom an infant is attached gives rise initially to intense separation anxiety, and eventually to withdrawal and resignation by the infant. This can have long-term traumatic consequences. James Robertson, a paediatrician, provided visual evidence of this. His harrowing documentary made with his wife Joyce was entitled 'A two year old goes to hospital'. The vivid portrayal of little Laura's traumatic reaction to an eight-day separation from her parents was influential in changing hospital practices to allow parents to visit. At the same time, Winnicott, a prominent paediatrician, took a strong position on the centrality of the mother–infant bond, and described the effects of less severe maternal unavailability, which also resulted in disrupted attachment (Karen, 1990).

Ainsworth, Blehar, Waters and Wall (1978) radically changed the field by providing an experimental situation called the 'Strange Situation Procedure', which was able to identify secure, insecure (avoidant and ambivalent) and disorganised attachments in infants from 12 months of age. She developed an experimental paradigm based on a series of structured separations and reunions with mothers. This was a breakthrough approach and has helped move the field from a focus on counting behaviours to looking at the relationship. Ainsworth's central premise was that the responsive mother provides a secure base: 'warm, sensitive care does not create dependency; it liberates and enables autonomy' (Karen, 1990, p. 39). The infant needs to know that his primary caregiver is steady and dependable.

In general, about two-thirds of infants in the population are described as 'securely attached'. What happens to the remaining one-third? While the securely attached child is more flexible, curious and socially competent, the insecurely attached child often behaves in ways that further alienate him from adults and peers. The insecure child may avoid closeness (avoidant), or may be highly anxious, demanding, crying and clinging and in this way elicits reactions that repeatedly reconfirm his view of the world—that no one is reliably 'there'. A secure child is able to express anger, hurt, jealousy and resentment, confident of a sensitive response. The insecure child does not have this confidence, as he has often experienced a mother unable to handle her own negative feelings, who either becomes dismissive or overreacts.

The attachment category, called 'disorganised', was a later development, and has been found to be linked with more severe forms of poor parenting

(Greenberg, Cicchetti & Cummings, 1990). A child in this category seeks proximity with his mother in distorted, confused ways. During the experimental situation he may approach her with his back towards her, or freeze suddenly in the middle of a movement or sit for a time and stare into space. His reactions, unlike the strategies of avoidant and ambivalent babies, seem to suggest the collapse of strategy, a disorganisation. At times, these infants become alternatively controlling or play the role of caregiver.

Attachment difficulties at 12 months have been correlated with poorer self-esteem, cognitive abilities, persistence in solving problems, and the ability to show sympathy to distress of peers. The mother's own attachment style in her family of origin has also been related to her infant's attachment to her (DeMulder & Radke-Yarrow, 1991). While opponents of attachment theory argue that genes contribute to much of what we become, for example shyness or sociability, or that mother–infant fit has not been sufficiently taken into account, there is growing evidence that maternal interactional styles contribute to attachment patterns (Zeanah et al., 1993).

Four types of attachment and parenting styles
A number of studies have explored the parenting style that is believed to contribute to the attachment status of an infant, although further research is necessary to confirm this relationship and explore ameliorating factors (Lamb, Thompson, Gardner, Charnov & Connell, 1985). Erickson (1998) and Moore and Dean (1998) described in detail the emerging consensus:

❑ **Secure attachment.**

Securely attached children use parents as a stable source. These children experience a sense of competency by learning that they can signal that they need attention and that this signal is effective. This results from a sensitive and connected caregiver, tuned in to the infant.

❑ **Insecure avoidant attachment.**

Avoidant attachment occurs when parents are unresponsive to the needs of their child. Parental rebuffs or even rejection are common, and the parent may withdraw when the infant is sad. This leads to the child appearing distant, having flat affect and exhibiting aggressive behaviours, or a lack of empathy.

❑ **Insecure resistant/ambivalent attachment.**

Erratic, unpredictable care by parents results in the child becoming preoccupied, anxious, not able to freely explore and consequently unable to build competence. These children expect adults to fail them, which reinforces their sense of inadequacy and may result in dependency and constant helpseeking.

❑ **Disorganised attachment.**

Disorganised attachment occurs when parents are threatening towards the infant. The child becomes confused and anxious and has a tendency towards dissociative behaviour. The 'safe' person for the infant is also a person of perceived 'threat'. Children in their attempts to deal with this paradox may behave in a controlling manner with their parents and at times take on the parental role themselves. Table 1 summarises some of this material.

Table 1   Childhood attachment and parental style

Child's attachment category			
Secure	Insecure Avoidant	Insecure Ambivalent	Insecure Disorientated
A	B	C	Da
Child's behaviour with parent			
Autonomous Explores readily	Avoids closeness (may be angry)	Demanding and/or angry Clinging	Disorganised Becomes controlling/ caregiving
Stereotypic parental style			
Responsive Sensitive	Rejecting Avoids emotional demands	Intermittently available	Maltreatment (by some)

Adapted from Byng-Hall and Moore (1998).
aThis classification can co-occur with A and C.

❏ Emotional intelligence.

Daniel Goleman (1996) reviews the existing literature and highlights the role early mother–infant interactions may have in the development of a concept he terms 'emotional intelligence'. This interesting construct refers to the ability to relate in the world as an adult and has five components:

- Self-awareness of different emotions, for instance confusion, hunger or loneliness.
- Self-regulation (the ability to handle distressing emotions).
- Motivation (pessimism versus optimism).
- Empathy.
- Social skills, including the ability to read non-verbal cues.

Development of this ability to relate as adults is suggested to have its origins in our earliest relationships, further accentuating the importance of mother–infant interactions.

POSTNATAL DEPRESSION AND CHILD DEVELOPMENT

❏ Face-to-face interactions.

As we have described previously (Milgrom, 1994), current research suggests that many postnatally depressed mothers have difficulty interacting with their infants. Depressed mothers gaze less at their infants (Field *et al.*, 1985), rock their infants less, are less active and decisive (Murray, 1988), have less well-timed responsiveness and demonstrate lower levels of warm acceptance

(Bettes, 1988). Clinically, depressed mothers have been variously characterised as emotionally flat, insensitive, disengaged and uninvolved (Gelfand & Teti, 1990; Goodman, 1992).

Others have suggested that it is important to approach these findings with caution. Mother–infant interactions following depression may differ and some mothers may be withdrawn whereas others may be intrusive (Cohn & Tronick, 1989; Cox, 1988; Murray, 1988). Gender differences may also be important and depressed mothers were reported to be more intrusive with sons (Hart, Field & del Valle, 1998). A proportion of depressed mothers have been found to be skilful and sensitive (Milgrom, 1991). Our clinical experience also confirms that some women include their infants in their depressive withdrawal whereas others disconnect from their infants. Murray et al. (1996) similarly found little difference in observed behaviour between two-month-old infants in their face-to-face interactions with depressed mothers. They suggested that previous studies included groups of women who were highly disadvantaged (as compared to their community sample) and that deficits in interaction interact with this factor. However, taken together, they conclude that research findings suggest that depressed mothers show deficits in their interactional behaviours (Murray & Cooper, 1997b).

Our own research on 30 depressed mothers and infants of three months of age also reveals that differences in interactions do exist at three months, although they are small, and that these differences become accentuated over time. We found that depressed mothers from a broad socio-economic group were significantly less able to respond to minimal infant cues, compared to non-depressed mothers, at both three and six months postpartum. In addition, depressed mothers used less physical affection in their interactions at both these times (Milgrom, 1991).

Of particular importance is not only the behaviour of the depressed mother, but also whether the infant begins to show disturbances in his interchanges. Infants are intensely sensitive to the quality of their interpersonal environment when it is disrupted experimentally, even in brief and mild ways (Murray & Cooper, 1997a). We found that when comparing infants of non-depressed and depressed mothers, microanalysis of the interaction showed that infants learned to significantly avert their gaze by six months of age, if their mother was depressed (Westley, 1992). Field and her colleagues (1985) showed that from as early as three months of age infants of depressed mothers generalise their depressed style of interaction to non-depressed adults. In addition, three-month-old infants of non-depressed mothers react vehemently to conditions of simulated maternal depression, showing protest and cycles of wary and 'look away' behaviour (Cohn & Tronick, 1989). It is not surprising, therefore, that infants of depressed mothers have been described as more drowsy, more distressed and fussy, looking at their mothers less and tending to engage in more self-directed activity (Cox, 1988). Infant difficulty has also been observed by Cutrona and Troutman (1986), with descriptions of increased infant crying in depressed groups and infants appearing more tense, more fussy and tending to become distressed more quickly under stress (Whiffen & Gotlib, 1989). Some infants appear to show avoidance and withdrawn behaviour, whereas others evidence more protest behaviour (Field, Healy, Goldstein & Gotherz, 1990).

An important question raised by the research above is the extent to which difficult infant behaviour is in fact a result of maternal behaviour or whether it is due to inherent temperamental differences. Infants classified as temperamentally 'difficult' were not found to be more common in our study of infants of depressed women compared to those of non-depressed controls (Milgrom & McCloud, 1996). The primary role of maternal rather than infant individual differences was also suggested by Cooper and Murray (1997). Two-month-old infants' behaviour during interactions with their mother (but *not* with a researcher) was significantly predictive of maternal depression and early maternal communication difficulties. Furthermore, infant behavioural disturbance at 18 months showed no association with neonatal characteristics, but was significantly predicted by maternal postnatal depression (PND).

A further consideration is whether infant variables themselves impact on the occurrence of maternal depression. Poor motor control or irritable behaviour in a normal sample of healthy full-term neonates of well mothers was found to be associated with an increased risk of subsequent PND by a factor of approximately four in a prospective study (Murray & Cooper, 1997). Although difficult neonatal behaviour may (together with other factors) precipitate the onset of maternal depression, there was no evidence that differences in infant functioning in the neonatal period predicted the quality of maternal face-to-face interactions with the infant at two months. By this time, the mother's mental state, together with her social circumstances, were most predictive of mother–infant interaction.

In summary, infant temperament may act as a trigger in combination with other stressors to influence PND, but there is no evidence to suggest that it is a primary causal factor of depression or of difficulties in the mother–infant interaction. On the other hand, there is substantial evidence that maternal mental state in depression is associated with difficulties in the mother–infant interaction characterised by a less sensitive focus on the infant, affective discordance, and abrupt breaks in attention and engagement in interaction.

❑ **Long-term effects on children of depressed mothers.**

The long-term outcome for children of depressed mothers appears compromised. There is some evidence that maternal depression during the first year of life influences children's later cognitive and language development, and this does not seem to be explained by individual infant differences but appears to be mediated by the quality of the early mother–infant interaction (Murray, 1992; Murray et al., 1996). In a review of children followed up to four and five years, Murray and Cooper (1997) reported two British studies that described adverse child cognitive outcome associated with maternal depression. However, it was pointed out that this relationship was confined either to children of mothers with poor education, or to boys, and that their own earlier study, by contrast, revealed no long-term cognitive deficits (Murray et al., 1996). The effect on cognitive development may therefore interact with other factors, yet to be elucidated. Nevertheless, there is a growing body of literature linking the quality of early mother–infant interaction in the general population and later language and social competence (Saxon, 1997; Beckwith & Rodning, 1996).

While the evidence that maternal depression results in cognitive difficulties in children is still controversial, evidence of ongoing interactional difficulties between mothers and children following an episode of postpartum depression is more prominent in the literature. A reduced quality of mother–child interactions has been shown to be still in evidence 19 months after birth, both for infants of mothers who were still depressed and for infants of mothers who had recovered (Stein et al., 1991). There are a number of other reports showing an association between PND and insecurity of attachment at 12–18 months, using the Ainsworth Strange Situation Procedure (Lyons-Ruth, Zollo, Connell & Gunebaum, 1986; Murray, 1992; Teti, Gelfand, Messinger & Isabella, 1995), although no association was found in one study (Campbell & Cohn, 1997). Increased emotional and behavioural disturbances in the form of sleeping, eating problems, temper or separation problems have also been reported (Milgrom, 1999). Murray (1992) identified behavioural disturbances in 18-month-old children of depressed compared to non-depressed women, although the effect in her study was again more prominent in boys (Murray, 1997). Paradoxically, follow-up of three-year-old children, whose mothers had a brief PND, revealed more behavioural disturbance than for children whose mothers had experienced prolonged PND, or whose mothers had not been depressed (Wrate, Rooney, Thomas & Cox, 1985).

EXPANDING OUR MODEL TO EXPLAIN THE CONSEQUENCES OF POSTNATAL DEPRESSION ON THE INFANT

How does PND result in long-term consequences for infants? The central importance of the mother–infant interaction to child development has been described. Maternal difficulties engaging in early face-to-face interaction may be an important negative force for later infant development, influencing the infant's ability to attend, process information and regulate emotions. Our model serves to further explain ways in which factors associated with PND might influence a poor mother–infant interaction.

❑ **Direct effects.**

As described previously, the symptoms of PND commonly include flat affect, lack of interest, anxiety and psychomotor retardation. These behaviours directly interfere with a mother's ability to engage her infant in the type of interaction described previously. Sensitivity to her infant, eye contact, joyful interaction, stimulation and immediate responsiveness do not come easily to a mother preoccupied with her sadness and immobilised by her depression.

❑ **Indirect effect: vulnerability factors.**

It is possible that depression does not directly influence interactions, but that it interacts with other variables to adversely affect mother–infant relationships. Many psychosocial difficulties have been described in depressed mothers, such as having had a poor relationship with their own mother during childhood, and having given birth to their first child at a younger age than women who do not experience depression. These experiences in early life and subsequent

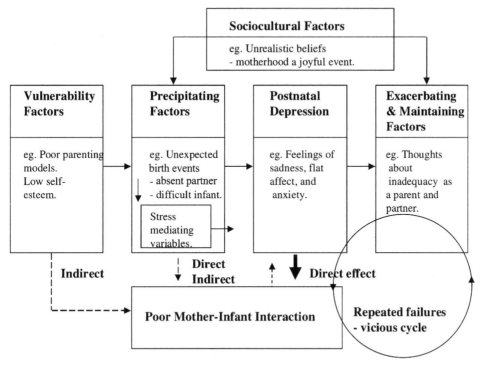

Figure 1   Extension of the biopsychosocial model of postnatal depression to effects on infants

multiple stressors are likely to predict a reduced competence in parental care and interactive abilities (Raphael-Leff, 1991).

❑ **Indirect effect: precipitating factors.**

These include a wide range of stressors such as a difficult birth or a newborn's temperamental difficulty. Infant temperament or external stresses on an infant can inhibit or facilitate the capacity to interact: '. . . the infant too, because of illness or object loss may in turn be unable to respond to or initiate overtures towards the adult . . .' (Jernberg, 1984, p. 39). Maternal competence of depressed women with 3–13-month infants has been found to be inversely related to stressors such as infant difficulty (Teti, Gelfand & Pompa, 1990).

Our model highlights the central importance of the role of the maternal cognitive style in mediating the effects of stress on postnatal adjustment (Cutrona & Troutman, 1986; Whitton, Appleby & Warner, 1996). Stressful life events will be experienced and reacted to differently, depending on the maternal coping style, and this in turn may influence how a mother interacts with her infant. Factors such as having a partner with long work hours may have an effect that is mediated through maternal coping style. A mother's perceived satisfaction with partners has been found to be correlated with positive mother–infant interactions (Klaus & Kennell, 1982). Maternal self-efficacy in the role of the mother also appears to be a crucial mediator of relations between psychosocial variables and the mother's behaviour with her child. Thus, social support may have a protective function by enhancing maternal self-efficacy beliefs. Similarly, although maternal depression was described earlier as associated with the development of an insecure mother–child attachment, up to 50% of infants have been reported to form secure attachments with their depressed mothers. This could be due to the variation found in maternal self-efficacy scores. Those who have low estimations of their own efficacy tend to give up easily in the face of difficulties such as a demanding infant or their depressed mood. Other stress-mediating variables may include parenting skills, parenting alliance or maternal resources (Abidin, 1992).

❑ **Indirect effect: exacerbating factors and the vicious cycle.**

One explanation for the finding that disturbed mother–infant interactions are resistant to change (Meager & Milgrom, 1996) might be that women with low confidence in their parenting behave in ways that lead to low rates of reinforcement from their infants, resulting in a vicious cycle of repeated interactive failures. An important notion therefore is that interactional difficulties gather their own momentum and persist even when circumstances improve. The vicious cycle may take the following form: a mother feels guilty about the possible effect of her depression on her infant. She then thinks 'My baby would be better off without me. I'm no use.' As a result she may withdraw, and in time her infant learns also to avert his gaze. This mother then feels confirmed in her role of being a failure as a parent. She thinks 'See, my baby does not like me' and withdraws further. An unrewarding relationship can then be a further contributing factor to her depression (Cox, 1988).

Although more research is necessary to explore the antecedents and consequences of mother–infant difficulties associated with postpartum disorders, enough evidence exists to support the strategy of early intervention. Early treatment may not only prevent mother–infant difficulties but also generational repetition since patterns of interaction are learned very early in life. A prospective study with a different type of 'at-risk' dyad revealed that, by three years of age, children who had been abused were already interacting with their baby siblings (aged 6–11 months) with poor sensitivity and aggression (Main, 1984). The current literature that exists to support the strategy of early intervention is outlined below.

EVIDENCE OF THE ABILITY TO CHANGE THE MOTHER–INFANT INTERACTION

Murray and Cooper (1997) posed the question: does treatment of PND directed solely at elevation of maternal mood, in the absence of any specific attention to the mother–infant relationship, indirectly improve the quality of mother–infant engagement and infant outcome? The result from their recent studies failed to find improvements in the quality of the mother–infant interaction either with the use of counselling, psychodynamic therapy or cognitive-behavioural treatment for maternal depression. However, parental reports of relationship problems decreased. While Murray and Cooper suggest that the degree of disturbance in mother–infant relationships was not sufficient in her community sample to show change, it is more likely that the mother–infant interaction needs to be more intensively and specifically targeted by programs treating maternal depression.

What evidence is there that it is possible to improve a problematic mother–infant interaction? A number of approaches have proven successful, targeting different aspects:

1. Direct intervention aimed at the parent–infant interchange.
2. More traditional psychotherapeutic approaches aiming to change the mother's subjective experience.
3. Psycho-educational approaches.

Targeting the parent–infant interchange

Tiffany Field (1982) pioneered the modification of disturbed interactions by enhancing behaviours in high-risk dyads that are often seen in more harmonious, synchronous interactions. Her data suggests that mothers of high-risk infants can be taught other ways to interact. She noted that in normative samples face-to-face interactions typically feature mothers slowing down, exaggerating and repeating their behaviours, contingently responding and imitating or highlighting the infant's behaviours. Mothers also take turns, not interrupting and respecting the infant's occasional break from the conversation, with the infant typically looking attentive and sounding contented. The atypical or disturbed interaction might, by contrast, feature a gaze-averting, squirming, fussing infant and a mother who appears to be somewhat overactive, intrusive, controlling and frustrated. Since adult behaviour is more amenable to change than is the infant's behaviour, attempts to modify interactions have typically focused on altering the adult's behaviour.

Field (1982) found that she could increase infant attention to mothers by skills training that included: instructing mothers to imitate all infant behaviours and repeat phrases, such as 'g'day, g'day, g'day'; encouraging silence during infant pauses and teaching 'facilitative manipulations' such as asking mothers to count slowly to themselves as they interacted so as to allow for infant pauses and observation of infant behaviour. These procedures were referred to as direct 'interactional coaching' of mothers on aspects of interaction. Other aspects of interactive coaching involved teaching mothers age-appropriate games, coaching mothers 'in vivo' during an interaction via an earpiece microphone and showing videotapes of mothers playing with their babies, for the mothers to view with or without a running commentary. In her later work, Field (1997) tailored interventions to the type of presenting difficulty. For instance, withdrawn mothers were instructed how to attract and maintain the infant's attention. In addition, she highlighted the therapeutic role of touching and infant massage for high-risk infants, including those of depressed women (Malphurs et al., 1996). The short-term effects of these manipulations included longer periods of eye contact by infants, fewer distress vocalisations and less squirming. The long-term effects are unclear, however.

Field's approach has been developed by others to train parents to respond sensitively to their fragile premature newborns (Barrera, Kitching, Cunningham,

Doucet & Rosenbaum, 1990; Rauh, Achenbach, Nurcombe, Howell & Teti, 1988) and for a range of parents of high-risk infants (McDonough, 1993). Hans, Bernstein and Percansky (1991) targeted adolescent parent–infant relationships and found that the parents who received the intervention were substantially more likely to remain in school, become employed, and have avoided a subsequent pregnancy at 12 months post-baseline compared with a national sample of adolescent parents (Ruch-Ross, Jones & Musick, 1992). Censullo (1994) formalised the 'Interaction Coaching for Adolescent Parents and their Infants' (ICAP), to provide a standardised method for practitioners to use in early interventions with teenage parents and their babies, as well as other high-risk infant–mother pairs. The ICAP procedure begins with the observation and assessment of the strengths and weaknesses of both parent and infant during social interaction. Interaction coaching techniques include teaching the parents to identify their infant's unique cues, and then adapting their responses to fit their infant's preferences, through the use of pauses, imitation and modulation of their face, voice, touch and position. Practice through trial and error is encouraged. An important part of the process is to help parents recognise success, no matter how subtle, which encourages them to continue, setting into play a repetitive cycle of success. According to Werner (1990) this process, which enhances maternal self-esteem and self-efficacy, has the potential to prevent the negative effects associated with exposure to early risk factors, and to encourage normal developmental outcomes.

McDonough (1993) has extended the interaction guidance approach using a family problem-focused, psychotherapeutic model. She claims success with difficult-to-engage families such as those 'overburdened' by poverty, poor education, family mental illness, substance abuse, and lack of social or partner support. Family strengths are highlighted using videotape replays, and family therapy complements direct feedback of videotaped parent–infant play. Both the behaviour of the infant and the parent's own style of interaction are viewed and discussed. Support, practical advice and education are included, with strong reinforcement of caregiver responsivity, sensitivity, reciprocity, reading infant behavioural cues and affective attunement. She reports an impressive case anecdote of success with a failure-to-thrive infant that was part of a project aimed at gathering treatment efficacy data.

Traditional psychotherapeutic approaches

Women with PND often have had poor relationships with their mothers. Selma Fraiberg (1980) coined the phrase 'Ghosts from the Nursery' to refer to those feelings that arise to disturb new parent–infant relationships. Infants reawaken powerful memories of earlier family relationships and these may form an obstacle to the developing new relationships, unless some work is done with parents to assist them in placing the memories into a more realistic context.

Fraiberg (1980) takes a partly traditional psychodynamic approach to intervention and focuses her efforts on understanding the subjective experience of mothers with babies, rather than directly changing maternal or infant behaviour. This exploration, however, is coupled with concrete assistance, emotional support and developmental guidance. Outcome measures have shown an increase in maternal empathy and playful interaction using this approach in groups (Lieberman & Pawl, 1988).

Other psychotherapeutic techniques, such as Muir's 'Watch, wait and wonder technique' (1992) and Lieberman and Pawl's 'Infant–parent psychotherapy' (1993), combine interactional guidance techniques with psychodynamic techniques. The focus is on the interaction of the parents with their babies in a play setting. The therapist is also usually in the room but takes care not to interact with the baby. Intervention in these forms of psychotherapy includes making overt what is happening in the interaction. This is done by the use of interpretive techniques, to link the mother's past experience with her current behaviours and to identify what is being projected onto the infant (Muir, 1992). Parent–infant psychotherapy is usually done with a dyad, but may be combined with casework to manage families and to involve fathers (Wright, 1986).

'Brief mother–baby psychotherapy' is another approach described by Cramer and colleagues (Cramer & Stern, 1988; Cramer et al., 1990; Cramer, 1997). The focus of this psychodynamic treatment is also the mother's representation of her infant and of her relationship with that infant in terms of the projections made, which relate to unresolved conflicts dating from the mother's own childhood. Cramer argues that core conflictual themes are activated and enacted in the relationship with the mother's own infant. Interpretation linking the past to the present and the mother's representations to the current interactions results in change. This treatment was evaluated for its effectiveness for children aged six months to two years with problems such as sleeping difficulties, feeding problems and disturbances in attachment. Cramer et al. (1990) found marked improvements in the mother's representations of herself, her infant and their relationship; in the quality of the mother–infant interactions; and in the symptoms for which the child was referred. Interestingly, comparison of Cramer's dynamic psychotherapy with the 'interaction guidance' treatment described by McDonough (1993) showed equivalent degrees of improvement on all maternal, infant and interactive outcome measures.

Psycho-educational approaches

Infant temperament
All infants are born with certain emotional dispositions. Parental education about temperamental differences is a useful approach to enhancing parent–infant interactions. Scales such as the Australian Revised Infant Temperament Scale can be used to elicit information about infants' recent and current behaviour to help identify temperament. This scale focuses on the infant's approachability, reactivity and irritability and was described in Chapter 3 (Sanson, Prior & Oberklaid, 1985).

The Brazelton Neonatal Assessment Scale (NBAS) has also been used psycho-educationally for infants under one month of age. It was devised originally as a research instrument to elicit early temperamental differences based on 28 infant responses. It was later used to facilitate parents' capacity to observe their new-born's capabilities and to explore the meanings that they ascribe to these capabilities. The NBAS has also been used to increase parents' self-esteem and competence through positive reinforcement using observations such as 'Look how much you have already noticed about your baby!' and 'See how she calmed when you talked to her!' Following his use of NBAS, a father who had said 'I don't think my baby likes me, she cries when I hold her' was able to elicit visual following, have the baby respond with a head orientation to her name and see crying as one of six states of soothability. This father then exclaimed excitedly: 'She really looked at me!' (Cordone & Glikerson, 1989). Belsky (1985) cautions about the use of NBAS as a one-off tool, and has found no ongoing benefits at one, three or nine months. He suggests that NBAS is likely to have limited success as an intervention tool without repeated 'booster' treatments that build upon or go beyond mere exposure to NBAS. He also added that, since marital/partner relationships can enhance or undermine parenting, direct attention to the parental relationship should accompany targeted attempts at the parent–infant interaction.

BABY H.U.G.S.: AN INTERVENTION PROGRAM DESIGNED FOR DEPRESSED WOMEN AND THEIR INFANTS*

A developing relationship is like a river—small obstacles or deviations early in its history will profoundly affect the future course of the water flow. This analogy is useful to highlight the importance of early intervention in those instances where parent–infant interactions are in difficulty.

Our own program targets parent–infant difficulty by using elements from the three major approaches to early intervention described in this chapter. In addition, CBT is used to deal with maternal cognitions that may affect mother–infant interactions. The concept for this program was initially described in two languages (Milgrom, 1994, 1996) and has been refined based on our clinical experiences as a module to be added to the main treatment program.

Baby H.U.G.S. targets

❏ **The parent–infant interchange.**

Direct work on the parent–infant interchange is the major focus of this module and is coupled with psycho-education and insight into parents' emotional responses to infant cues. Play and observation are encouraged, followed by an awareness of parental feelings that may get in the way. Sometimes parents ascribe to their infants what they find unacceptable about themselves. Information can be equally powerful: for instance, a mother who interprets her infant's turning away as wilful can be taught about the normal pauses in the infant's interactions (Meares, Penman, Milgrom-Friedman & Baker, 1982).

❏ **Infant temperament.**

Helping parents to observe the type of babies that they have, and to recognise that different responses are necessary for different temperamental styles, is another approach to enhancing mother–infant interaction.

* H.U.G.S. is an acronym for Happiness, Understanding, Giving and Sharing. The name H.U.G.S. was initially given to a toddler group designed by Alys Key Family Care, Heidelberg, Australia, to facilitate interactions, and was adapted and developed further for infants by Professor Jeannette Milgrom, as the 'Baby' H.U.G.S. program.

❑ **Parental attitudes, beliefs and cognitions.**

Challenging the labelling of infants which is not based on fact and encouraging thinking based on the reality of the infant is also an important focus point of intervention.

Cutrona and Troutman (1986) highlight the central role of parental cognitions in PND, suggesting that it may be necessary to change the way a parent thinks about her or his child. Abusive mothers, when listening to taped sounds of an infant crying, describe the infant as more angry than do control mothers suggesting that these parents attribute a distorted meaning to their infant's behaviour (Friedrich, Tyler & Clark, 1985). It also appears that in the general population set beliefs about infants are common. Consistency of maternal attitudes to child rearing from pregnancy to eight months postpartum has been reported by Davids and Holden (1970).

We found that when non-depressed women were asked to use 10 adjectives to describe their infants there was remarkable consistency between the positive and negative adjectives that the mothers used at two days and at three months postpartum (Milgrom & Green, 1999). These fixed cognitions often do not take into account the reality of the infant and can be challenged with cognitive techniques when maladaptive.

❑ **Partner/spouse relationships and social networks.**

Strategies for strengthening support systems for women with PND are considered essential. A number of intervention programs have stressed that social isolation must be reduced in order to reduce parent–infant difficulties (McDonough, 1985). In addition, women with PND often report partnership difficulties (Cox, 1988) and these may influence their relationship with their infants. Oates and Heinicke (1985) demonstrated that, in a non-clinical sample, fathers' positive experience of marriage predicted the quality of mother–infant interaction at six months. This module is designed to draw on the material in the main program to reinforce social networks and explore marital difficulties as a critical part of intervention.

In summary, the above targets such as modifying cognitions and involving partners are achieved by incorporating relevant sessions from the Getting Ahead of Postnatal Depression program and the Couples program described in Chapter 7. The additional three-session module that follows focuses directly on the parent–infant interaction and is available as an add-on therapeutic intervention (see notes on 'How to incorporate the module into the main program' p. 199).

Efficacy

There is a need to increase research on the efficacy of intervention strategies such as the Baby H.U.G.S. program. Few reports in the literature evaluate treatment groups for mothers with PND that focus on mother–infant relationships. Yet such groups may be particularly attractive to depressed mothers.

A PROGRAM FOR PARENT–INFANT DIFFICULTIES

NOTES FOR THE THERAPIST

This additional three-week module is based on the Baby H.U.G.S. program (Milgrom, 1994; Milgrom, 1996) for women to attend group sessions with their babies. It is designed for those women with depression who are having difficulties relating to or coping with their infants under 12 months.

❑   **'H.U.G.S.'**

This stands for Happiness, Understanding, Giving and Sharing.

❑   **The program.**

The program consists of sessions that are structured to invite interaction between parents and infants. The facilitators encourage this interaction to be positive, and provide skills training for achieving positive communication between parents and infants. As one of the most striking features of a successful interaction is the joy that accompanies the interaction, a playful non-judgemental context is cultivated. The basic premise for the group is that it is possible to intervene directly with the mother–infant dyad and improve skills in communication, parent observation and responsiveness.

The aim of these sessions is to foster parental skill in interacting with infants by focusing on:

1. Observing infant behaviour.
2. Understanding the cues that infants give.
3. Exploring parental responses and interpretation of infant cues.
4. Challenging parental perceptions.
5. Promoting the pleasure of parenting with play and physical contact.
6. Allowing expression of observations, anxieties or negative feelings towards their infants in a non-judgemental setting.

It is anticipated that improved mother–infant interactions will promote the development of parent–infant attachment, infant development and maternal self-esteem. Although the program is not directly aimed at infant management difficulties such as sleeping, feeding and separation, these issues often emerge and improve. Some psycho-educational material is provided in the third session for those women who want to pursue these issues.

❑   **Background reading.**

In addition to counselling or therapeutic skills, the facilitator of a H.U.G.S. program needs to develop a basic knowledge of infant development and adaptive or maladaptive interactions. A suggested reading list for those without an infancy background is provided at the end of this section as a starting point, and can be usefully coupled with observation of parents and infants in a play situation.

❑ **Am I failing my child?**

As many women feel a profound sense of failure in admitting that they are having difficulties with their infants, it is important not to accentuate this feeling. Rather, this module is presented as an opportunity to develop the relationship with their infants as well as a forum for sharing feelings of not coping, not bonding with their baby, or the sheer frustration of the endless demands a baby makes. It is also important to highlight the need for support from other family members or friends.

Group leaders need to present themselves as allies and attempt to empower parents. A useful approach to countering the guilt and fear that some depressed women experience in terms of the possible damage that their mood disturbance may have on their child is to focus on the resilience of infants and the ability of early intervention to get relationships back on course.

❑ **Who to include.**

Not all depressed mothers have difficulty coping with their infants. Of those who are experiencing problems, these range from intrusiveness, lack of attachment or eye contact, anxiety, poor awareness of babies' interactive needs, separation issues and lack of stimulation or withdrawal. This module has been designed to address a range of these issues by improving parent–infant interactions.

For those women who are not having specific difficulties with their infants, the module can be a useful adjunct to the main group program by extending the concept of 'increasing pleasant activities' to include infants. Infants will also benefit from the emphasis on face-to-face interactions, since maternal depression is often accompanied by flattened affect, inhibited motor activity and poorer interpersonal responsiveness. These behaviours may all compromise infant development (Murray & Cooper, 1997).

Although the focus is on the mother–infant dyad, participation of the father is encouraged since the importance of spouse support and direct paternal involvement in infant care is increasingly recognised.

❑ **How to incorporate the module into the main program.**

Options:

1. This module can be part of the main treatment program by adding it on at the end, just before Session 9. The module as described assumes this has occurred.
2. Alternatively, an adapted shorter program with a focus on parent–infant interactions can be produced by the following

combination: begin with Session 1 of the main group program, as this allows for the development of a group process and the sharing of birth and pregnancy experiences. The introductory session is also an opportunity to focus on how life has changed since the baby has arrived, and what expectations women had of their baby prior to the birth. This three-session module can then follow as the core intervention. You may wish to spend more than three sessions to cover the material more fully and combine it with cognitive intervention techniques described in the main treatment program (Sessions 6, 7 and 8). These approaches help parents challenge the negative thoughts that they may hold about their baby. Session 5 on unrealistic expectations of parenting can follow, to bring all this material together by understanding family of origin influences on current parenting practices. This sequence of sessions can be concluded with Session 2 of the main program, 'Pleasant activities—how can I find the time?' (making sure to include infant-focused activities), and Session 9 to 'sum up'. Finally, as has been suggested earlier, irrespective of which treatment approach is used, the couples work described in Chapter 7 is recommended in addition, for all depressed women who have a partner.

SUGGESTED READING LIST

Auckett, A. (1991). *Baby massage, hill of content.* New York: Newmarket Press.
Caplan, F., & Caplan, T. (eds) (1995). *The first twelve months of life.* New York: Bantam.
Fraiberg, S. (ed.) (1980). *Clinical studies in infant mental health* (Chs. 1–5). New York: Basic Books.
Lier, L. (1988). Mother–infant relationship in the first year of life. *Acta Paediatrica Scandinavica,* 344(77), 31–42.
Milgrom, J. (1994). Mother–infant interactions in postpartum depression: An early intervention program. *Australian Journal of Advanced Nursing,* 11(4), 29–38.
Murray, L., & Cooper, P. (1997). *Postpartum depression and child development* (especially Section II). New York: Guilford Press.
Van de Pol, C. (1992). *How to love being a parent.* Diggers Rest, Australia: Saturn.

SESSION 1: LET'S PLAY—PLAY AND PHYSICAL CONTACT

NOTES FOR THE THERAPIST

In this first session, baby massage, feelings about physical contact and age-appropriate play are introduced. The aim is to bring to the forefront the pleasure that is evident when a mother and her infant are successfully interacting, as well as the importance of non-verbal communication. It is also an opportunity to observe relationship difficulties between mother–infant dyads that can be targeted in later sessions.

❑ **Creating a light-hearted and comfortable atmosphere.**

Ideally, the room needs to be set up in a 'baby-friendly' way, usually with blankets and toys on the floor and cushions to sit on, or armchair-type seating, allowing easy transition to floor play. Large, light spaces work best. The aim is to maximise the interactions that occur between mothers and babies while the group is in progress. Providing tea, coffee and biscuits after the group has ended allows time for feeding, changing babies or just recharging before the organisational feat of packing up and going home. Group leaders can explore with mothers what else might be needed to make everyone as comfortable as possible.

INTRODUCTION AND SESSION CONTENT

❑ **Purpose of module.**

Allow each member of the group to state what they wish to get out of the module, as this provides useful information for group facilitators to highlight various aspects of the sessions. Following this discussion, the aims and objectives of the H.U.G.S. program are outlined:

'During these sessions we will be working together:

- *To open the way for exploring new ways of managing infants, while looking after one's own needs.*
- *To facilitate positive interactions between parents and infants.*
- *To share observations and anxieties, in a supportive setting.*
- *To allow for fun, laughter and a positive accepting atmosphere.'*

Let's play

Refer to Session 2, Getting Ahead of Postnatal Depression program to remind participants of the importance of balancing the day with activities that need to be done, and those that are pleasurable. Introduce the idea of play as a 'pleasant activity' that can be done with their infant.

'Play with your baby is vital. All the games babies play help them learn the essentials of getting about in this world in a fun way. Your baby enjoys finding out about you and the world in this way. Play also gives you an opportunity to connect with your baby whilst having fun.'

Explore games parents currently play and introduce new age-appropriate games. Select one or two age-appropriate games and demonstrate these in the session. Examples are given in Box 2 and develop a resource file of other games.

'In your interaction games with your child, bear in mind that all children are natural-born players. All children at play are learning and working very hard.'

BOX 2

Games we can play

1. Peek-a-boo. This game relies on the fact that the baby is intrigued by human faces. Later on, the game means that the child has a memory of someone he loves and that person's image is fixed enough in his mind and secure enough in his feelings for him to try a short separation under his control. He has a sense of his parent's permanence, as well as that of objects, and even anticipates the joy of recalling her or him.
2. The come-and-get-me game requires a pursuing parent and a scrambling, frantically pursued baby.
3. The pick-up-the-things-I-drop game.
4. Tactile games emphasising toes and fingers. Often they are completed by a sensational tickling finish and accompanied by a rhyme such as 'This Little Piggy Went to Market', while a parent takes each toe and recites what it does.
5. Your imitation of your child's movements can make your older infant laugh and try to imitate you. Watching you imitate him adds a consciousness of his own movements. A mirror hypnotises him for the same reason.
6. Naming games involving the child's nose, toes, feet, hands, eyes and mouth emphasise body parts and self-concepts. If you suck his exploring finger, he may try sucking it again himself, then offer it to you for an encore.

Adapted excerpts from Caplan and Caplan (1995).

Half of the session is then used to encourage play between mothers and their infants with suggestions of different types of play, depending on the infant's response. Toys may be introduced to demonstrate their use as stimulation or distraction. Positive feedback to mothers is important and this session also allows mothers to meet and get to know each others' babies.

Reading suggestion: Excerpts from Caplan and Caplan (1995), *The first twelve months of life* (pp. 67-73). New York: Bantam Books.

❑ **Other variations.**

If the play session is going well, suggest to parents that they improvise to get a desired outcome with their baby.

'Play a game to:

● *Calm your baby. OR*
● *Excite your baby. OR*
● *Teach your baby a task that is developmentally appropriate.'*

Infant responses to the above variations are discussed, highlighting differences between babies and what works for a particular baby. The concepts of infant temperament (some babies are more placid and others more difficult to soothe), and being in tune with the mood of your baby, are introduced.

Baby massage

❑   **Describe the benefits of massage.**

'Physical contact is enjoyed by most babies and allows you and your baby to spend an enjoyable physical time together.

Not everyone is equally comfortable with physical contact. Let us explore touch and its effect on us by breaking into pairs and mothers massaging each others' hands. Notice what you liked or whether the experience was uncomfortable in any way.'

❑   **Exercise.**

'Face your partner and relax your arms and hands. Flop your hands about to relax. Slowly massage each other's hand (in turn), using a gentle stroking motion over the entire palm and back of the hand and applying gentle pressure to each finger. Swap partners and repeat.'

At the end of the exercise, discuss how each mother responded to the massage and what she liked and didn't like. How will this make baby massage enjoyable or difficult?

❑   **Planning your infant massage.**

- Encourage mothers not to massage on days when they feel stressed, angry or too busy to enjoy this time with their baby. These feelings are easily communicated through touch, and perhaps a walk in the pram might be better.
- Parents are encouraged to massage their baby every day for a week, even if it is only for a few minutes, until the baby can tolerate an increased massage time.
- Babies may not enjoy a massage under two months of age, and if either their baby or themselves are not enjoying the massage then it should be discontinued and tried again in a month or so.

HANDOUT 1

What to do during a baby massage session

(Photocopy the text below)

❑   **What to do during a baby massage session.**

Unless you can make an extra session available for baby massage, it is best just to describe the procedure at this stage and set baby massage as homework. If possible, show a brief videotape of baby massage to help women develop this routine.

(a) 'Ensure that the room is warm enough, private and familiar.
(b) Ensure that you are organised before you start:

1. *Take the phone off the hook.*
2. *Lock the back door.*
3. *Have clean clothes ready.*
4. *Have towel and oil ready (olive oil or edible oil may be used).*
5. *Fill the bath if you wish to bathe your baby following the massage.*

(c) *Sit comfortably—either leaning against a wall or pillows, or kneeling over your baby. This position allows you to have good control of your baby and he gets skin contact from your legs.*

(d) *Remember to relax your arms and hands. Flop your hands as you have learned to do to relax your hands.*

(e) *Making sure your hands are warm, slowly undress your baby. Brush oil on his body with the flat of your hand.*

(f) *As you massage your baby, the only pressure needed is the weight of your hands. Use gentle sweeping strokes.'*

- Encourage parents not to press too hard or too tight.
- Encourage mothers to sing or talk to their baby and have them tell the baby what they are doing, e.g. *'I am stroking your little arm, do you like that?'*
- Encourage mothers to explore different techniques, strokes and positions and to discover which ones the baby enjoys.

❑   **Discussion.**

'How did you find the activities today? What will it be like to introduce regular baby massage into your week?'

HOMEWORK

- To increase the amount of physical contact time between parent and baby, by using massage. Photocopy the poem in Box 3 for parents to place on their fridge.
- To engage in age-appropriate parent–baby games, and explore alternative, interesting and new ways of managing and relating to their infant.

❑   **Postscript.**

The benefits of mother–baby play can be the subject of a number of sessions and extended to include movement to music. Babies love rhythm, music and movement and this approach has been developed into a useful adjunct to therapy with mothers and babies within the Infant Clinic (Loughlin, 1992). By increasing the time available for play, women can overcome their initial hesitations and develop new ways of interacting with their infants. Interventions should occur in a gentle, non-threatening manner by slowly introducing new games and modifying play activities if the infant is not enjoying the interaction.

BOX 3

Let me sit with my baby

And play for a while
and forget all
my unfinished work
with a smile.
For every tomorrow
holds work to be done,
but lullaby moments
and peek-a-boo fun,
are life's tender treasures
meant just for today,
for babies grow up . . .
and the years
slip away.

SESSION 2: LET'S LEARN ABOUT YOUR BABY—OBSERVING AND UNDERSTANDING YOUR BABY'S SIGNALS

NOTES FOR THE THERAPIST

Group aims

The focus of this group is on infants, and mothers may need to be reminded that they can, in parallel, be looking after their own needs by incorporating suggestions made in the main group, such as having their own time for relaxation.

This session involves structured exercises with different activities used to highlight non-verbal interactive behaviours including stress responses. The emphasis is on parental observation of cues given by infants to communicate their needs. Observations and interpretations of infant behaviours are explored in a fun setting. Temperamental differences are noted. Appreciation of the skills of infants is highlighted as this can help some mothers to recognise how their infant is expressing himself.

Encourage parents to focus on positive behaviours in their child and ensure that negative aspects are challenged, using the cognitive framework covered previously in the main treatment program.

Describe objective 1: learning about individual differences

'In this session we are going to learn about the different individual personalities of your babies and their preferred style of relating.'

Before starting, briefly review how play and baby massage are progressing at home and how this might reflect something about their baby's temperament. Then continue with Session 2 as described below.

❑   **Let's learn about your baby.**

Each mother may be asked to use adjectives to introduce her infant to the group and describe his personality. This is explored in the context of what has already been learned of the infant in the play session, and the concept of temperamental differences and 'fit' with the parent. Negative labels are challenged and parents are encouraged to describe positive attributes of their infant. In this session, parental cognitions and attitudes about their infants emerge, and challenging can occur by using other group members to offer alternative descriptions and looking for cognitive distortions. Start with the concept of temperament to normalise a range of behaviours.

'We all know that temperament varies from birth. For instance, some babies are more difficult to soothe and others are more placid.

I would like you each to introduce your baby to the group as an individual personality, using as many adjectives and ways of describing him as you can.'

- Examine adjectives such as 'happy' or 'demanding' and reword as <u>behaviours</u> such as 'gurgles a lot' or 'cries a lot'. That is, how do we know that a baby is happy or demanding?
- Discuss the differing temperaments of babies. Facilitators may wish to draw upon a temperament scale to highlight the different behaviours that result from different temperaments. Sanson and Oberklaid (1985) describe behaviours that load towards different temperamental dispositions such as 'approachable' or 'adaptable'. These are described in the resource table opposite, and help mothers to accurately describe infant behaviour.
- Any negative aspects that are brought out are challenged and reframed using observations and suggestions made by the group members. For example, a mother might use labels such as he is a 'good' or 'bad' baby. Further exploration might reveal that she observes that 'he frowns all the time.' Alternative interpretations include the possibility that 'he appears to be concentrating.' An

Table 2   Dimensions of temperament

Label	Description	Low score	High score
Activity level	The level and extent of motor activity	Not active	Very active
Rhythmicity	The regularity with which behaviours such as sleeping and feeding occur	Rhythmic, regular	Arhythmic, irregular
Approach–withdrawal	The nature of the response to a new person or stimulus	First response is approach	First response is withdrawal
Adaptability	The ease with which a child adapts to changes in the environment	Very adaptable	Not adaptable
Intensity	The energy level of a response or reaction	Not intense	Very intense
Threshold or responsiveness	The strength to stimulation necessary to evoke a discernible response	High threshold	Low threshold
Mood	The amount of friendly, happy behaviour as contrasted with unfriendly, unhappy behaviour	Positive, happy	Negative, unhappy
Distractibility	The degree to which extraneous stimuli alter ongoing behaviour, such as crying	Distractible, soothable	Not distractible or soothable
Persistence or attention span	The amount of time devoted to an activity, and the effect of distraction on the activity	Persistent, long attention span	Not persistent, short attention span

From Sanson, Prior and Oberklaid (1985).

'irritable' baby may also be observed to be highly 'observant' and 'sensitive'.
- Use cognitive techniques learned earlier to identify cognitive distortions, e.g. 'My baby is always unsettled.' Is this an overgeneralisation? Is the baby really unsettled 24 hours a day?

❑   **Describe objective 2: learning to read your baby.**

'In this part of the session we will increase your skills as parents in the first stage of successful interaction and communication, that is, understanding your infant's cues. To do this, we will:

- *Observe our babies.*
- *Try to understand "baby talk" by focusing on the cues or signals that babies give.*
- *Explore the various meanings that your baby's communications (cues) may have.'*

❑   **Exercise 1.**

Instruct mothers to adopt the 'en face' position with their baby, which involves directly facing each other at about 30 centimetres apart, with the baby on the mother's raised knee. Alternatively, place the baby on the floor or in a bouncinette.

'Try to get your baby to talk to you.'

- Allow each member to talk about their infant's behaviour. Encourage members to elaborate on their observations of how their baby communicates, what they are trying to tell them, and what behaviours they base their conclusions on.

Typical questions

'What do you observe about your baby?'
'What do you observe about yourself?'
'What is your baby telling you?'

Reflect back to the mother about what you are seeing.

At times you might suggest a change of behaviour to the mother to see if the baby responds differently.

- This exercise can often be used to demonstrate that behaviours are open to differing interpretations.
- Focus on a fun atmosphere and explore the concept of misreading cues at times. How far one explores depends on the group and how mothers are responding.
- Develop a video library of videos of mothers playing with babies, so that if infants are asleep videos of other parents interacting with their babies may be used to work with.

❑   **Lecture.**

Important ways you and your baby communicate: eye gaze, tone, touch, emotional interplay.

'What happens between you and your baby when you "talk" together? Interactions have been likened to a dance where you each take turns, are "tuned in" to each other and occasionally you move together. At times you know it is time to stop and "pause" from the dance. How do you and your baby dance—with your:

- *Eyes.*
- *Voice.*
- *Tone.*
- *Touch?*

How do your babies tell us what they want:

- *With increased excitement to tell us they want more?*
- *They look away if they want a pause?*
- *Vocalisation?*
- *Crying?'*

(Add mothers' suggestions on the whiteboard.)

'Can babies wait?

- *Babies cannot wait.*
- *They do best if our responses to them are immediate and appropriate to their cues.*
- *This is not possible all the time; ''good-enough'' is our goal.'*

A typical conversation with your baby might go like this: *'Your baby smiles and so you look, smile and coo at your baby. The baby looks at you then coos. Your voice and face become more animated and the baby also becomes increasingly excited and moves all his limbs. Then the baby tires*

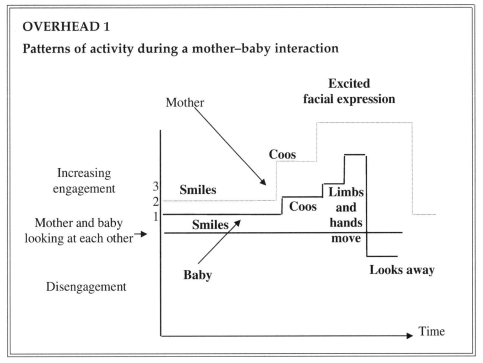

OVERHEAD 1

Patterns of activity during a mother–baby interaction

Adapted from Penman et al. (1983).

and starts to look away. You decrease your activities, waiting for a signal that the baby is ready to start again. You may still smile and look at him to create a readiness for more play.'

❑ **Exercise 2.**

'Let us explore our babies' responses to our non-verbal communication.'

- Body language: hold your baby in different ways.
- Use different tones of voice, saying 'hello' repeatedly and watch your baby's reaction.
- Look at your baby's behaviour when you imitate him.
- Use different facial expressions (sad to happy and responsive).

❑ **Exercise 3: stress responses.**

'Let us explore how our babies respond if:

1. We keep our faces blank and unresponsive.
2. We ignore our baby's signals that they are ready for a "pause".
3. We intrude in his space using too loud a voice or constant stimulation.'

❑ **Discussion.**

'What have we learned today?'

Things that you can do to facilitate interactions:

- Follow the leader (your baby).
- Respond immediately.
- Reduce interfering activity when you are playing.
- Imagine how your baby feels.
- Bring fun into your games.
- Touch your baby.
- Wait expectantly for your baby to be ready.

Learn your baby's preferences. Adjust stimulation to your baby's needs at the time.

HOMEWORK

Play 'en face' for 15 minutes a day by trying to incorporate this play into your day. For example, this can be at nappy-changing time, bath time, etc.
    Keep a diary of:

1. A good time.
2. A difficult time.
3. What your baby did.
4. How you felt.

❑ **Postscript.**

As with Session 1, many skills are introduced and can usefully be consolidated by extending the number of sessions aimed at the parent's interchange with the infant. Observing the infant with guided exercises as described above, and learning to appreciate the skills and temperament of their babies, can take some time. If more time is available and seems indicated, try modelling or coaching with immediate feedback, e.g. *'Try talking quietly now.'*

SESSION 3: LET'S EXAMINE OUR FEELINGS—PARENTAL RESPONSES TO INFANT CUES

NOTES FOR THE THERAPIST

❑ **Group aims.**

A major aim of this session is to separate parental issues from the needs of infants. This is often facilitated by exploring cognitions that parents attribute to infant behaviour and challenging them. For instance, a mother may describe her infant as always wanting something from her. Other group members may help her observe her infant's curiosity in his environment, and his attempts to engage in interactions. His frustration at not being responded to at times leads to him fussing. She may be encouraged to acknowledge her feelings of being overwhelmed by any attempts to be drawn out of her depressed mood; and helped to explore ways in which she can respond to some of her baby's needs, and solicit help from her partner when she is overwhelmed.

In this session we therefore progress from helping parents observe their infants to:

- Exploring their interpretation of their infant's behaviour.
- Becoming aware of the emotions aroused in the mother by her infant.

❑ **Describe objectives.**

Let us learn about your responses

'Today we will try to identify the difficult thoughts and feelings that can develop in relation to your babies' behaviours, the emotions that develop from general contact with the baby, and how to understand them.'

Establish a warm trusting atmosphere whereby members feel that they can honestly discuss how the communication from their baby makes them feel. Discuss openly which particular behaviours are rewarding and which are stressful.

❑ **Let us use last week's homework as a starting point.**

'Last week we observed and interpreted what "baby talk" means; this final stage focuses on how this makes us feel as parents. How did your homework

go? How did you feel when you were unsure of what your baby was saying? How did you feel if you did not know what was wrong when your baby cried? How did you feel if your baby did not respond during the play session? What difficult times did you have during the week? Did your feelings sometimes cause you to misinterpret your infant's cues?'

- Explore the various thoughts and feelings aroused and why women might react the way that they do.
- Explore issues of: what is a *'good enough mother?'* Feelings of inadequacy, failure, guilt, anger and frustration may all be brought up.

❑   **Interpreting infant behaviour: theirs or ours?**

- Explore the concept that sometimes we put words to the behaviour of our baby which come from our own feelings, or from our past, rather than from what the baby may be actually saying (refer back to Sessions 6, 7 and 8 of the Getting Ahead of Postnatal Depression program, which introduces ways of challenging cognitive distortions).
- Explore past experiences and relationships that parents have had and the influence that these have on their responses to their infants. The following topics can be good discussion starters:

    — Infants reawaken memories of childhood.
    — Parental models of care are based on early learning experiences.

(Refer back to Session 5 of the Getting Ahead of Postnatal Depression program to remind women about what they shared of their family of origin experiences.)

This part of the program can elicit powerful feelings and memories of earlier conflicts. At times, mothers will need another avenue, such as individual counselling, to fully deal with issues that arise. Again, if time is available, increased group sessions can fruitfully explore these issues.

❑   **From behaviours to feelings: now what do I do?**

Use examples brought up by the homework to highlight parental responses and parental feelings that are not a direct consequence of the baby's behaviour.

For example, *'He cries a lot and I feel helpless and angry.'* Use the group to recognise the need to separate parental feelings (e.g., anger) from appropriate responses to the infant (e.g., feed, soothe, rock baby).

❑   **Management issues.**

'In our time together in this module we have focused mainly on how to improve the communication between us and our baby. This is the

foundation of our relationship. Sometimes this will help with baby manage-
ment problems we may have such as:

- *Leaving our baby.*
- *Sleeping through the night.*
- *Breastfeeding.*
- *Understanding infant developmental stages.*
- *How to organise childcare and time-out.*

At other times you may need to seek advice from books, maternal and child
health nurses or doctors to deal with these issues.'

❑   **Discussion.**

Allow women to identify if any of the above are issues for them and
how they will manage the issues, e.g. self-help or seek help.
   Option: provide brief psycho-educational material on basic infant
management (Green, 1988).

❑   **An interactional framework.**

'Our relationships grow as a result of what happens between us and our
baby on a day-to-day basis. Free up a space to bring the fun back in your
time with your baby if it has gone missing or become crowded out by life's
demands. Make room for you and your baby by getting as much support as
you need so that you are more available and ready to play.'

- *Social support: encourage brainstorming on networking and using com-*
  munity resources.
- *Encourage sharing infant tasks with partners.*
- *Allow for time-out and couple time to recharge.*

HOMEWORK

Give parents the following handout as a reminder of things to do
and what they learned in the group.

HANDOUT 2

Things to remember

1. **Have fun with your baby**
2. **Dance with your baby**
   - **Observe your infant**
   - **Interpret your baby's behaviour**
   - **Be aware of emotions aroused in yourself**
   - **Remember the skills discussed to build communication**
   - **Appreciate the skills of your baby**
3. **Challenge your negative thoughts**
   - **Rethink feelings that are not based on fact**

Handout 2 continued

- Encourage rational thinking based on the reality of your baby's behaviour. Then deal with the behaviour and your own feelings separately
4. Influences from the past
   - Infants reawaken powerful memories of earlier family relationships. Separate your baby from them
5. Your marriage and social support
   - Support your marital relationship with couple time and sharing infant tasks
   - Strengthen support networks
   - Have time-out by arranging support for yourself

❑   Postscript.

Group facilitators may wish to assess the improvement or status of the mother–infant interaction before and after the module using a modified version of the Milgrom–Burn Scale.

RESOURCE

Assessing the interaction: the Milgrom–Burn scale

See Box 1, Chapter 3.

The most challenging aspect of this session can be the material that emerges when parents attribute their own behaviour to the parental models that they acquired on the basis of their own childhood experience. At times, this may be distressing and require further follow-up. Again, it is the material in this session, in particular, that may need to be continued into another session.

Chapter 9

INDIVIDUAL TREATMENT: A FLEXIBLE APPROACH

With contributions from Jennifer Ericksen and Carol Richards

INTRODUCTION

As described previously, postnatal depression (PND) affects at least 10% of women who have given birth. To these women, the arrival of a new baby is not the exciting, wonderful event that they had expected. PND often affects the new mother insidiously so that she no longer recognises herself, her abilities or the extent of her distressing feelings. Most women with PND need to be allowed to tell their 'story'. Each story is different and might describe difficulties in the mother's ability to cope, recent stresses such as a loss, or problems within the mother–infant relationship. To some, the fact of becoming a mother arouses feelings about issues that have occurred in the past, often related to their own mothering.

Individual treatment offers a more flexible approach than group treatment, as the package can be tailored to the individual's situation (see Case 1). Some women are resistant to group participation and prefer individual treatment. Other women may struggle with problems that are so traumatic that the problems are better dealt with in individual counselling, since being a member of a group may be experienced as putting sensitive issues too much 'in the spotlight'.

Individual therapy may also be more suitable for women who have additional problems. Women with limited intellectual capacity or with limited ability to understand or express themselves, in the language of therapy, usually benefit from individual treatment geared to their level or provided with the use of a professional interpreter. However, using family members as interpreters is not recommended. Women with sensory deficits can also be treated in this way (see Case 2). Individual therapy allows for the setting of realistic goals given the situations and resources of the individuals involved.

In addition, it has been our experience that it can take some weeks to collect women for group intervention, and there are times when it

---

CASE 1
A case study of multiple losses[a]

Louise was a 32-year-old woman with PND. Her BDI score was 28. Louise spent five months in hospital waiting for the birth of her second child. She had a normal delivery of a much planned and wanted son. Andrew was eight weeks old when Louise first sought help. She had tried for four years to have Andrew yet didn't feel close to him. She felt stunned, unable to do things around the house, didn't want to see friends, go shopping or visit anyone. Her daughter, Jane, aged four, was causing chaos at home, with oppositional behaviour.

On her first visit to our clinic, Louise appeared happy. She smiled a lot, seemed very capable with Andrew, interacting quite appropriately with him. She was willing to talk about everything and constantly referred to the long time she had spent in hospital during her pregnancy. Louise was married and 'adored' her partner, whose praises she sang.

When asked if she would like to tell her story, the following unfolded. Louise had had two miscarriages, then a very premature infant girl (Jane) who was now four years old. She then had two further pregnancies, resulting in two premature babies, one male who died four hours after birth and one female who died six hours after birth. In both cases she had decided not to have the babies ventilated, so carried with her the thought that they may have lived if she had chosen to leave on the machine. She then had Andrew, who was born at 31 weeks gestation.

The therapist allowed Louise time to tell her story and to cry for her lost babies (she had not had counselling), and looked at photos of her two dead babies who had been named and were intensely missed by Louise. When asked if she thought Andrew was going to die, Louise was quite startled before acknowledging this fear.

Louise needed time to understand that her depression reflected a need to grieve for her dead babies before she was able to feel joy for her living baby. She was also helped to understand why Jane was so difficult. Jane had been separated from her mother so many times, and Jane needed time to grieve also and to understand Andrew was here to stay. Louise began to feel better in the first two weeks of counselling as she came to understand that there were reasons for her feelings.

---

[a]This and the following cases are examples of the diverse nature of issues that a woman with PND may have experienced. Each of these women had the courage to share their stories and they are among the thousands of women who suffer from PND who have sought help and recovered. It is from women such as these that we learn more about PND. Each mother is as unique as her story is different, and the impact of her illness can be profound. To quote one of our mothers: *'A mother is crying—is someone listening?'*

is detrimental for women suffering from PND to wait. Individual therapy also caters for women who are unable to make a regular commitment to weekly group times owing to their own or their children's health, or other reasons. Finally, the individual approach described below is suitable for health professionals who prefer a general counselling approach, with optional usage of cognitive-behavioural therapy (CBT) modules. It also provides a greater opportunity to develop a therapeutic relationship.

The individual treatment approach as outlined in this chapter has been found by us to be efficacious for a wide cross-section of presenting problems and diagnostic categories. It consists of the following phases.

CASE 2
A case study of a therapeutic approach in the context of special needs

Kerry is a 36-year-old woman who is deaf and required someone to sign (Auslan) for her. This was not possible in our group situation as it complicated the group process. Kerry had three children: a boy of 13 years who was able to hear; a girl of 10 years who was deaf, had multiple disabilities and did not live with her mother; and Dylan aged five months, who was not deaf. A maternal child health nurse thought that Kerry's depression was due to her deafness, which had been present from birth. Kerry finally sought help for her depression and an interpreter was used by the therapist who elicited the following story.

Kerry's depression stemmed from guilt—her de facto partner was 10 years younger than her and also deaf. In fact, most of Kerry's friends were also deaf and the circles Kerry mixed in had a predominance of deaf people, all of whom used sign language. Kerry assumed that many people were talking about her relationship and that she was not married. Coupled with this, her partner's parents, who were from a different culture, did not believe that Dylan was their son's child, and would not accept him, nor Kerry herself. The gossip and rejection were the basis of Kerry's depression. Once Kerry could understand her feelings, she was able to work through her depression, and explore other issues, such as having hearing children.

Phase 1: Extended assessment **(two to four sessions)**

In all therapeutic interventions, assessment of the individual's situation is the starting point for the therapeutic alliance. In Chapter 3, we described key areas of functioning to be assessed in new mothers, including the level of depression and anxiety. With an individual approach, this assessment can be broadened and provides therapeutic benefits. For instance, it may be the first opportunity a woman has had to debrief in detail about a traumatic birth experience, or a traumatic past event. These women may be concerned for their own or their baby's well-being. The first session can often be a time when women 'dump' their feelings of going mad, fears of being a bad mother or their guilt of not wanting their baby. The therapist may be the first person she may tell these things to, and feel she is really being listened to. Often family and friends' advice to 'snap out of it' or 'it will pass' is not helpful.

Individual therapy can then provide customised treatment according to the needs of the mother as determined by clinical and psychometric assessment. It is important to let the mother know from the first session that she can be helped and that she will get better. She needs to be given some idea of the length of treatment, and what she can expect from the therapist. During this phase it is helpful to find out how much prior information about PND this mother has received, and to take into account any conflicting information that she has been given.

Finally, as the mother–infant relationship is very important in PND, it is useful to have knowledge of what problems may arise in this area and of problems in infant development. If at any time a therapist feels concerned, enlisting the help of a maternal and child health nurse can be invaluable.

Phase 2: Goal setting **(one to two sessions)**

By the end of the assessment sessions, it is helpful to formulate the main areas of concern for the woman and her partner, and to set some provisional goals. To ensure that goals are achievable it is essential that the therapist has some knowledge of how demanding motherhood can be. Goal setting needs to take into account the time required for the mother to care for her baby, particularly as she may be slowed down by her depression, and therapists need to be particularly careful not to set too much 'homework'.

Phase 3: Treatment **(number of sessions depends on goals)**

Once goals have been identified, treatment with a problem-solving emphasis and relevant components of the CBT approaches in the Getting Ahead of Postnatal Depression program can be provided. A basic counselling approach can also be used to explore further areas of general concern for women suffering from PND. Just being given time to talk to someone on a regular basis, who listens, reframes and assists in goal setting and decision making, is beneficial.

Couple sessions, as detailed in Chapter 7, are usefully combined with individual treatment. This important component of treatment allows the father to be involved and given information on how to support his partner. It may also be the first opportunity he has for someone to listen to how difficult and confusing life has become for him.

For women with interactional difficulties, the program for parent–infant difficulties is recommended (see Chapter 8). As highlighted with the case examples, although all the mothers are suffering from PND, they have their own individual stories, only some of which may include difficulties with their babies. Add to this the differing points of view of the fathers, and the complexity of treating mothers with PND becomes apparent. In the more complex cases, particularly with an infant at risk, individual counselling may be the preferable option (see Case 3).

PHASE 1: EXTENDED ASSESSMENT

Objective

1. To develop rapport with a new mother, allowing her time and freedom to tell 'her story'.
2. To provide information about PND and to help the mother develop a clearer understanding of PND.
3. To enable the mother to accept that she has PND.

CASE 3
Case study: an infant at risk

Jill, a 28-year-old married woman, was referred to our clinic by her maternal and child health nurse, for depression and difficulties managing her eight-week-old daughter, who was her first child. On the initial consultation, Jill seemed very depressed and showed a lack of interest in her baby although the baby seemed very aware of her mother. Jill talked of a planned pregnancy, a supportive partner and of her 'beautiful baby' Jessie. At the initial consultation the therapist listened to Jill and tried to help Jill feel at ease. At the second consultation, Jill was very upset and crying and disclosed to the therapist that she loved Jessie but was afraid to love her in the way that she wanted to. Jill also talked about deep feelings inside that made her want to hurt Jessie. She confided that she had felt that if she squeezed Jessie harder when she was feeding her, she could break her ribs and had at times squeezed quite hard. She found herself frequently handling Jessie roughly when putting her in her cradle.

The therapist, after discussing the issues with Jill, contacted Shane, her partner, and explained to him the difficulties that Jill was having and the need to involve child protection. A meeting with Jill, the therapist and a protection worker followed. At this meeting, the protection worker explained to Jill that it was in Jessie's best interest that she had sought help by telling someone of her fears. The protection worker was helpful and supportive of Jill, who agreed to continue to get help for her depression and at the same time to try to work through her feelings about hurting Jessie. It also emerged that Shane was having tremendous difficulties coping with the situation and was distressed that he could not 'fix' the problem between Jill and Jessie. Supportive counselling for him helped him to accept what he could and could not do to help.

4. To create an atmosphere in which the mother feels accepted, understood and valued so that she can explore feelings, thoughts and behaviour.
5. To reach a clearer understanding of the major concerns in the mother's life, including problems in the mother–infant relationship and her support system.

Referral source

A recent mother may have been referred by another health professional, such as a general practitioner, community health nurse or social worker. In this case, the mother may be aware that she has PND. On the other hand, the mother may be self-referred and not be aware that she has PND.

Notes on first session

The first session is particularly important. Not only has the mother made a difficult decision in asking for help, but often she is feeling afraid of the first interview. The relationship between the therapist and the mother may have already begun over the phone when the appointment was made. The central task of the therapist is to understand that this mother is unique, that no two mothers have the same experience in childbirth and that this mother–infant relationship has its own special characteristics. If the mother believes that the therapist accepts her and her infant as they are, then it allows her the freedom to open up and work through her depression. Women need to feel safe to show their frailties without judgement, and this is critical to remember when placing individual mothers in groups. Other issues to keep in mind have also been elaborated in the introduction to this chapter.

It is important that the therapist informs the mother that she can be helped and that she will get better. Do not, at this stage, tell the mother a time when she will be better, but rather inform her that the treatment will be in three phases. After attending even the first counselling session, the mother can expect to have a better understanding not only of PND but also of herself.

Collecting general information (often in the first session)

As stated in the introduction, the first session with the mother is important and will affect whether the mother returns for further appointments. A good rapport is essential. Mothers often need to be oriented to the setting and asked *why* they believe they need help at this time. Some time is spent in familiarisation with the mother and the way she is currently feeling and coping. Asking the mother about *how she is feeling* and her symptoms is very important in this initial phase of rapport building, and crucial to the success of the therapeutic intervention. The therapist's attentiveness and receptiveness to both the mother and the baby are helpful and can be done by asking generally about the family and their situation. This sets the background to later more in-depth questions. Listening and encouraging the mother to communicate as well as showing empathy and concern sets the tone. Certain skills help to develop the relationship and are described later (refer to section at the end of this chapter on 'Counselling and postnatal depression').

Using counselling techniques to summarise what has been said, reflect it back, label feelings and ask whether you have understood the mother correctly creates a helpful atmosphere and positive therapeutic relationship. The therapist should be supportive and act like a facilitator rather than an 'expert'. During the sessions the therapist can take the opportunity to join with the mother in the care of the infant (e.g., help to entertain the baby, if necessary).

Some of the steps in which assessment can be facilitated are described below.

❑   **Orientation to Clinic.**

'Hello, my name is _____ *. I am a* _____ *.*
I have had a letter/phone call from _____ *and*

my understanding is _____.'
   'Is that your understanding of why you are here today?' *Perhaps you would like to tell me what has brought you here.'*

❏   **How she came to be seeking help.**

'Can you tell me a little bit about what has brought you here?'
'How did you find your way to this clinic?'

Some discussion about how the mother has come to be seeking treatment is a good starting point. What is her understanding of why she is here? Information about her social networks and her understanding of the problem may be revealed, as may feelings of guilt or fears of going mad.

❏   **General information.**

At this point, it is a good time to get any necessary information such as demographic information (if required) and family information. General questions about her family, her partner, the baby's grandparents, the number of children she has and their ages help to build rapport and provide important basic information. In the first session it is not necessary to do too much or gather too much data. Just allowing the mother to begin her story is sufficient.
   It is important to ask what the name of her baby is and to show interest in him/her. Remembering the infant's age will enable the therapist to be aware of developmental issues.

❏   **Maternal description of symptoms.**

Mothers usually want to discuss the symptoms and difficulties that they are experiencing early on in the assessment process. This is why they have presented. More detailed and background information can be elicited after this has been accomplished.

'How have you been feeling since the birth of your baby?'
'Have you noticed any changes in yourself?'

Focus on symptoms such as difficulties in sleeping, appetite, concentration, feelings of worthlessness, loss of interest, lowered mood or irritability, and thoughts about death.

'Have you experienced any other worrying symptoms?'

As a way of understanding more about the nature and degree of the mother's depression, standardised assessment tools can be administered as described in Chapter 3. The Beck Depression and Beck Anxiety Inventories, together with a standardised interview for depression, are very useful tools. Therapists should be familiar with the DSM-IV criteria for mood and anxiety disorders. Begin by asking the mother if there are any particular areas in her life that she believes have contributed to her depression.

'How do you understand what is happening to you?
'Are there any factors that you think might be contributing to the way that you are feeling or managing?'
'What have you found helps at all?'

❑   **Birth and pregnancy.**

All therapists have their own way of working in order to further put mothers at ease. Some questions that might be asked are factual. For example, it is often useful to hear the mother's version of the pregnancy and birth.

'Would you mind if I asked you some questions that you have probably not been asked before?'

The birth history is very important and may give you clues to the way the mother is feeling.

'How have you been since _____ was born?'
'When did you start to feel this way?'

Allowing the mother to tell her own story often elicits more information than if the therapist asked set questions. The information required includes health and experiences during pregnancy:

- Was the pregnancy planned?
- Was this the mother's first pregnancy?
- What happened to other pregnancies?
- Has the mother been trying to have a baby for a long time?
- Were there difficulties with conception?

❑   **Education about what is postnatal depression.**

Some brief information about the symptoms of PND and its incidence is timely at this stage (refer to Session 1 of the Getting Ahead of Postnatal Depression program). It can help to reassure the mother that she is understood, is in good hands and that help will follow. Some mothers will not be ready yet to acknowledge that they may have PND and they may try to minimise their symptoms or to attribute the symptoms to some other cause.

'If only my baby would sleep better, then I would be able to feel better, have more energy and manage.'

HANDOUT

Symptoms of postnatal depression

Refer to Overhead 1/Session 1 of the Cognitive-Behaviour Therapy Group program

---

'Do you recognise any of these symptoms?'

The assessment phase of the individual therapy program gives women time to adjust to the idea that they are not feeling as they should and that they might need some help to do so. It will also provide information on current coping strategies.

❑   **Couple relationship.**

'Are you currently in a relationship?'
'Can you tell me about your partner?'
'How is your partner coping?'
'How would you describe your relationship?'

If the woman is not in a relationship, then some information about the baby's father can be obtained. Issues about access, financial and social support may be worth exploring.

❑   **Risk status.**

The therapist should always ascertain risk factors and assess the mother's state of mind. If the mother is suicidal, some strategies may need to be put in place immediately. The therapist may find it necessary to contact the woman's partner to talk with him. He may be totally unaware of his partner's feelings. For confidentiality reasons it is useful to advise the mother before contacting her partner, explaining why such actions are necessary. In addition, the therapist may find it necessary to involve a child protection agency when counselling a woman with PND if it is considered that the infant is at risk.

Mandatory reporting of children at risk exists in many states and the therapist can use the protection worker as a support to get the help the mother requires. It should be viewed as a positive action rather than a threat that adds further fears to an already depressed woman. The parents should be told of your intention and be a part of the case plan.

The importance of developing a good rapport and gaining the woman's trust is paramount. This trust then helps overcome difficulties such as mandatory reporting of a child at risk and contacting the woman's partner.

Thus, if mandatory reporting exists, the therapist does not have any choice but to make a report. It is wise to contact the woman's partner and to inform the parents what you intend and why. This should be done in a positive way and seen as a step toward wellness. If the therapist views it as a positive step and conveys that to the woman, the therapeutic relationship need not be harmed.

In summary, if the therapist has any concerns for the mother or baby and fears harm may come to either, the therapist may need to involve others, such as:

- The woman's partner.
- A maternal and child health nurse.

- Child protection agency.
- Community supports.
- Extended family.

❑   **Brief history** (often in the second session)

The following questions are often not asked until the second assessment session when some rapport has developed.

❑   **Family of origin.**

'Can you tell me about the family you grew up in?'

Drawing a genogram is useful and provides an opportunity to ask difficult questions about mother, father and siblings, then and now.

'What was your childhood like?'
'How do you remember your family life?'
'Were there any major events in your life, as you were growing up?'
'Did you have any emotional difficulties when you were growing up?'
'How would you describe your relationship with your parents?'
'Have you ever experienced physical, sexual or emotional abuse?'

❑   **School and employment history/life aspirations.**

'How do you remember your school life'?
'Tell me about your working life.'

Information about school and employment is helpful in completing a picture of the woman, her achievements, aspirations, capabilities and background.

❑   **Past medical and psychological history.**

'Have you had any medical or psychological difficulties in the past?'
'Have you had professional assistance with these?'
'Have you had any problems with alcohol, drug abuse or eating disorders?'

Previous problems and treatment are also important to know about. Medical conditions that can have similar symptoms to depression (such as hypothyroidism) need to be considered.

❑   **Maternal history of depression.**

Try to get some insight into the mother's previous history of depression.

'Have you ever suffered from depression before?'
'Can you remember having times in your life when you felt down for a few weeks at a time?'
'Did you get any treatment at these times?'
'What did you find helpful?'
'How do you generally manage when things do not go so well for you?'

❑   **Fertility.**

Some women will have had difficulties becoming pregnant and may have been involved with assisted fertility procedures that can require some debriefing. Many women find procedures that they have undertaken very intrusive, and need help to recover from the experience. Some women may have been trying to conceive for long periods, which they found difficult. For others, unplanned pregnancies may result in problematic emotional and social consequences.

Information in this area can be obtained as a prelude to asking about this pregnancy.

Expanding on previous information (after reviewing material obtained to date)

Some information can be expanded upon, now that a context has been described and the therapeutic relationship established.

❑   **Pregnancy.**

Explore pregnancy, birth expectations and experiences more fully.

'Was this a planned pregnancy?'
'How did you find being pregnant?'
'How did you feel about being pregnant?'

❑   **Birth and hospital experiences.**

Feelings about treatment in hospital and in the early weeks after taking the baby home can be very revealing.

'Tell me about the birth of _____.'
'How did you feel about the delivery?'
'How did you feel about your doctor and your treatment in hospital?'
'How did your partner cope?'
'How were you feeling in hospital?'

❑   **Expectations of motherhood.**

'What was it like for you in hospital?'
'What was it like bringing your baby home?'
'How do you feel about your baby?'
'Is motherhood what you expected?'
'What do you find most difficult?'
'What are the good things?'
'Are there any things that you find worrying you?'

❑   **Early relationships: mother's own mothering.**

A mother's memories of her own family's expectations and experience of mothering can be influencing how she feels. This can include:

• Her relationship with her own mother.
• Childhood and adolescence.

'How would you describe your relationship with your own mother?'
'What was your childhood like?'
'How do you remember your own experiences of being mothered?'
'Have you asked your mother how she felt when she had you?'
'Do you feel differently now you are a mother?'

Other assessment targets (Sessions 3 or 4)

At this point in Phase 1, the therapist has generally spent one or two sessions with the mother and is starting to understand her story. To complete the assessment phase, a number of other areas of information may need to be covered and are described below. Not every question has to be asked, nor does the questioning have to occur in the order described. Clinical judgement will determine if questions under a particular heading are relevant, and to what extent, if there are concerns in that area. Some questions may be asked in this assessment phase and others noted and explored more fully in Phase 2, when the main areas of concern are elaborated and goals are set for change.

❑   **Social supports.**

Supports can include family and friends, and it is helpful to compare a mother's expectations and the reality of her situation.
'This is a time when there may be people around you who will offer help to you. Have you been aware of people who may be able to help or support you or who are interested in you and your baby?'
'How do you feel about other people helping you?'
'Have you asked them for help?'
'Here is a handout of the possible sources of support for you to think about in your particular life situation and to perhaps help you expand your current network.'

HANDOUT

Possible sources of support
- Mother
- Mother-in-law
- Siblings
- Neighbours
- Professional help
- Friends
- Church groups
- Relatives
- Community centres
- 'Other'

'What type of help/support would you find useful at this time?'
- Company
- Telephone contact
- Visits
- Help with baby
- Professional help
- Help with other siblings
- Help with housework
- Shopping
- Babysitting
- 'Other'

Probe—encourage mothers to start thinking about increasing the use of social supports and to set time aside for themselves.

Encourage mothers to share information with their partners.

'What do you think your husband thinks postnatal depression is?'
'Did you show the handout on symptoms of postnatal depression to your husband/partner?'
'Did you discuss it together?'
'Did he see some of the symptoms in you?' 'When did he first notice them?'
'How do you feel your husband has responded to your condition?' (Probe for supportiveness, emotional and practical.)

❑ **Changes in life since the birth of the baby, especially in the marital/partner relationship.**

- Couples find that their relationships often change dramatically after a baby, especially their sex lives.

  'Have there been any specific areas of tension between you and your husband?'
  'How has your relationship with your husband changed since the baby's arrival? In what way?'
  'Have you and your husband discussed the differences between your parenting styles? Are there any differences?'

- Feelings about self, including transition from working.

  'What are your feelings about yourself at present?' (Probe for self-esteem/mothering skills.)

  Some women find it very different not having their own money; this may create a 'power shift' in their relationship with their partners.

  'How did it feel leaving work? Do you plan to return? What do you miss most?'

❑ **Understanding contributing factors.**

A mother's beliefs of why she has developed depression is informative, and can include <u>major stressful life events</u>, or her own coping style and personality (e.g., perfectionism).

'Are there any issues that you think may be contributing to your feelings at present?'
'Is there anything that particularly worries you about being a mother or about your baby?'
'Have you ever had any previous traumatic experiences as you were growing up that are relevant?'

❑ **The mother–baby relationship.**

Explore maternal feelings, including how she has bonded towards her baby, and management problems such as feeding, sleep and her routine.

Questions that can be asked include:

'How do you remember your baby in hospital?'
'Did you have any particular problems?'
'How has the baby settled at home?'
'Do you have anything that is worrying you at present about your baby?'
'How do you feel about your baby?'
'How many times a day are you feeding your baby?'
'Are you bottle- or breast-feeding?'
'Are you experiencing any difficulties?'
'Are you able to enjoy your baby?'
'How many hours a day is your baby sleeping?'
'Do you spend much time holding your baby?'
'When your baby cries, do you usually know the reason?'
'How does your partner relate to your baby?'

❏   **Partner functioning.**

'How is your partner coping with the conflicting pressures of work and home?'
'How is he dealing with finding you depressed most days?'
'Does he have any supports?'

PHASE 2: GOAL SETTING

Objective

To identify major contributing issues to a mother's PND, and to set realistic goals for the woman to achieve to enable change to take place by:

1. Assisting the mother to recognise her particular problems and her own strengths.
2. Encouraging the mother to take steps towards changing problem areas.
3. Helping the mother to realise that change takes time.
4. Encouraging the mother to problem solve and find solutions of her own.
5. Enabling the mother to practice achievable change towards her goals.

During the assessment process, the point of the questions is to elucidate the major issues for a particular mother. From the answers to questions, a clinical judgement is made about what issues need to be expanded. During the goal-setting phase, two to three issues are selected as the major areas of concern that will become the target of treatment. Information about these areas is expanded. Once the issue is well understood, the therapist should encourage the mother to make realistic goals and think of the possibility of taking small steps toward them. Realistic goals are particularly important as many women already feel they are failing and do not need this reinforced. For example, the main issues becoming apparent for future emphasis may be:

1. No social supports.
2. Mother–infant issues.
3. Anxiety.
4. Marital tensions or relationship breakdown as in Case 4.
5. Low self esteem.

CASE 4
Case study reflecting issues of assisted fertility and the impact on the couple relationship

It is important that the therapist does not assume that all major underlying issues for the mother have been discussed, if a mother has had previous help for her depression. Vanessa, 32, presented at the clinic when her baby was six months old. Her depression was getting worse, she had returned to work and it had been assumed that her tearfulness was due to leaving Paul, her infant. When asked to talk about her pregnancy and the birth of Paul, she mentioned briefly that her husband (John) had left her prior to the birth of Paul. He had attended the delivery of Paul and returned to live with Vanessa after the birth. Vanessa reported that the relationship was really supportive and there were not really any problems now. When asked by the therapist why her husband had left, she claimed that she had asked him to, as there had been a lot of arguments over her pregnancy. With probing, Vanessa revealed the following.

  She and her husband had been trying to have a baby for 10 years. John always claimed that he could not produce a child. Paul had been conceived with the assistance of IVF. Both partners had agreed to IVF; however, there had been little counselling for the couple, who used the program twice. Paul had been conceived with donor sperm which John had at first agreed to, but then felt he couldn't accept. John claimed he was happy with his son, but Vanessa didn't think that he meant it. There was a communication breakdown in the relationship and, without counselling, the relationship broke down and John left. Vanessa had told no one about the donor sperm and was unable to talk to John as she was afraid to hear what he had to say. Vanessa continued in counselling and as her depression lifted she was able to see that she and John needed to talk to each other and they were referred for couple counselling.

Therapists can **keep a record sheet** of goals.

Example of a record sheet

Provisional goals (main issues of concern)

Goal 1: _____

Discussed with mother	☐
Decision making regarding strategies	☐
Action/treatment	☐
Evaluation	☐
Problem solved	☐

Provisional treatment plan

On the basis of information that has been learned about a mother and her situation, it is now possible to devise a treatment plan to meet provisional goals. For example, a mother may identify two major areas of concern as goals of treatment:

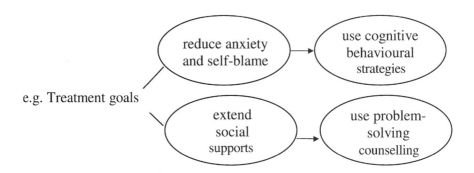

PHASE 3: TREATMENT

Adapting relevant modules from the CBT program

Selected modules from the Getting Ahead of Postnatal Depression program, described in previous chapters, can be used if maternal goals include changing behaviour, anxiety or assertiveness and cognitions, such as thoughts of failure. Common maternal issues are described in Box 1, together with relevant modules that can be adapted from the Getting Ahead of Postnatal Depression program. Similarly, if identified issues are within the couple relationship, then Chapter 7 serves as a useful approach to couples work, as shown in Box 2.

In individual treatment, counselling skills can be usefully combined with the cognitive-behavioural modules for a variety of targets, as shown in Box 3 and elaborated in the next section.

Examples of questions that can be asked to monitor progress, or consolidate changes made, include the following:

- Monitoring progress in the mother's symptoms and partner support.

  'How have you been managing over the last week?'
  'How have you been feeling?' (Probe for more information such as anxious feelings or any previously identified problems.)
  'Have there been any changes since last week?'
  'How is your husband managing?'
  'Has he noticed any changes in you?'
  'How is he responding to your symptoms?'

BOX 1

Common maternal issues

• Low self-esteem	→	Adapt Session 4 group program 'Psycho-education on self-esteem and love letter', also Session 7 'Challenging my internal critic'
• Family of origin problems	→	Adapt Session 5 group program 'Unrealistic expectations of parenting influences from the past' and section on 'My family of origin'
• Few social supports and activities	→	Adapt Session 2 group program 'Pleasant activities: 'How can I find the time?'
• Previous miscarriages/ terminations/losses	→	Adapt Session 5 by considering 'Issues from the past' not as related to family of origin but to previous losses
• Perfectionistic personality	→	Adapt Sessions 6 and 7 group program 'My internal dialogue: the missing link' and 'Developing a more helpful thinking style'
• Anxiety	→	Adapt Session 3 group program 'Relaxation on the run'
• Expectations of motherhood	→	See Session 1 group program
• Marital problems	→	Use Chapter 7
• Mother–baby issues	→	Adapt Session 5 group program section on 'Challenging unhelpful thoughts and unrealistic expectations of parenting'. Continue with Chapter 8 for serious difficulties

USE HANDOUTS FROM GROUP PROGRAM AS APPROPRIATE

BOX 2

Common paternal issues

• Lack of understanding of symptoms/blame		
• Adjusting to responsibilities of parenthood		
• Accepting that partner needs help		
• Not knowing how to help and when		
• Getting the support that they need	→	Use Chapter 7 as
• Family of origin issues		a guide for three
• Juggling work and family demands		couples sessions
• Feelings of isolation		
• Living with a depressed person		

> **BOX 3**
>
> **Counselling targets**
>
> In addition to CBT modules, counselling approaches can be used for:
> - Identifying strengths and resources
> - Stimulating and encouraging
> - Monitoring progress
> - Ventilating feelings
> - Elucidating issues
> - Exploring alternative solutions to problems
> - Problem solving
> - Decision making
> - Building and extending existing coping skills
> - Improving communication between family members
> - Increasing a mother's knowledge of resources, PND and child development
> - Changing, maintaining and consolidating behaviour changes: see examples in the text

'What are your feelings about yourself at present?' (Probe for self-esteem.)

- Monitoring mother's depression.

  'Have you been experiencing any other worrying symptoms?'
  'How much sleep are you managing?'
  'What sort of things have you managed to arrange for yourself to allow time-out?'

- Consolidating social support increases.

  Help mothers to understand that it is a strength to ask for help when it is needed, and to plan toward the future by developing both short- and long-term goals.

  'Have you been able to ask for help when you needed it, or to accept help when it has been offered?'
  'How did that work out?'
  'How did you feel about having someone help?'
  'What did you do?'
  'Are there other opportunities to get a little bit of time/space for yourself?'
  'Have you talked to your husband about this?'

- Keep exploring mother–baby issues.

  'How is your baby going?'
  'How are you feeling about your baby at present?'

  Follow up any issues in the areas of:

  — Feeding.
  — Sleeping.

— Holding the baby.
— Crying.
— Routine.

'Are things any different this week with your baby?'
'What have you tried? What seems to be most useful?'

Counselling and postnatal depression

Women with PND often recount that the most helpful part of therapy was being heard and understood. Skills in listening facilitate the development of a warm relationship, communicate empathy and help the mother to focus on her issues. The therapeutic relationship forms the basis of all three phases described. A warm, trusting relationship is a prerequisite for helping. It is the helping relationship that underlies the therapeutic process, as described in Box 4.

BOX 4

The therapeutic process

Phase 1: **Assessment**

Warmth and empathy
Rapport
Gathering information   →   focusing

Phase 2: **Goal setting**   ↓

Elaboration and clarification
Themes and patterns   →   goals

Phase 3: **Treatment**   ↑

Behaviour change
Encouragement   →   solutions
Problem solving

Basic counselling skills are required at each phase of individual treatment outlined in this chapter. Egan (1994) describes the skills that are helpful; these have been linked to the phases of the individual approach we have presented, and are expanded and summarised below. A three-stage model of the counselling process adapted from Kagan (1986, p. 193) is used as a basis for describing the basic counselling skills that are relevant to each stage of the individual approach outlined. For example, of vital importance to the first phase (Extended Assessment) is *listening*, which is an active process in a counselling relationship. It goes beyond attending to and receiving a message, and includes communicating that the facts and feelings have been heard and understood. Paraphrasing, reflecting thoughts and feelings, and summarising, are all ways of letting the mother know that she has been understood, accepted and empathised with. Empathy is the ability to see a situation from the mother's point of view or frame of reference. Non-verbal behaviour is also important and can communicate interest and attention.

In the second phase (Goal Setting), skills facilitating *understanding* are important. They help people to see things more objectively and from new perspectives, as well as enabling them to set realistic goals for themselves. Furthermore, using basic counselling helps mothers to explore issues and understand them fully *before* any action is taken. This ensures their full involvement in the process.

BOX 5: Phase 1 (extended assessment)

Skills for exploration and problem definition

- Attention giving
- Active listening:
  Communicating empathy, acceptance, paraphrasing, reflecting thoughts and feelings, summarising.
- Focusing:
  Helping mother to be specific
- Moving conversations on

BOX 6: Phase 2 (goal setting)

Skills for understanding and goal development

- Helping mother to clarify and elaborate
- Offering new perspectives, alternative frameworks
- Listening for themes, patterns, helping mother see them
- Comforting
- Goal setting

BOX 7: Phase 3 (treatment)

Skills for action

Changing behaviours and developing skills can occur via counselling or can be combined with our cognitive-behavioural modules.

FINAL SESSION*

The final session should focus on relapse prevention.

'Although you are now feeling much better in yourself, you might still have some times when things are not so good. Have you thought about this? How would you manage? What resources are available to you after treatment?'

'Are you planning another baby? Many people worry about becoming depressed again after subsequent pregnancies. What are your feelings about this?'

'What would you do?'

'Have you got any feedback to give us about the therapy that you have received? What have you found most helpful during therapy? What advice would you give to someone else with postnatal depression?'

Refer to Cognitive-behavioural therapy modules: Sessions 9 and 10, for termination ideas and relapse prevention.

SUMMARY

Phase 1:   Assessment—Exploration
- Orientation
- How they came to be seeking help
- General information about partner and children
- Maternal description of symptoms and coping strategies
- Education about postnatal depression

Subsequent two to three sessions
- Maternal history (previous depression)
- Major life events, family of origin
- Mother's childhood and adolescence (school life, employment history, life aspirations, past medical or psychological difficulties)
- History of couple relationship
- Pregnancy and birth experience
- Changes in life since baby
- Maternal supports (expectations and reality)
- Mother–infant management and bonding issues
- Predisposing factors and maternal theories
- Mother's experience of mothering

Phase 2:   Goal setting
- Expanding major issues of concern and goal development
- Monitoring progress in mother's symptomatology

Phase 3:   Treatment
- Action using both counselling skills and selected CBT modules

---

* The counselling treatment approach can also be conducted in groups and is elaborated and available as a working manual from the authors. In addition, detailed counselling examples of how to deal with specific issues that arise for postnatally depressed women is provided by Handford (1997).

Chapter 10

CONCLUDING COMMENTS ON CLINICAL ISSUES

The group program described in this book has been found to be an effective treatment approach for many women with postnatal depression (PND). However, successful delivery of the program, whether in its group format or adapted for individuals, requires consideration of a number of non-specific factors. For instance, helping mothers manage their day so that they can attend the group may be critical. In addition, given the likelihood that for every 10 women one will become postnatally depressed, it is important to consider the role not just of treatment but also of prevention. Finally, we need to consider future research directions to explore what we do not yet understand regarding the experience of PND.

MAKING THE GROUP PROGRAM WORK

❏ **Arranging childcare.**

Should infants accompany their mothers during the treatment program? If not, how is this best managed? Mothers suffering from PND are less likely to want to be separated from their babies and many have concerns about the vulnerability of their infants. In addition, many depressed mothers have a preconception that they are poor parents and are concerned with mothering the 'right' way, particularly in the presence of professionals and other mothers. However, the infant may act as a stressor to the mother and the mother may be unable to participate fully in a group program, or process new information and attempt alternative solutions, if she is attending to her baby. This raises a dilemma for the treating team or professional, given that mothers with PND generally exhibit disturbed mother–infant interactions that require early intervention. Any program considered should address the needs of both the mother and the child. We advocate encouraging mothers to leave their infants at home to attend the main group program or, alternatively, arrange on-site childcare. This proximity has the advantage that if the mother or infant become distressed at separation they can check on each other (see Box 1). We also advocate that some therapeutic work is done with the infant present (see Chapter 8). With individual treatment, however, it is usually easiest not to separate maternal and infant sessions, but to deal with material as it arises. We have found that, in the individual sessions, having the infant present is useful and manageable.

BOX 1

One model for on-site childcare

Mothers pitch in to cover the costs of two babysitters who use an adjoining room, which had been made 'baby friendly'. Floor rugs, mobiles and toys are available. Large, light rooms work best and adjoining outdoor areas are ideal so that unsettled babies can be taken outside, often in their pusher, if necessary. The babysitters settle, feed or play with infants. If the infant becomes too distressed, the mother is called out of the group to tend to her infant and can return to the group as soon as possible.

❏ **Managing time and demands.**

New mothers have enormous demands placed on their time and resources. Often traditional support services have failed to appreciate the pressure of time that new mothers experience. A common erroneous assumption is that because mothers stay at home they have time on their hands. It is extremely important that the treating professional considers that the mother has not a moment to waste. Waiting for a consultation can be stressful, as can organising the day to make an appointment. Her entire day is filled with demands and she would rather be home in time for the next feed, rather than being stuck in the traffic with a hungry, screaming infant in the back of the car. It seems facile to be writing about such a consideration, but it is particularly crucial for mothers experiencing PND. An experience with a screaming infant in the back of the car is enough to reduce a depressed mother to tears and to cripple her ability to cope for the remainder of the day. A common story is that by the end of the day the endless routine of feeding, washing and changing can be so draining for a sleep-deprived, depressed mother that she is likely to phone her husband at work, demanding that he come home because she is unable to continue caring for the baby.

This highlights two important issues:

- Be absolutely strict about starting and finishing times.
- Help mothers plan how they are going to organise their day to be able to attend treatment. In many cases, it will be important to help the mother resolve issues about childcare, transport, housework and so forth before she starts coming to therapy. Home help services to assist with housework or home delivery of groceries and vegetables may be what is required to free up the mother to attend therapy.

❏ **Making cognitive-behavioural therapy (CBT) work for women with PND.**

Helping tired mothers

Mothers attending to the needs of a young baby will necessarily and normally be sleep deprived, often existing on three to four hours of broken sleep at a time. Apart from the difficulties that depressed individuals may experience falling asleep, depressed women with infants experience this problem after each night feed rather than just at the beginning of the night. Mothers with PND are more likely to report feeling best in the morning and worse as the day progresses. By contrast, individuals suffering from depression at other times in their lives report feeling worst in the morning. Adapting a depression program for these mothers needs to take into account the difficulties of processing new information owing to the combination of sleep deprivation and depressive symptomatology. The treatment program needs to begin slowly, with ample opportunity to process and practice new information and skills, and the time of day carefully considered.

Gender-sensitive therapy

There is an emerging literature on gender differences in the experience of depression. Boughton (1998) argued that CBT programs are generally constructed in a manner more suited to deal with difficulties in men. She argued that behavioural tasks commonly do not take into account gender differences, such as women's greater preoccupation with relationship difficulties rather than 'doing something practical about the problem'. She hypothesised that self-esteem differences in men and women have differing genesis: men are more achievement based whereas women are more identity/relationship based. Therefore, deficits in self-esteem in women may need a different emphasis in treatment. She also pointed out that current quantitative research does not often evaluate gender differences. A counter-argument, however, is that many CBT programs have been developed and evaluated using groups of women, partly owing to the more common presentation of problems such as anxiety. With other problems, such as headaches, it may even be that CBT works better for women than men (Martin, 1998). Thus, while CBT appears to be a valid approach for work with women, it is important to focus particularly on identity and relationship issues. In addition to skills development, an emphasis on group process is a good avenue for taking into account some of the special needs of women, in feeling listened to and understood rather than being task oriented. In the Getting Ahead of Postnatal Depression program, we have attempted to adapt traditional CBT approaches for depressed mothers. In particular, we allow for ample discussion time, and take into account the presence of the infant and partner at this important transitional phase in the life cycle.

❑ **The dangers of manuals.**

  Is it the techniques described in a manual that are therapeutic or the group process? What are the downfalls of sticking to a protocol, irrespective of the patient's experience? Wilson (1998) reported that despite clinicians' intuitive beliefs that individualised treatment is superior to standardised approaches, patients treated according to validated manuals do better. Others, however, caution about the dangers of manuals being applied in a mechanical way, without consideration of other factors.

  Hoffman (1998) reminds us that manuals, or the models from which they emanate, are only a map or metaphor. She further suggests that 'soft' areas such as psychotherapy require both a scientific framework and a philosophy that can explain the non-linear complexity of human events. Ultimately, clinical judgement and an open mind need to be coupled with a formalised approach to treatment.

Furthermore, the benefits of treatment may be partially related to factors other than those specified in the manual, such as the quality of the therapeutic relationship, adherence to the treatment manual, the competence of the therapist or the client's belief in the treatment (Shapiro, 1995). Benefits of treatment may also depend on how much the client engages in tasks. For instance, in a general depressed population, cognitive-behavioural therapists' ratings of patient compliance with homework assignments after two treatment sessions accounted for 13% of final improvement of depressive symptoms (Startup & Edmonds, 1995). This issue is a vexed one as we have previously alluded to postnatally depressed mothers commonly having difficulty completing homework, owing to competing time demands. If this occurs, we suggest reducing homework expectations to some extent.

Another problem with following manuals rigidly is that, at times, improvement in depression will occur quickly and some women will not be interested in completing the 12-week package. In general, we encourage women to persevere, in order to acquire skills that will help them to problem solve issues that arise, and teach them strategies to use, should a relapse occur. On other occasions, it is more important to terminate treatment and congratulate the woman on her gains.

Other problems in the administration of a packaged program include how to deal with those who drop out, not because they have improved, but because they are dissatisfied with the treatment. Again, clinical judgement is required to determine if any alternative support needs to be offered or if this mother is poorly motivated to follow through with any type of therapeutic intervention.

Finally, it is important for the therapist to keep in mind the importance of accessing social support, time-out and self-care, as has been emphasised throughout the manual. Thus, at the end of treatment, some mothers may still need further help to arrange these supports and need extra input from the therapist. Onward referrals to other professionals or self-help groups may be necessary. Often the program has helped a mother on the 'road to recovery', and it is then helpful to work beyond the manual and network her back into her community, matching the level of support to her needs.

PREVENTION

The prevalence of PND in the community, and the significant proportion of women already suffering from depression when they become pregnant, highlight the need for developing preventive measures. This may prevent needless suffering as well as being cost effective, especially in times of scarce resources when treatment costs are difficult to meet (Holden, 1994b). At present, however, there is little evidence as to whether antenatal intervention will reduce the incidence of PND. Three major approaches that have been used are as follows:

- Using screening procedures antenatally to detect those at risk of depression or already suffering from depression.

- Exploring types of interventions that are likely to reduce PND or its occurrence.
- Early diagnosis and intervention to shorten the length of the illness.

❏ **Detecting those at risk of depression.**

Of the risk factors outlined in Chapter 1, a history of severe depression is likely to increase risk about threefold (Marks, Wieck & Checkley, 1992). Other factors that reliably predict PND include presence of marital problems, difficulties in childhood and current relationships, social adversity and conflicts about parenthood (O'Hara & Zekoski, 1988). We have also found recently that personality factors such as cognitive style account for a large proportion of the variance in predicting postpartum adjustment (Annakis et al., 1998). Despite this information, regular screening of at-risk groups does not occur.

Kumar (1994) also highlighted that screening for psychiatric conditions in most antenatal clinics was often unsystematic and left to junior staff, and that there was no requirement in the UK to record whether psychiatric outpatients were pregnant. Much is needed to be done to improve the sensitivity and specificity of screening procedures for psychiatric disorders, including PND. Kumar also raised the important issue of the lack of professional expertise to assess a mother's competence, safety and motivation to care for her child now and in the future. Most countries have developed protective services that generally assess neglect only after it has occurred. Thus, we need not only early detection of those at risk of PND, but also of women likely to have parenting difficulties, so that appropriate supports can be put in place.

❏ **Prophylactic interventions.**

Kumar (1994) suggested three approaches with an emphasis on more severe disorders, although he did not evaluate the efficacy of these approaches:

1. *Pre-conception counselling:* To advise on risks of recurrence of depression, risks to the unborn infant of remaining on antidepressant medication and its effect on fertility.
2. *Support during pregnancy:* This may involve liaison between general practitioners, psychologists, psychiatrists, social workers or nursing staff, as well as planning for postpartum care, which may include mother–baby units for severe cases.
3. *Evaluating risk to the infant or fetus:* Examples of risk factors to assess include prescribed or self-ingested medications, suicidal ideation and malnutrition.
4. *Psychotropic medication:* More research is also required to confirm whether biological markers may identify women likely to benefit from early anti-depressant therapy (Wisner & Wheeler, 1994) or prophylactic progesterone (Dalton, 1989).

❏ **Primary versus secondary prevention.**

Holden (1994b) refers to the relevance of three levels of prevention to PND:

1. *Primary prevention:* This approach aims to prevent the incidence of PND by measures either directed at the whole population or targeted selectively at

high-risk groups. For instance, efforts directed at this approach would aim to change social attitudes for problems such as the low status of motherhood and the lack of supportive rituals after childbirth. In addition, limited affordable quality childcare, media idealisation of the realities of parenting, and stresses on the families of women suffering from PND could be targeted. Universal measures could also be aimed at educating school children and a wide range of health professionals (midwives, obstetricians, general practitioners) in interpersonal skills and in the psychological needs of women and challenges of parenting.

2. *Secondary prevention:* This refers to early diagnosis and intervention to shorten the length of the illness. Preventive approaches could include early antenatal contact, providing information about resources and supports, continuity of care, and putting mothers in touch with other mothers or groups. Very early contact in the delivery room and providing emotional support were found in a randomised control trial to reduce labour time and complications (Kennell, Klaus & McGrath, 1991). Privacy, rest and empathic listening in the postnatal ward were also advocated. Despite the number of people who seem to be working in the perinatal psychiatry field these days, there is surprisingly little published material on this topic (Barnett, 1997). In one of the few existing studies, intensive counselling in pregnancy has been found to be effective in preventing postnatal depression when continued postnatally (Elliott, 1988). This finding, however, has not been replicated in subsequent studies. Stamp, Williams and Crowther (1995) attempted antenatal intervention but found no postpartum benefits. However, women attended an average of only three meetings, compared to seven in Elliott's study. A smaller pilot study indicated that antenatal classes focusing on parenting and coping strategies resulted in decreased anxiety but not depression postpartum (Buist, Westley & Hill, 1998). While antenatal preparation is an obvious target of intervention, there is no convincing evidence to date that imparting information about PND antenatally is successful at changing the incidence. A more promising approach may be to focus on relationship support prenatally.

   Gordon and Gordon (1960) reported that women who were encouraged during pregnancy to confide in their husbands and enlist his practical help not only received more help, but also were less likely to become depressed. They added two 40-minute sessions to traditional antenatal classes in which women and their partners were advised not only to seek information and practical help but also to make friends with couples experienced in childcare, to avoid moving house, to get plenty of rest, to discuss plans and worries in depth, to cut down unnecessary activities and arrange babysitters. Holden (1994b) reviewed evidence that the marital relationships of women who received this type of individual antenatal counselling remained stable, whereas those in a control group had deteriorated by six months postpartum.

3. *Tertiary prevention:* This involves limiting the disability caused by the illness by providing focused immediate treatment such as the approach described in this book.

RESEARCH: FUTURE DIRECTIONS

Research on PND has touched on most of the main areas of interest of those wanting to understand the problem and develop solutions. In all these areas, however, a start has been made to answering questions rather than definite conclusions being reached. With respect to epidemiological research, for example, data is available on the prevalence of PND and the factors affecting prevalence but there are still many possibilities worthy of investigation. A pilot study that we completed, for example, revealed a much higher prevalence rate of PND (31.6%) in a rural community compared to an urban community (Johnston, Martin & Milgrom, 1998). Similarly, studies of the symptoms of PND have begun to focus on the question of whether PND can be differentiated from depression occurring at times other than following childbirth. These studies need expansion to include questions such as how the symptoms of PND cluster together, and whether subtypes of PND can be identified.

Quite an extensive literature exits on the aetiology of PND, particularly identifying risk factors. Nevertheless, many questions remain, such as how these risk factors relate to each other, and the mechanism(s) by which they lead to PND. Developing an inclusive model of PND, as we have done, allows us to proceed to develop and test more specific mechanisms that are suggested by the model. Also, what are the protective factors for those who do not develop PND? It may not just be the absence of vulnerability factors that is important, but also the presence of specific protective factors such as social support. Some of the consequences of PND have been explored for the mothers and their families. Further, longitudinal studies are needed, however, exploring fully the short- and long-term effects of PND on mothers, their infants, their partners as well as on the sibs of their infants. For instance, how does infant developmental stage interact with severity of PND?

Researchers have begun evaluating both psychological and pharmacological treatment approaches to PND but this literature is at a very early stage of development. The range of measures needs to be expanded to determine the effects of treatment on both targeted and non-targeted variables. Do treatment programs have unanticipated benefits, but also do they have any adverse effects on mothers and their families? Research using dismantling strategies is needed to ascertain which components of multifaceted treatment programs are necessary and which are not. Furthermore, how do cultural factors influence treatment approaches? The central goal of psychotherapy research is not only to understand change mechanisms but also to find out what is helpful, for whom and under what circumstances (Shapiro, 1995). Maintenance issues require investigation: do treatment gains deteriorate across time? Because of the number of women affected by PND, we not only need to develop a concerted approach to treatment, but also to attempt to reduce the costs of treatment. Studies comparing high and low intensive treatments need to be assessed, as do preventive measures. With respect to prevention, what is the most appropriate level of intervention—mothers who have just developed PND? Mothers identified as at risk of PND? Or more population-focused campaigns that educate the public about issues such as myths pertaining to motherhood, the high incidence of PND, the need for supporting the new mothers and so forth?

Based on the evidence to date, secondary and tertiary prevention may be the most realistic approaches. Our model suggests that biopsychosocial stressors in vulnerable women combine to result in the experience of depression. It may therefore not be possible to *prevent* PND but only to set in motion procedures that minimise the impact and duration of the depressive condition while taking measures to improve the supportiveness of the social environment. Moreover, as we suggest that cognitive, behavioural and affective factors maintain the problem, the preventive effects of CBT for a second episode of PND would be important to evaluate in future studies.

CONCLUDING COMMENT

We started this book by emphasising the magnitude of the problem that PND represents. We believe that it is reasonable to claim that a significant proportion of women have experienced depression following childbirth across cultures, throughout history. Their suffering has impacted on their lives, their babies and their partners. Yet, until recently, little attention has been devoted to this extensive set of problems: research has been limited, and services to identify and remediate PND have been minimal in most health care systems. We hope that this book, which offers a model of PND and a 'tried and tested' treatment program, will contribute one small step towards helping women suffering from PND, and their families.

REFERENCES

Abidin, R. R. (1986). *Parenting stress index manual* (2nd ed.). Charlottesville, VA: Pediatric Psychology Press.

Abidin, R. R. (1992). The determinants of parenting behavior. *Journal of Clinical Child Psychology, 21*(4), 407–412.

Abramson, L. Y., Seligman, M. E. P., & Teasdale, J. D. (1978). Learned helplessness in humans: Critique and reformulation. *Journal of Abnormal Psychology, 87*(1), 49–74.

Ainsworth, M. D. (1979, April). Attachments beyond infancy. *American Psychologist,* 709–716.

Ainsworth, M. D. S., Blehar, M. C., Waters, E., & Wall, S. (1978). *Patterns of attachment: A psychological study of the strange situation.* Hillsdale, NJ: Erlbaum.

American Psychiatric Association (1994). *Diagnostic and statistical manual of mental disorders* (4th ed.). Washington, DC: American Psychiatric Press.

Annakis, V., Milgrom, J., & Stanley, R. (1998). *A predictive model of postpartum adjustment.* Paper presented at the 33rd Annual Conference of the Australian Psychological Society, Melbourne, Australia.

Appleby, L., Gregoire, A., Platz, C., Prince, M., & Kumar, R. (1994). Screening women for high risk of postnatal depression. *Journal of Psychosomatic Research, 38*(6), 539–545.

Appleby, L., Warner, R., Whitton, A., & Faragher, B. (1997). A controlled study of fluoxetine and cognitive-behavioural counselling in the treatment of postnatal depression. *British Medical Journal, 314,* 932–936.

Areias, M. E. G., Kumar, R., Barros, H., & Figueiredo, E. (1996a). Comparative incidence of depression in women and men during pregnancy and after childbirth. *British Journal of Psychiatry, 169,* 30–35.

Areias, M. E. G., Kumar, R., Barros, H., & Figueiredo, E. (1996b). Correlates of postnatal depression in mothers and fathers. *British Journal of Psychiatry, 169,* 36–41.

Atkinson, A. K., & Rickel, A. U. (1984). Depression in women: The postpartum experience. In A. U. Rickel, M. Gerrard, & I. Iscoe (Eds), *Social and psychological problems of women: Prevention and crisis intervention* (pp. 197–218). Washington: Hemisphere.

Augusto, A., Kumar, R., Calheiros, J. M., Matos, E., & Figueiredo, E. (1996). Postnatal depression in an urban area of Portugal: Comparison of childbearing women and matched controls. *Psychological Medicine, 26,* 135–141.

Bakeman, R., & Brown, J. (1981). Early interaction: Consequences for social and mental development at three years. *Child Development, 51,* 437–447.

Ballard, C. G., Davis, R., Cullen, P. C., Mohan, R. N., & Dean, C. (1994). Prevalence of postnatal psychiatric morbidity in mothers and fathers. *British Journal of Psychiatry, 164,* 782–788.

Ballard, C. G., Davis, R., Handy, S., & Mohan, R. N. C. (1993). Postpartum anxiety in mothers and fathers. *European Journal of Psychiatry, 7,* 117–121.

Ballinger, C. B., Buckley, D. E., Naylor, G. J., & Stansfield, D. A. (1979). Emotional disturbance following childbirth: Clinical findings and urinary excretion of cyclic AMP (adenosine 3'5' cyclic monophosphate). *Psychological Medicine, 9,* 293–300.

Bardon, D., Glaser, Y. I. M., Prothero, D., & Weston, D. H. (1968). Mother and baby unit: Psychiatric survey of 115 cases. *British Medical Journal, 2,* 755–758.

Barnett, B. (1991). *Coping with postnatal depression.* Port Melbourne: Lothian.

Barnett, B. (1997). *Antenatal intervention to reduce the risk of postnatal depression: A review.* Paper presented at the First Conference of the Marcé Society Australasian Branch, Brisbane, Australia.

Barrera, M., Kitching, K., Cunningham, C., Doucet, D., & Rosenbaum, P. (1990). A three year early home intervention follow-up study with low birth weight infants and their parents. *Topics of Early Childhood Special Education, 10,* 14–21.

Beatrice, G., & Milgrom J. (1999). *Personality factors associated with postnatal depression.* Submitted for publication.

Beck, A. T. (1967). *Depression: Clinical, experimental, and theoretical aspects.* New York: Harper & Row.

Beck, A. T., Epstein, N., Brown, G., & Steer, R. A. (1988). An inventory for measuring clinical anxiety: Psychometric properties. *Journal of Consulting and Clinical Psychology, 56,* 893–897.

Beck, A. T., & Greenberg, R. L. (1974). Cognitive therapy with depressed women. In V. Franks & V. Burtle (Eds), *Women in therapy: New psychotherapies for a changing society.* New York: Brunner/Mazel.

Beck, A. T., & Steer, R. A. (1987). *Manual for the revised Beck Depression Inventory.* San Antonio, TX: Psychological Corporation.

Beck, A. T., Ward, C. H., Mendelson, M., Mock, J., & Erbaugh, J. (1961). An inventory for measuring depression. *Archives of General Psychiatry, 4,* 53–63.

Becker, J. (1974). *Depression: Theory and research.* Washington, DC: Winston.

Becker, R. E., & Heimberg, R. G. (1985). Social skills training approaches. In M. Hersen & A. S. Bellack (Eds), *Handbook of clinical behavior therapy with adults* (pp. 201–226). New York: Plenum.

Beckwith, L., Cohen, S. E., Kopp, C. Y., Parmelee, A. H., & Marcy, T. G. (1976). Caregiver–infant interaction and early cognitive development in preterm infants. *Child Development, 47,* 579–587.

Beckwith, L., & Rodning, C. (1996). Dyadic processes between mothers and preterm infants: Development at ages 2 to 5 years. *Infant Mental Health Journal, 17*(4), 322–333.

Belsky, J. (1985). Experimenting with the family in the newborn period. *Child Development, 56*(2), 407–414.

Belsky, J., & Rovine, M. (1990). Patterns of marital change across the transition to parenthood: Pregnancy to three years postpartum. *Journal of Marriage and the Family, 52,* 5–19.

Berg-Cross, L., & Cohen, M. S. (1995). Depression and the marital relationship. *Psychotherapy in Private Practice, 14*(1), 35–51.

Bettes, B. A. (1988). Maternal depression and motherese: temporal and intonational features. *Child Development, 59*(4), 1089–1096.

Bonnin, F. (1992). Cortisol levels in saliva and mood changes in early puerperium. *Journal of Affective Disorders, 26*(4), 231–239.

Boughton, S. (1998). *Gender differences in the experience of depression.* Thesis completed for the Master of Family Therapy, School of Public Health, Faculty of Sciences, La Trobe.

Bowlby, J. (1953). *Child care and the growth of love.* Harmondsworth, UK: Penguin.

Boyce, P. (1991). *Limitations and use of the Edinburgh Postnatal Depression Scale and Beck Depression Inventory after childbirth: Use and misuse of the Edinburgh Postnatal Depression Scale.* Keele, UK; University of Keele.

Boyce, P. (1994). Personality dysfunction, marital problem and postnatal depression. In J. Cox & J. Holden (Eds), *Perinatal psychiatry: Use and misuse of the Edinburgh Postnatal Depression Scale* (pp. 82–97). London: Gaskell.

Boyce, P. M., Stubbs, J. M., & Todd, A. (1993). The Edinburgh Postnatal Depression Scale: Validation for an Australian sample. *Australian and New Zealand Journal of Psychiatry, 27,* 472–476.

Brazelton, T. B., Koslowski, B., & Main, M. (1974). Origins of reciprocity: The early mother–infant interaction. In M. Lewis & L. Rosenbloom (Eds), *Effect of the infant on its caregiver* (pp. 49–79). New York: Wiley.

Brockington, I. F., & Kumar, R. (Eds) (1981). *Motherhood and mental illness.* London: Academic Press.

Broom, G. L. (1984). Consensus about the marital relationship during the transition to parenthood. *Nursing Research, 33,* 223–228.

Brown, G. W. (1993). The role of life events in the aetiology of depressive and anxiety disorders. In S. C. Stanford & P. Salmon (Eds), *Stress: From synapse to syndrome* (pp. 23–50). London: Academic Press.

Brown, S., Lumley, J., Small, R., & Astbury, J. (1994). *Missing voices: The experience of motherhood.* Melbourne: Oxford University Press.

Brown, W. A. (1979). *Psychological care during pregnancy and the postpartum period.* New York: Raven Press.

Buist, A. (1996). *Psychiatric disorders associated with childbirth: A guide to management.* Sydney: McGraw-Hill.

Buist, A., Norman, T. R., & Dennerstein, L. (1993). Plasma and breast milk concentrations of dothiepin and northiaden in lactating women. *Human Psychopharmacology Clinical and Experimental, 8*(1), 29–33.

Buist, A., Westley, D., & Hill, C. (1998). Antenatal prevention of postnatal depression. *Archives of Women's Mental Health, 1,* 1–7.

Burns, D. (1980). *Feeling good.* New York: NAL Penguin.

Byng-Hall, J., & Moore, M. (1998). *Creating a coherent story in family therapy: Important implications of attachment research.* Workshop presented by Australian Association for Infant Mental Health and the New South Wales Family Therapy Association, Sydney, Australia.

Cairns, R., Cairns, B. D., Xie, H., Leung, M., & Hearne S. P. (1998). Across generations: Academic competence and aggressive behaviours in young mothers and their children. *Developmental Psychology, 34*(6), 1162–1174.

Campbell, S. B., & Cohn, J. F. (1991). Prevalence and correlates of postpartum depression in first-time mothers. *Journal of Abnormal Psychology, 100,* 594–599.

Campbell, S. B., & Cohn, J. F. (1997). The timing and chronicity of postpartum depression: Implications for infant development. In L. C. Murray & P. Cooper (Eds), *Postpartum depression and child development* (pp. 165–197). New York: Guilford Press.

Campbell, S. B., Cohn, J. F., Flanagan, C., Popper, S., & Meyers, T. (1992). Course and correlates of postpartum depression during the transition to parenthood. *Development and Psychopathology, 4,* 29–47.

Caplan, F., & Caplan, T. (1995). *The first twelve months of life.* New York: Bantam.

Carro, M. G., Grant, K. E., & Gotlib, I. H. (1993). Postpartum depression and child development: An investigation of fathers as sources of risk and resilience. *Development and Psychopathology, 5,* 567–579.

Censullo, M. (1994). Strategy for promoting greater responsiveness in adolescent parent/ infant relationships: Report of a pilot study. *Journal of Pediatric Nursing, 9*(5), 328–332.

Censullo, M., Lester, B., & Hoffman, J. (1985). Rhythmic patterning in mother–newborn interaction. *Nursing Research, 34,* 342–346.

Clark, D. M. (1990). Cognitive therapy for depression and anxiety: Is it better than drug treatment in the long term? In K. Hawton & P. Cowen (Eds), *Dilemmas and difficulties in the management of psychiatric patients* (pp. 55–64). New York: Oxford University Press.

Clark, D. M., & Fairburn, C. G. (Eds) (1997). *Science and practice of cognitive behaviour therapy.* New York: Oxford University Press.

Cohn, J. F., & Tronick, E. Z. (1988). Mother–infant face-to-face interaction: Influence is bidirectional and unrelated to periodic cycles in either partner's behaviour. *Developmental Psychology, 24*(3), 386–392.

Cohn, J. F., & Tronick, E. Z. (1989). Specificity of infants' response to mothers' affective behaviour. *Journal of the American Academy of Child and Adolescent Psychiatry, 28,* 242–248.

Conte, H. R., & Karasu, T. B. (1992). A review of treatment studies of minor depression: 1980–1991. *American Journal of Psychotherapy, 10*(1), 58–74.

Cooper, P. J., Campbell, E. A., Day, A., Kennerley, H., & Bond, A. (1988). Non-psychotic psychiatric disorder after childbirth: A prospective study of prevalence, incidence, course and nature. *British Journal of Psychiatry, 152,* 799–806.

Cooper, P. J., & Murray, L. (1995). Course and recurrence of postnatal depression: Evidence for the specificity of the diagnostic concept. *British Journal of Psychiatry, 166,* 191–195.

Cooper, P. J., & Murray, L. (1997). The impact of psychological treatments of postpartum depression on maternal mood and infant development. In L. Murray & P. J. Cooper

(Eds), *Postpartum depression and child development* (pp. 201–220). New York: Guilford Press.

Cooper, P. J., Murray, L., Hooper, R., & West, A. (1996). The development and validation of a predictive index for postpartum depression. *Psychological Medicine, 26,* 627–634.

Coopersmith, S. (1987). *SEI Self-esteem inventories.* Palo Alto, CA: Consulting Psychologists Press.

Cordone, I. A., & Glikerson, L. (1989). Family administered neonatal activities: An innovative component of family centred care. *Zero to three, 10*(1), 23–28.

Cox, A. D. (1988). Maternal depression and impact on children's development. *Archives of Diseases in Childhood, 63*(1), 90–95.

Cox, J.L. (1983). Postnatal depression: A comparison of African and Scottish women. *Social Psychiatry, 18,* 25–28.

Cox, J. L., (1986). *Postnatal depression: A guide for health professionals.* Edinburgh: Churchill Livingstone.

Cox, J. L. (1996). Perinatal mental disorder: A cultural approach. *International Review of Psychiatry, 8,* 9–18.

Cox, J. L., Connor, J. M., & Kendell, R. E. (1982). Prospective study of psychiatric disorders of childbirth. *British Journal of Psychiatry, 140,* 111–117.

Cox, J. L., & Holden, J. M. (Eds) (1994). *Perinatal psychiatry: Use and misuse of the Edinburgh Postnatal Depression Scale.* London: Gaskell.

Cox, J. L., Holden, J. M., & Sagovsky, R. (1987). Detection of postnatal depression: A development of the 10-item Edinburgh Postnatal Depression Scale. *British Journal of Psychiatry, 150,* 782–786.

Cox, J. L., Murray, D., & Chapman, G. (1993). A controlled study of the onset, duration and prevalence of postnatal depression. *British Journal of Psychiatry, 163,* 27–31.

Coyne, J. C., Kessler, R. C., Tal, M., Turnbull, J., Wortman, C. B., & Greden, J. F. (1987). Living with a depressed person. *Journal of Consulting and Clinical Psychology, 55,* 347–352.

Cramer, B. (1997). Psychodynamic perspectives on the treatment of postpartum depression and child development. In L. Murray & P. J. Cooper (Eds), *Postpartum depression and child development* (pp. 237–261). New York: Guilford Press.

Cramer, B., Robert-Tissot, C., Stern, D., Serpa-Rusconi, S., DeMuralt, M., Besson, G., Palacio-Esoasa, F., Bachmann, J. P., Knauer, D., Berney, C., & D'Arcis, U. (1990). Outcome evaluation in brief mother–infant psychotherapy: A preliminary report. *Infant Mental Health Journal, 11,* 278–300.

Cramer, B., & Stern, D. (1988). Evaluation of changes in mother–infant brief psychotherapy: A single case study. *Infant Mental Health Journal, 9,* 20–45.

Cutrona, C. E. (1982). Nonpsychotic postpartum depression: A review of recent research. *Clinical Psychology Review, 2,* 487–503.

Cutrona, C. E. (1983). Causal attributions and perinatal depression. *Journal of Abnormal Psychology, 92,* 161–172.

Cutrona, C. E. (1984). Social support and stress in the transition to parenthood. *Journal of Abnormal Psychology, 93,* 378–390.

Cutrona, C. E., & Troutman, B. R. (1986). Social support, infant temperament, and parenting self-efficacy: A mediational model of postpartum depression. *Child Development, 57,* 1507–1518.

Dalton, K. (1971). Prospective study into puerperal depression. *British Journal of Psychiatry, 118,* 689–692.

Dalton, K. (1977). *The premenstrual syndrome and progesterone therapy.* Chicago: Heinemann.

Dalton, K. (1989). *Depression after childbirth* (2nd ed.). Oxford: Oxford University Press.

Davids, A., & Holden, R. H. (1970). Consistency of maternal attitudes and personality from pregnancy to eight months following childbirth. *Developmental Psychology, 2*(3), 364–366.

Davis, M., & Wallbridge, D. (1981). *Boundary and space: An introduction to the work of D. W. Winnicott.* Melbourne: Penguin.

De Battista, C., & Schatzberg, A. F. (1995). Somatic therapy. In I. D. Glick (Ed.), *Treating depression.* San Francisco: Jossey-Bass.

DeMulder, E., & Radke-Yarrow, M. (1991). Attachment with affectively ill and well mothers: Concurrent behavioural correlates. *Development and Psychology,* (3), 227–242.

Dennerstein, L., Varnavides, K., & Burrows, G. (1986). Postpartum depression: A review of recent literature. *Australian Family Physician, 15*(11), 1470–1472.

Dix, C. (1986). When lovers become parents. In C. Dix (Ed.), *The new mother's syndrome* (Ch. 7, pp. 104–116). New York: Pocket Books.

Dragonas, T., Thorpe, K., & Golding, J. (1992). Transition to fatherhood: A cross-cultural comparison. *Journal of Psychosomatic Obstetrics and Gynaecology, 13*, 1–19.

Dunnewold, A. L. (1997). *Evaluation and treatment of postpartum emotional disorders.* Sarasota, FL: Professional Resource Press.

Egan, G. (1994). *The skilled helper: A systematic approach to effective helping* (4th ed.). Pacific Grove, CA: Brooks/Cole.

Elliott, S. A. (1984). Pregnancy and after. In S. Rachman (Ed.), *Contributions to medical psychology* (pp. 93–116). Oxford: Pergamon Press.

Elliott, S. A. (1988). Psychological strategies in the prevention and treatment of postnatal depression. In M. Oates (Ed.), *Clinics in obstetrics and gynaecology* (Vol. 3, No. 4, pp. 879–903). London: Baillière Tindall.

Elliott, S. A., Sanjack, M., & Leverton, T. J. (1988). Parents groups in pregnancy: A preventative intervention for postnatal depression? In B. H. Gottlieb (Ed.), *Marshalling social support, formats, processes and effects* (pp. 87–110). London: Sage.

Engel, G. L. (1980). The application of the biopsychosocial model. *American Journal of Psychiatry, 137*, 535–544.

Erickson, M. (1998). Strategies for breaking intergenerational cycles of child abuse and neglect. Report prepared by V. Carty & S. Jones. *Australian Association for Infant Mental Health Newsletter, 10*(2), 1–9.

Eysenck, H. J. (1994). The outcome problem in psychotherapy: What have we learned? *Behaviour Research and Therapy, 32*, 477–495.

Fawcett, J., & York, R. (1986). Spouses' physical and psychological symptoms during pregnancy and the postpartum. *Nursing Research, 35*, 144–148.

Feinberg, M. (1992). Comment: Subtypes of depression and response to treatment. *Journal of Consulting and Clinical Psychology, 60*(5), 670–674.

Field, T. M. (1982). Interaction coaching for high-risk infants and their parents. In H. A. Moss, R. Hess & C. Swift (Eds), *Early intervention programs for infants: Prevention in Human Services* (Vol. 1, No. 4, pp 5–21). New York: Haworth Press.

Field, T. M. (1997). The treatment of depressed mothers and their infants. In L. Murray & P. J. Cooper (Eds), *Postpartum depression and child development* (pp. 221–236). New York: Guilford Press.

Field, T. M., Dempsey, J. R., & Shuman, H. H. (1981). Developmental follow-up of pre- and post-term infants. In. S. L. Friedman & M. Sigman (Eds), *Preterm birth and psychological development.* New York: Academic Press.

Field, T., Healy, B., Goldstein, S., & Gotherz, M. (1990). Behaviour state matching and synchrony in nondepressed versus depressed dyads. *Developmental Psychology, 24*, 7–14.

Field, T., Sandberg, D., Garcia, R., Nitza, V., Goldstein, S., & Guy, L. (1985). Pregnancy problems, postpartum depression and early mother–infant interactions. *Developmental Psychology, 21*(6), 1152–1156.

Finlay-Jones, R., & Brown, G. W. (1981). Types of stressful life event and the onset of anxiety and depressive disorders. *Psychological Medicine, 11*, 803–815.

Fleming, A. S. , Flett, G., Ruble, D., & Shaw, D. (1988). Postpartum adjustment in first-time mothers: Relations between mood, maternal attitudes, and mother–infant interactions. *Development Psychology, 24*(1), 71–81.

Fleming, A. S., Klein, E., & Corter, C. (1992). The effects of a social support group on depression, maternal attitudes and behavior in new mothers. *Journal of Child Psychology and Psychiatry, 33*(4), 685–698.

Flick, L. H., & McSweeney, M. (1987). Measures of mother–child interaction: A comparison of three methods. *Research in Nursing and Health, 10*, 129–139.

Fraiberg, S. (1980). *Clinical studies in infant mental health.* New York: Basic Books.

Frank, E., Prien, R. F., Jarrett, R. B., Keller, M. B., Kupfer, D. J., Lavori, P. W., Rush, A. J., & Weissman, M. M. (1991). Conceptualization and rationale for consensus definitions of terms in Major Depressive Disorder: Remission, recovery, relapse, and recurrence. *Archives of General Psychiatry, 48*, 851–855.

Frankenburg, W., & Dodds, J. (1967). The Denver Developmental Screening Test. *Journal of Paediatrics, 71*, 181–191.

Friedrich, W. A., Tyler, J. D., & Clark, J. A. (1985). Personality and psychophysiological variables in abusive, neglectful and low-income control mothers. *Journal of Nervous and Mental Disease, 183*(8), 449–460.

Gelfand, D. M., & Teti, D. M. (1990). The effects of maternal depression on children. *Clinical Psychology Review, 10*, 329–352.

Gerrard, J., Holden, J. M., & Elliott, S. A. (1993). A trainer's perspective of an innovative training programme to teach health visitors about the detection, treatment and prevention of postnatal depression. *Journal of Advanced Nursing, 18*, 1825–1832.

Gibaud-Wallston, J. A. (1977). Self-esteem and situational stress: Factors related to sense of competence in new parents. (Doctoral dissertation, George Peabody College for Teachers, 1977). *Dissertation Abstracts International, 39*, 379B. (University Microfilms No. DDK78–09936.)

Gilley, T. (1993). *Access for growth: Services for mothers and babies.* Melbourne: Brotherhood of St Laurence.

Glick, I. D. (Ed.) (1995). *Treating depression.* San Francisco: Jossey-Bass.

Glover, V. (1992). Do biochemical factors play a part in postnatal depression? *Progress in Neuro-Psychopharmacology and Biological Psychiatry, 16*(5), 605–615.

Goldberg, D. P., Cooper, B., Eastwood, M. R., Kedward, H. B., & Shepherd, M. (1970). A standardized psychiatric interview for use in community surveys. *British Journal of Preventive Social Medicine, 24*, 18–23.

Goldberg, D. P., & William, P. (1988). *A user's guide to the General Health Questionnaire.* Windsor, UK: NFER-Nelson.

Goleman, D. (1996). *Emotional intelligence.* London: Bloomsbery.

Goodman, S. H. (1992). Understanding the effects of depressed mothers on their childen. In E. F. Walker, R. H. Dworkin, & B. A. Cornblatt (Eds), *Progress in experimental personality and psychopathology research* (pp. 47–109). New York: Springer.

Gordon, R. E., & Gordon, K. K. (1960). Social factors in prevention of postpartum emotional adjustment. *Obstetrics & Gynecology, 15*, 433–438.

Gordon, J., Swan, M., & Robertson, R. (1995). 'Babies don't come with a set of instructions': Running support groups for mothers. *Health Visitor, 68*(4), 155–156.

Gotlib, I. H., Whiffen, V. E., Wallace, P. M., & Mount, J. H. (1991). Prospective investigation of postpartum depression: Factors involved in onset and recovery. *Journal of Abnormal Psychology, 100*, 122–132.

Greenberg, M. S., & Silverstein, M. L. (1983). Cognitive and behavioral treatments of depressive disorders: Interventions with adults. In H. L. Morrison (Ed.), *Children of depressed parents: Risk, identification, and intervention* (pp. 189–220). New York: Grune & Stratton.

Greenberg, M. T., Cicchetti, D., & Cummings, E. M. (Eds) (1990). *Attachment in the preschool years: Theory, research and intervention.* Chicago: University of Chicago Press.

Gregoire, A. J. P., Kumar, R., Everfill, B., Henderson, J., & Studd, J. W. W. (1996). Transdermal oestrogen for treatment of severe postnatal depression. *Lancet, 347*, 930–933.

Grossman, F. K., Eichler, L. S., & Winickoff, S. A. (1980). *Pregnancy, birth and parenthood.* San Francisco: Jossey-Bass.

Gruis, M. (1977). Beyond maternity: Postpartum concerns of mothers. *American Journal of Maternal Child Nursing, 2*(3), 182–188.

Hamilton, M. A. (1967). Development of a rating scale for primary depressive illness. *British Journal of Social and Clinical Psychology, 6*, 278–296.

Handford, P. (1997). *Self-help groups for women with postpartum depression and anxiety: A group facilitator's manual* (2nd ed.). Vancouver: Pacific Postpartum Support Society.

Handley, S. L., Dunn, T. L., Waldron, G., & Baker, J. M. (1980). Tryptophan, cortisol and puerperal mood. *British Journal of Psychiatry, 136*, 498–508.

Hans, S., Bernstein, V., & Percansky, C. (1991). Adolescent parenting programs: Assessing parent–infant interaction. *Evaluation and Program Planning, 14*, 87–95.

Harkness, S. (1987). The cultural mediation of postpartum depression. *Medical Anthropology Quarterly, 1*, 194–209.

Harris, B. (1993). Post-partum thyroid dysfunction and postnatal depression. *Annals of Medicine, 25*(3), 215–216.

Harris, B. (1994). Biological and hormonal aspects of postpartum depressed mood: Working towards strategies for prophylaxis and treatment. *British Journal of Psychiatry, 164,* 288–292.

Harris, B. (1996). Hormonal aspects of postnatal depression. *International Review of Psychiatry, 8*(1), 27–36.

Harris, B., Johns, S., Fung, H., Thomas, R., Walker, R., Read, G., & Riad-Fahmy, D. (1989). The hormonal environment of postnatal depression. *British Journal of Psychiatry, 154,* 660–667.

Hart, S., Field, T., & del Valle, C. (1998). Depressed mothers' interactions with their one-year-old infants. *Infant Behavior and Development, 21*(3), 519–525.

Harvey, I., & McGrath, G. (1988). Psychiatric morbidity in spouses of women admitted to a mother and baby unit. *British Journal of Psychiatry, 152,* 506–510.

Hayworth, J., Little, B. C., Bonham Carter, S., Raptopoulos, P., Priest, R. G., & Sandler, M. (1980). A predictive study of postpartum depression: Some predisposing characteristics. *British Journal of Medical Psychology, 53,* 161–167.

Hendrick, V., Altshuler, L. L., & Suri, R. (1998). Hormonal changes in the postpartum and implications for postpartum depression. *Psychosomatics, 39*(2), 93–101.

Highet, N. (1998). *Evaluation of community treatments for post partum depression.* Thesis submitted for the award of Doctor of Psychology, Division of Social Sciences, Humanities and Education, Murdoch University, Western Australia.

Hinchcliffe, M., Hooper, D., & Roberts, F. J. (1975). A study of the interaction between depressed patients and their spouses. *British Journal of Psychiatry, 126,* 164–172.

Hoffman, L. (1988). Setting aside the model in family therapy. *Journal of Marital and Family Therapy, 24*(2), 145–156.

Holden, J. (1994a). Using the Edinburgh Postnatal Depression Scale in clinical practice. In J. Cox & J. Holden (Eds), *Perinatal psychiatry: Use and misuse of the Edinburgh Postnatal Depression Scale* (pp. 125–144). London: Gaskell.

Holden, J. (1994b). Can nonpsychotic depression be prevented? In J. Cox & J. Holden (Eds), *Perinatal psychiatry: Use and misuse of the Edinburgh Postnatal Depression Scale* (pp. 54–81). London: Gaskell.

Holden, J. M., Sagovsky, R., & Cox, J. L. (1989). Counselling in a general practice setting: Controlled study of health visitor intervention in the treatment of postnatal depression. *British Medical Journal, 298,* 223–226.

Hollon, S. D., Shelton, R. C., & Davis, D. D. (1993). Cognitive therapy for depression: Conceptual issues and clinical efficacy. *Journal of Consulting and Clinical Psychology, 61,* 270–275.

Holmes, T. H., & Rahe, R. H. (1967). The Social Readjustment Rating Scale. *Journal of Psychosomatic Research, 11,* 213–218.

Hopkins, J., Campbell, S. B., & Marcus, M. (1987). Role of infant-related stressors in postpartum depression. *Journal of Abnormal Psychology, 96*(3), 237–241.

Hopkins, J., Marcus, M., & Campbell, S.B. (1984). Postpartum depression: A critical review. *Psychological Bulletin, 95*(3), 498–515.

Hunt, B. (1998). *The father's inner world: Birth and trauma.* Proceedings of the Fifth Annual Meeting of The Australian Association for Infant Mental Health, Sydney.

Jacobson, E. (1929). *Progressive relaxation.* Chicago: University of Chicago Press.

Jadresic, E., Araya, R., & Jara, C. (1995). Validation of the Edinburgh Postnatal Depression Scale (EPDS) in Chilean postpartum women. *Journal of Psychosomatic Obstetrics and Gynaecology, 16,* 187–191.

Jebali, C. (1991). Working together to support women with postnatal depression. *Health Visitor, 64*(12), 410–411.

Jermain, D. M. (1992). Psychopharmacologic approach to postpartum depression. *Journal of Women's Health, 1,* 47–52.

Jernberg, A. (1984). Theraplay: Child therapy for attachment fostering. *Psychotherapy, 21,* 39–47.

Jinadu, M. K., & Daramola, S. M. (1990). Emotional changes in pregnancy and early puerperium among the Yoruba women of Nigeria. *International Journal of Social Psychiatry, 36,* 93–98.

Johnston, E., Martin, P. R., & Milgrom, J. (1998). Comparison of postnatal depression in a rural and urban area. Paper presented at 33rd National Conference, Australian Psychological Society, Melbourne. Abstract in *Australian Journal of Psychology, 50,* (1998 Supplement), 96.

Jones, A., Watts, T., & Romain, S. (1995). Facilitating peer group support. *Health Visitor, 68*(4), 153.

Kagan, C. (1986). *A manual of interpersonal skills for nurses: An experiential approach/Carolyn Kagan, Josie Evans, Betty Kay* (p. xiii). London: Harper & Row.

Karen, R. (1990). Becoming attached. *Atlantic Monthly,* February, 35–50.

Kelly, J. V. (1967). The influence of native customs on obstetrics in Nigeria. *Obstetrics and Gynecology, 30,* 608–612.

Kendell, R. E., Chalmers, L., & Platz, C. (1987). The epidemiology of puerperal psychosis. *British Journal of Psychiatry, 150,* 662–673.

Kennell, J., Klaus, M., & McGrath, S. (1991). Continuous emotional support during labour in a US hospital: A randomised controlled trial. *Journal of the American Medical Association, 265,* 2197–2201.

Kitzinger, S. (1989). Childbirth and society. In I. Chalmers, M. Enkin, & M. J. N. C. Keirse (Eds), *Effective care in pregnancy and childbirth* (pp. 99–109). New York: Oxford University Press.

Klaus, M. H., & Kennell, J. (1982). *Parent–infant bonding.* St Louis: Mosby.

Kovacs, M., Rush, A. J., Beck, A. T., & Hollon, S. D. (1981). Depressed outpatients treated with cognitive therapy or pharmacotherapy: A one-year follow-up. *Archives of General Psychiatry, 38,* 33–41.

Kumar, R. (1994). Prevention of adverse effects of perinatal maternal mental illness on the developing child. In J. Cox & J. Holden (Eds), *Perinatal psychiatry: Use and misuse of the Edinburgh Postnatal Depression Scale.* London: Gaskell.

Kumar, R., & Robson, K. (1978). Neurotic disturbance during pregnancy and the puerperium: Preliminary report of a prospective survey of 119 primiparae. In M. Sandler (Ed.), *Mental illness in pregnancy and the puerperium.* Oxford: Oxford University Press.

Kumar, R., & Robson, K. M. (1984). A prospective study of emotional disorders in child bearing women. *British Journal of Psychiatry, 144,* 35–47.

Lamb, M. E., Thompson, R. A., Gardner, W., Charnov, E. L., & Connell, J. P. (1985). *Infant–mother attachment: The origins and developmental significance of individual differences in strange situation behavior.* Hillsdale: Erlbaum.

Lane, A., Morris, K. M., Turner, K. M., & Barry, S. (1997). Postnatal depression and elation among mothers and their partners: Prevalence and predictors. *British Journal of Psychiatry, 171,* 550–555.

Lazarus, R. S., & Folkman, S. (1984). *Stress, appraisal and coping.* New York: Springer.

Leff, J. (1990). The 'new cross-cultural psychiatry': A case of the baby and the bathwater. *British Journal of Psychiatry, 156,* 305–307.

Lier, L. (1988). Mother-infant relationships in the first year. *Acta Paediatrics Scandinavica Supplementum, 344*(77), 31–42.

Lewinsohn, P. M. (1974). A behavioral approach to depression. In R. J. Friedman & M. M. Katz (Eds), *The psychology of depression: Contemporary theory and research.* New York: Wiley.

Lewinsohn, P. M., Antonuccio, D. O., Steinmetz, J. L., & Teri, L. (1984). *The coping with depression course: A psycho-educational intervention for unipolar depression.* Eugene, OR: Castalsa.

Lewinsohn, P. M., & Gotlib, I. H. (1995). Behavioral theory and treatment of depression. In E. E. Beckham & W. R. Leber (Eds), *Handbook of depression* (pp. 352–375). New York: Guilford Press.

Lewinsohn, P. M., Hoberman, H. M., & Rosenbaum, M. (1988). A prospective study of risk factors for unipolar depression. *Journal of Abnormal Psychology, 97*(3), 251–264.

Lewinsohn, P. M., Hoberman, H., Teri, L., & Hautzinger, M. (1985). An integrative theory of depression. In S. Reiss & R. R. Bootzin (Eds), *Theoretical issues in behavior therapy* (pp. 331–359). San Diego: Academic Press.

Lewinsohn, P. M., Munoz, R. F., Youngren, M. A., & Zeiss, A. M. (1992). *Control your depression.* New York: Simon & Schuster.

Lewinsohn, P. M., Sullivan, J. M., & Grosscup, S. J. (1980). Changing reinforcing events: An approach to the treatment of depression. *Psychotherapy: Theory, Research and Practice, 47,* 322–334.

Lieberman, A. F., & Pawl, J. H. (1988). Clinical applications of attachment theory. In J. Belsky & T. Nexworksi (Eds), *Clinical implications of attachment.* Hillsdale, NJ: Erlbaum.

Lieberman, A. F., & Pawl, J. H. (1993). Infant–parent psychotherapy. In C. Zeanah Jr (Ed.), *Handbook of infant mental health* (pp. 427–442). New York: Guilford Press.

Lloyd, C. (1980). Life events and depressive disorder reviewed: Events as predisposing factors. *Archives of General Psychiatry, 37,* 541–548.

Loughlin, E. (1992). Being. *Dance Therapy Collections, 1,* 4–6.

Lovestone, S., & Kumar, R. (1993). Postnatal psychiatric illness: The impact on partners. *British Journal of Psychiatry, 163,* 210–216

Lyons-Ruth, K., Zollo, D., Connell, D., & Gunebaum, H. V. (1986). The depressed mother and her one-year-old infant: Environment, interaction, attachment and infant development. In E. Z. Tronick & T. Field (Eds), *Maternal depression and infant disturbance: New directions for child development,* No. 34 (pp. 61–82). San Francisco: Jossey-Bass.

Main, M. (1984). Predicting rejection of her infant from mother's representation of her own experience, *Child abuse and neglect, 8*(2), 203–217.

Malphurs, J., Larrain, C., Field, T., Pickens, J., Peleas-Nogueras, M., Yando, R., & Bendall, O. (1996). Altering withdrawn and intrusive interaction behaviours of depressed mothers. *Infant Mental Health Journal, 17,* 152–160.

Marks, M. N., Wieck, A., & Checkley, S. A. (1992). Contribution of psychological and social factors to psychotic and non-psychotic relapse after childbirth in women with previous histories of affective disorder. *Journal of Affective Disorders, 29,* 253–264.

Martin, P. R. (1996). Cognitive-behavioural treatment of postnatal depression: Results of a programme evaluation. Paper presented at 19th National Conference of the Australian Association for Cognitive and Behavioural Therapy, Sydney. Abstract in *National Association for Cognitive and Behavioural Therapy, 54.*

Martin, P. R. (1998). Headaches trigger factors: To avoid or not to avoid, that is the question. Paper presented at 33rd Annual Conference of the Australian Psychological Society, Melbourne, Australia. *Australian Journal of Psychology, 50* (1998 Supplement), 102.

May, A. (1995). Using exercise to tackle postnatal depression. *Health Visitor, 68*(4), 146–147.

Mayberry, L. J., & Affonso, D. D. (1993). Infant temperament and postpartum depression: A review. *Health Care for Women International, 14,* 201–211.

McDonough, S. C. (1985). Intervention programs for adolescent mothers and their offspring. In M. Frank (Ed.), *Infant intervention programs: Truths and untruths.* New York: Haworth Press.

McDonough, S. C. (1993). Interaction guidance: Understanding and treating early infant–caregiver relationship disturbances. In C. Zeanah Jr (Ed.), *Handbook of infant mental health* (pp. 414–426) New York: Guilford Press.

McLean, P. D., & Hakstian, A. R. (1979). Clinical depression: Comparative efficacy of outpatient treatments. *Journal of Consulting and Clinical Psychology, 47,* 818–836.

McLean, P. D., & Hakstian, A. R. (1990). Relative endurance of unipolar depression effects: Longitudinal follow-up. *Journal of Consulting and Clinical Psychology, 58,* 482–488.

McNair, D. M., Lorr, M., & Drappleman, L. F. (1992). *Manual for the Profile of Mood States* (rev. ed.). San Diego: Educational and Industrial Testing Service.

Meager, I., & Milgrom, J. (1996). Group treatment for postpartum depression: A pilot study. *Australian and New Zealand Journal of Psychiatry, 30,* 852–860.

Meares, R., Penman, R., Milgrom-Friedman, J., & Baker, K. (1982). Some origins of the 'difficult' child: The Brazelton scale and the mother's view of her new-born's character. *British Journal of Medical Psychology, 55,* 77–86.

Meisels, S. J. (1989). Can developmental screening tests identify children who are developmentally at risk? *Paediatrics, 83,* 578–585.

Meitz, A., & Milgrom, J. (1999). The effect of caregiver–infant ratio on the quality of infant experience in day care settings. Submitted for publication.

Meltzoff, A. N., & Moore, M. K. (1983). Newborn infants imitate adult facial gestures. *Child Development, 54*(3), 702–709.

Merchant, D. C., Affonso, D. D., & Mayberry, I. J. (1995). Influence of marital relationship and child-care stress on maternal depression symptoms in the postpartum. *Journal of Psychosomatic Obstetrics and Gynaecology, 16*(4), 193–200.

Milgrom, J. (1991). *Mother–infant interaction and postpartum depression.* Final Report of the Victorian Health Promotion Foundation, Melbourne, Australia.

Milgrom, J. (1994). Mother–infant interactions in postpartum depression: An early intervention program. *Australian Journal of Advanced Nursing, 11*(4), 29–38.

Milgrom, J. (1996). Program thérapeutique de groupe et interaction mère–bébé. *Devenir, 8*(1), 7–24.

Milgrom, J. (1998a). *Parenting stress: A follow-up study.* Submitted for publication.

Milgrom, J. (1998b). Postnatal depression: Symptoms, risk factors and management. *International Psychiatry Today, 8*(3), 1–6.

Milgrom, J. (1999). A 2-year follow-up of mothers and infants following postnatal depression. Submitted for publication.

Milgrom, J., & Burn, J. (1988). *Synchrony Coding Scale in maternal perceptions of infant temperament, maternal competency, mothering style and later mother–infant synchrony.* Unpublished thesis, Melbourne College of Advanced Education.

Milgrom, J., & McCloud, P. I. (1996). Parenting stress and postnatal depression. *Stress Medicine, 12*(3), 177–186.

Milgrom, J., & Green, S. (1999). *Factors influencing maternal perception of infant difficulty.* Submitted for publication.

Milgrom, J., & Meager, I. (1996). Group treatment for post-partum depression: A pilot study. *Australian and New Zealand Journal of Psychiatry, 30*(6), 750–758.

Milgrom, J., & Negri, L. (1999). *The use of the Edinburgh Postnatal Depression Scale in diagnosing depression in the community: An Australian sample.* Submitted for publication.

Milgrom, J., Negri, L., & Martin, P. R. (1997). *Cognitive-behavioural approaches to intervention in post-natal depression.* 20th National Conference, Australian Association for Cognitive Behavioural Therapy, Brisbane, Australia.

Milgrom, J., Westley, D. T., & McCloud, P. I. (1995). Do infants of depressed mothers cry more than other infants? *Journal of Paediatrics and Child Health, 31*(3), 218–221.

Milgrom-Friedman, J., Penman, R., & Meares, R. A. (1980). Some pilot studies of early attachment and detachment behavior. In E. J. Anthony (Series Ed.) & C. Chiland (Vol. Ed.), *Yearbook of the International Association for Child and Adolescent Psychiatry and Allied Professions: Vol. 6. The child in his family: Preventive child psychiatry in an age of transition* (pp. 79–83). New York: Wiley.

Miller, I. W., Norman, W. H., Keitner, G. I., Bishop, S. B., & Dow, M. G. (1989). Cognitive-behavioral treatment of depressed inpatients. *Behavior Therapy, 20*, 25–47.

Millis, J. B., & Kornblith, P. R. (1992). Fragile beginnings: Identification and treatment of postpartum disorders. *Health and Social Work, 17*(3), 192–199.

Moore, M., & Dean, S (1998). *Contemplating the face of trauma: Understanding the enduring consequences of abuse and neglect in infancy.* Workshop presented at the Australian Association for Infant Mental Health, 5th Annual Meeting, Sydney, Australia.

Muir, E. (1992). Watching, waiting and wondering: Applying psychoanalytic principals to mother–infant intervention. *Infant Mental Health Journal, 13*(4), 319–328.

Murray, L. (1988). Effects of postnatal depression infant development: Direct studies of early mother–infant interactions. In R. Kumas & I. F. Brockington (Eds), *Motherhood and mental illness 2* (pp. 159–185). Cambridge, UK: Butterworth.

Murray, L. (1992). The impact of postnatal depression on infant development. *Journal of Child Psychology and Psychiatry, 33*, 561.

Murray, L. (1997). Postpartum depression and child development. *Psychological Medicine, 27*, 253–260.

Murray, L., & Carothers, A. D. (1990). The validation of the Edinburgh Postnatal Depression Scale on a community sample. *British Journal of Psychiatry, 157*, 288–290.

Murray, L., & Cooper, P. J. (Eds) (1997a). *Postpartum depression and child development.* New York: Guilford Press.

Murray, L., & Cooper, P. J. (1997b). The role of infant and maternal factors in postpartum depression, mother–infant interactions, and infant outcome. In L. Murray & P. J. Cooper

(Eds), *Postpartum depression and child development* (pp. 111–135). New York: Guilford Press.

Murray, L., Fiori-Cowley, A., Hooper, R., & Cooper, P. J. (1996). The impact of postnatal depression and associated adversity on early mother infant interaction and later infant outcome. *Child Development, 67,* 2512–2516.

Murray, L., & Stein, A. (1989). The effects of postnatal depression on the infant. *Baillière's Clinical Obstetrics and Gynaecology, 3*(4), 921–933.

Negri, L. M. (1998). *Screening and treatment of women with post-partum depression.* Unpublished doctoral thesis, La Trobe University, Bundoora, Melbourne.

Nezu, A. M. (1987). A problem-solving formulation of depression: A literature review and proposal of a pluralistic model. *Clinical Psychology Review, 7,* 121–144.

Nicolson, P. (1989). Counselling women with post natal depression: Implications from recent qualitative research. *Counselling Psychology Quarterly, 2*(2), 123–132.

Nicolson, P. (1998). *Postnatal depression: Psychology, science and the transition to motherhood.* London: Routledge.

Nott, P. N. (1987). Extent, timing and persistence of emotional disorders following childbirth. *British Journal of Psychiatry, 151,* 523–527.

Nott, P. N., Franklin, M., Armitage, C., & Gelder, M. G. (1976). Hormonal changes and mood in the puerperium. *British Journal of Psychiatry, 128,* 379–383.

Oakley, A., Rajan, L., & Grant, A. (1990). Social support and pregnancy outcome. *British Journal of Obstetrics and Gynaecology, 97,* 155–162.

Oates, D. S., & Heinicke, C. M. (1985). Prebirth prediction of the quality of the mother–infant interaction: The first year of life. *Journal of Family Issues, 6*(4), 523–542.

Oei, T. P. S., & Shuttlewood, G. J. (1996). Specific and nonspecific factors in psychotherapy: A case of cognitive therapy for depression. *Clinical Psychology Review, 16*(2), 83–103.

O'Hara, M. N. (1994). Postpartum depression: Identification and measurement in a cross-cultural context. In J. Cox & J. Holden (Eds), *Perinatal psychiatry: Use and misuse of the Edinburgh Postnatal Depression Scale* (Ch. 10, pp. 145–168). London: Gaskell/Royal College of Psychiatrists.

O'Hara, M. W. (1986). Social support, life events, and depression during pregnancy and the puerperium. *Archives of General Psychiatry, 136,* 339–346.

O'Hara, M. W. (1995). *Postpartum depression: Causes and consequences.* New York: Springer.

O'Hara, M. W. (1997). The nature of postpartum depressive disorders. In L. Murray & P. J. Cooper (Eds), *Postpartum depression and child development* (pp. 3–31). New York: Guilford Press.

O'Hara, M. W., Neunaber, D. J., & Zekoski, E. M. (1984). Prospective study of postpartum depression: Prevalence, course and predictive factors. *Journal of Abnormal Psychology, 93*(2), 158–171.

O'Hara, M. W., Rehm, L. P., & Campbell, S. B. (1982). Predicting depressive symptomatology: Cognitive-behavioral models and postpartum depression. *Journal of Abnormal Psychology, 91*(6), 457–461.

O'Hara, M. W., Schlechte, J. A., Lewis, D. A., & Varner, M. W. (1991). Controlled prospective study of postpartum mood disorders: Psychological, environmental and hormonal variables. *Journal of Abnormal Psychology, 100*(1), 63–73.

O'Hara, M. W., Schlechte, J. A., Lewis, D. A., & Wright, E. J. (1991). Prospective study of postpartum blues: Biologic and psychosocial factors. *Archives of General Psychiatry, 48,* 801–806.

O'Hara, M. W., Stuart, S., Gorman, L. L., & Kochanska, G. (1998). *Interpersonal psychotherapy for postpartum depression.* Paper presented at the Annual Meeting of the American Psychological Association, San Francisco.

O'Hara, M. W., & Swain, A. M. (1996). Rates and risk of postpartum depression: A meta analysis. *International Review of Psychiatry, 8,* 37–54.

O'Hara, M. W., & Zekoski, E. M. (1988). Postpartum depression: A comprehensive review. In R. Kumar & I. F. Brockington (Eds), *Motherhood and mental illness 2* (pp. 17–63). London: Wright.

O'Hara, M. W., Zekoski, E. M., Philipps, L. H., & Wright, E. J. (1990). Controlled prospective study of postpartum mood disorders: Comparison of childbearing and non-childbearing women. *Journal of Abnormal Psychology, 99,* 3–15.

Olioff, M. (1991). The application of cognitive therapy to postpartum depression. In T. M. Vallis, J. L. Howes, & P. C. Miller (Eds), *The challenge of cognitive therapy: Applications to nontraditional populations* (pp. 111–133). Plenum Press: New York.

Painter, A. (1995). Health visitor identification of postnatal depression. *Health Visitor, 68*(4), 138–140.

Paul (1996). *Survival tips for husbands.* Paper presented at information night, Monash Medical Centre (Post and Ante Natal Depression Association (PanDa) Newsletter), Melbourne, Australia.

Pawlby, S., & Hall, F. (1980). Early interactions and later language development of children whose mothers come from disrupted families of origin. In T. Field, S. Goldberg, D. Stern, & A. M. Sostek (Eds), *High-risk infants and children: Adult and peer interactions.* New York: Academic Press.

Paykel, E., Emms, E. M., Fletcher, J., & Rassaby, E. S. (1980). Life events and social support in puerperal depression. *British Journal of Psychiatry 136*, 339–346.

Penman, R., Meares, R., Baker, K., & Milgrom-Friedman, J. (1983). Synchrony in mother–infant interaction: A possible neurophysiological base. *British Journal of Medical Psychology, 56*(1), 1–7.

Philipps, L. H. C., & O'Hara, M. W. (1991). Prospective study of postpartum depression: 4½-year follow-up of women and children. *Journal of Abnormal Psychology, 100* (2), 151–155.

Phillips, N. (1995). Dr. Know. *Mastermind Media, 4,* 4–5.

Pitt, B. (1968). Atypical depression following childbirth. *British Journal of Psychiatry, 114,* 1325–1335.

Pitts, F. (1995). Comrades in adversity: The group approach. *Health Visitor, 68*(4), 144–145.

Pridham, K. F., Berger Knight, C., & Stephenson, G. R. (1989). Mothers' working models of infant feeding: Description and influencing factors. *Journal of Advanced Nursing, 14,* 1051–1061.

Prien, R. F., & Kupfer, D. J. (1986). Continuation drug therapy for major depressive episodes. *American Journal of Psychiatry, 143,* 18–23.

Procidano, M. E., & Heller, K. (1983). Measures of perceived social support from friends and family: Three validation studies. *American Journal of Community Psychology, 11,* 1–24.

Raphael-Leff, J. (1991). *Psychological processes of childbearing.* London: Chapman & Hall.

Raskin, V. D., Richman, J. A., & Gaines, C. (1990). Patterns in depressive symptoms in expectant and new parents. *American Journal of Psychiatry, 147,* 658–660.

Rauh, V., Achenbach, T., Nurcombe, B., Howell, C., & Teti, D. (1988). Minimising adverse effects of low birthweight: Four year results of an early intervention program. *Child Development, 59,* 544–553.

Rehm, L. P. (1977). A self-control model of depression. *Behavior Therapy, 8,* 787–804.

Rehm, L. P. (1990). Cognitive and behavioral theories. In B. B. Wolman & G. Stricker (Eds), *Depressive disorders: Facts, theories, and treatment methods* (pp. 64–91). New York: Wiley.

Rehm, L. P., & Kaslow, N. J. (1984). Behavioral approaches to depression: Research results and clinical recommendations. In C. M. Franks (Ed.), *New developments in behavior therapy: From research to clinical application* (pp. 155–229). New York: Haworth Press.

Reighard, F. T., & Evans, M. L. (1995). Use of the Edinburgh Postnatal Depression Scale in a southern, rural population in the United States. *Progress in Neuro-Psychopharmacology and Biological Psychiatry, 19,* 1219–1224.

Richards, J. P. (1990). Postnatal depression: A review of recent literature. *British Journal of General Practice, 40,* 472–476.

Richman, J. A., Raskin, V. D., & Gaines, C. (1991). Gender roles, social support and postpartum depressive symptomatology. *Journal of Nervous and Mental Disease, 179,* 139–147.

Robinson, L. A., Berman, J. S., & Neimeyer, R. A. (1990). Psychotherapy for the treatment of depression: a comprehensive review of controlled outcome research. *Psychological Bulletin, 108,* 30–49.

Robinson, S., & Young, J. (1982). Screening for depression and anxiety in the postnatal period: Acceptance or rejection of a subsequent treatment offer. *Australian and New Zealand Journal of Psychiatry, 16,* 47–51.

Romito, P. (1989). Unhappiness after childbirth. In I. Chalmers, M. Enkin, & M. J. N. C. Keirse (Eds), *Effective care in pregnancy and childbirth* (pp. 1433–1446). New York: Oxford University Press.

Rosenbaum, M., & Merbaum, M. (1984). Self-control of anxiety and depression: An evaluative review of treatments. In C. M. Franks (Ed.), *New developments in behavior therapy: From research to clinical application* (pp. 105–154). New York: Haworth Press.

Rubble, D. N., Fleming, A. S., Hackel, L. S., & Stangor, C. (1988). Changes in the marital relationship during the transition to first time motherhood: Effects of violated expectations concerning division of household labor. *Journal of Personality and Social Psychology*, 55, 78–87.

Ruch-Ross, H., Jones, E., & Musick, J. (1992). Comparing outcomes in a statewide program for adolescent mothers with outcomes in a national sample. *Family Planning Perspectives*, 24, 66–96.

Rutter, D. R., & Durkin, K. (1987). Turn-taking in mother infant interaction: An examination of vocalisations and gaze. *Developmental Psychology*, 23(1), 54–61.

Sanson, A., Prior, M., & Oberklaid, F. (1985). Normative data on temperament in Australian infants. *Australian Journal of Psychology*, 37(2), 185–195.

Sanson, A., Oberklaid, F., Pedlow, R., & Prior, M. (1991). Risk indicators: Assessment of infancy predictors of pre-school behavioural maladjustment. *Journal of Child Psychology and Psychiatry*, 32(4), 609–626.

Sanson, A., Prior, M., Garino, E., Oberklaid, F., & Sewell, J. (1987). The structure of infant temperament: Factor analysis of the Revised Infant Temperament Questionnaire. *Infant Behaviour and Development*, 10, 97–104.

Sanson, A. V., Prior, M., & Oberklaid, F. (1985). Normative data on temperament in Australian infants. *Australian Journal of Psychology*, 37(2), 185–195.

Saxon, T. F. (1997). A longitudinal study of early mother–infant interaction and later language competence. *First Language*, 17, 271–281.

Schweitzer, R. D., Logan, G. P., & Strassberg, D. (1992). The relationship between marital intimacy and postnatal depression. *Australian Journal of Marriage and Family*, 13(1), 19–23.

Scott, D. (1992). Early identification of maternal depression as a strategy in the prevention of child abuse. *Child Abuse and Neglect*, 16, 345–358.

Scott, J. (1996). Cognitive therapy of affective disorders: A review. *Journal of Affective Disorders*, 37, 1–11.

Seale, R., Williams, S., & Reynolds, I. (1988). *Postnatal Depression Support Group Program*. Tresillian Family Care Centres, Petersham, New South Wales.

Seeley, S., Murray, L., & Cooper, P. J. (1996). The outcome for mothers and babies of health visitor intervention. *Health Visitor*, 69, 135–138.

Shapiro, D. A., (1995). Finding out how psychotherapies help people change. *Psychotherapy Research*, 5(11), 1–21.

Sharpley, C. F., & Rogers, H. J. (1984). Preliminary validation of the abbreviated Spanier Dyadic Adjustment Scale: Some psychometric data regarding a screening test of marital adjustment. *Educational and Psychological Measurement*, 44(4), 1045–1049.

Sigman, M., Cohen, S. E., Beckwith, L., & Parmelee, A. H. (1981). Social and familial influences on the development of preterm infants. *Journal of Paediatric Psychology*, 6(1), 1–13.

Simons, A. D., Levine, J. L., Lustman, P. J., & Murphy, G. E. (1984). Patient attrition in a comparative outcome study of depression: A follow-up report. *Journal of Affective Disorders*, 6, 163–173.

Spanier, G. B. (1976). Measuring dyadic adjustment: New scales for assessing the quality of marriage and similar dyads. *Journal of Marriage and the Family*, 38, 15–28.

Spitzer, R. L., Williams, J. B. W., Gibbon, M., & First, M. B. (1990). *Structured Clinical Interview for DSM-III-R: Patient Edition* (SCID-P, Version 1.0). Washington, DC: American Psychiatric Press.

Stamp, G. E., Williams, A. S., & Crowther, C. A. (1995). Evaluation of antenatal and postnatal support to overcome postnatal depression: A randomised controlled trial. *Birth Issues in Perinatal Care*, 22(3), 138–143.

Startup, M., & Edmonds, J. (1995). Compliance with homework assignments in cognitive-behavioral psychotherapy for depression: Relation to outcome and methods for enhancement. *Cognitive Therapy Research* 18, 567–576.

Stein, A., Gath, D. H., Bucher, J., Bond, A. D., & Cooper, P. J. (1991). The relationship between postnatal depression and mother–child interaction. *British Journal of Psychiatry*, 158, 46–52.

Stern, D. N. (1985). *The interpersonal world of the infant: A view from psychoanalysis and developmental psychology.* New York: Basic Books.

Stern, G., & Kruckman, L. (1983). Multi-disciplinary perspectives on post-partum depression: An anthropological critique. *Social Science and Medicine, 17,* 1027–1041.

Stuart, S. (1995). Treatment of postpartum depression with interpersonal psychotherapy. *Archives of General Psychiatry, 52*(1), 75–76.

Svartberg, M., & Stiles, T. C. (1991). Comparative effects of short-term psychodynamic psychotherapy: A meta-analysis. *Journal of Consulting and Clinical Psychology, 59*(5), 704–714.

Taylor, A., Dore, C., & Glover, V. (1996). Urinary phenylethylamine and cortisol levels in the early puerperium. *Journal of Affective Disorders, 37,* 137–142.

Taylor, E. (1989). Postnatal depression: What can a health visitor do? *Journal of Advanced Nursing, 14,* 877–886.

Teti, D. M., Gelfand, D. M., Messinger, D. S., & Isabella, R. (1995). Maternal depression and the quality of early attachment: An examination of infants, preschoolers and their mothers. *Developmental Psychology, 31,* 364–376.

Teti, D. M., Gelfand, D. M., & Pompa, J. (1990). Depressed mother's behavioural competence with their infants: Demographic and psychosocial correlates. *Development and Psychopathology, 2,* 259–270.

Thase, M. E. (1995). Cognitive behavior therapy. In I. D. Glick (Ed.), *Treating depression* (pp. 33–70). San Francisco: Jossey-Bass.

Thase, M. E., & Howland, R. H. (1995). Biological processes in depression: An updated review and integration. In E. E. Beckham & W. R. Leber (Eds), *Handbook of depression* (pp. 213–279). New York: Guilford Press.

Tronick, E. Z., Als, H., Adamson, L., Wise, S., & Brazelton, T. B. (1978). The infant's response to entrapment between contradictory messages in face-to-face interaction. *Journal of the American Academy of Child Psychiatry, 17,* 1–13.

Tronick, E. Z., & Weinberg, M. K. (1997). Depressed mothers and infants: Failure to form dyadic states of consciousness. In L. Murray & P. Cooper (Eds), *Postpartum depression and child development* (pp. 54–81). New York: Guilford Press.

Ussher, J. M. (1992). Research and theory related to female reproduction: Implications for clinical psychology. *British Journal of Clinical Psychology, 31,* 129–151.

Wadhwa, P. D., Dunkel-Schetter, C., Chicz-Demet, A., Porto, M., & Sandman, C. A. (1996). Prenatal psychosocial factors and the neuroendocrine axis in human pregnancy. *Psychosomatic Medicine, 58,* 432–446.

Wallace, P. M., & Gotlib, I. H. (1990). Marital adjustment during the transition to parenthood: Stability and predictors of change. *Journal of Marriage and the Family, 52,* 21–29.

Waller, N. G. (1993). Review of the Beck Depression Inventory. In J. C. Impara & J. C. Conoley (Eds), *Supplement to the twelfth mental measurements yearbook* (pp. 57–59). Lincoln, NB: Buros Institute of Mental Measurements.

Watson, J. P., Elliott, S. A., Rugg, A. J., & Brough, D. I. (1984). Psychiatric disorder in pregnancy and the first postnatal year. *British Journal of Psychiatry, 144,* 453–462.

Webster, M. L., Thompson, J. M. D., Mitchell, E. A., & Werry, J. S. (1994). Postnatal depression in a community cohort. *Australian and New Zealand Journal of Psychiatry, 28,* 42–49.

Werner, E. (1990). Protective factors and individual residence. In S. Meisels & J. Shonkoff (Eds), *Handbook of early intervention* (pp. 97–116). Cambridge, UK: Cambridge University Press.

Westley, D. T. (1992). *The effect of postnatal depression on the mother–infant interaction.* Unpublished master's thesis, Monash University, Clayton, Melbourne.

Whiffen, V., & Gotlib, I. (1989). Infants of postpartum depressed mothers: Temperament and cognitive status. *Journal of Abnormal Psychology, 98*(3), 274–279.

Whitten, A. Appleby, L., & Warner, R. (1996). Maternal thinking and the treatment of postnatal depression. *International Review of Psychiatry, 8*(1), 73–78.

Whitten, A., Warner, R., & Appleby, L. (1996). The pathway to care in post-natal depression: Women's attitudes to post-natal depression and its treatment. *British Journal of General Practice, 46,* 427–428.

Wickberg, B., & Hwang, C. P. (1996). Counselling of postnatal depression: A controlled study on a population based Swedish sample. *Journal of Affective Disorders, 39*(3), 209–216.

Wilson, L. M., Reid, A. J., Midmer, D. K., Biringer, A., Carroll, J. C., & Stewart, D. E. (1996). Antenatal psychosocial risk factors associated with adverse postpartum family outcomes. *Canadian Medical Association Journal, 154*(6), 785–799.

Wilson, T. (1998). *Cognitive-behavioural treatment of binge eating and bulimia.* Paper presented at 21st National Conference of the Australian Association for Cognitive and Behavioural Therapy, Melbourne, Australia.

Winnicott, D. W. (1965). *The role of maternal care in the maturational process and facilitating environment.* London: Hogarth Press.

Winnicott, D. W. (1974). *Playing and reality.* London: Pelican.

Wisner, K. L., & Wheeler, S. B. (1994). Prevention of recurrent postpartum major depression. *Hospital and Community Psychiatry, 45*(12), 1191–1196.

Wittchen, H. U., Robbins, L. N., Cottler, L. B., Sartorius, N., Burke, J. D., & Regier, D. (1991). Cross cultural feasibility, reliability and sources of variance of the Composite International Diagnostic Interview (CIDI). *British Journal of Psychiatry, 159*, 645–653.

World Health Organization (1993a). *Composite International Diagnostic Interview 1.1: Interviewer manual.* Washington, DC: American Psychiatric Press.

World Health Organization (1993b). *The ICD-10 classification of mental and behavioural disorders: Diagnostic criteria for research.* Geneva: World Health Organization.

Wrate, R. M., Rooney, A. C., Thomas, P. F., & Cox, J. L. (1985). Postnatal depression and child development. *British Journal of Psychiatry, 146*, 622–627.

Wright, B. M. (1986). An approach to infant–parent psychotherapy. *Infant Mental Health Journal, 7*(4), 247–263.

Zeanah, C. H., Benoit, D., Barton, M., Regan, C., Hirshberg, L., & Lipsitt, L. (1993). Representations of attachment in mothers and their one year old infants. *Journal of the American Academy of Child Adolescent Psychiatry, 32*(2), 278–286.

Zeiss, A. M., Lewinsohn, P. M., & Munoz, R. F. (1979). Nonspecific improvement effects in depression using interpersonal, cognitive, and pleasant events focused treatments. *Journal of Consulting and Clinical Psychology, 47*, 427–439.

Zelkowitz, P., & Milet, T. H. (1996). Postpartum psychiatric disorders: Their relationship to psychological adjustment and marital satisfaction in the spouses. *Journal of Abnormal Psychology, 105*, 281–285.

INDEX

Index compiled by A.C. Purton

Related titles of interest...

Cognitive Therapy in Groups
Guidelines and Resources for Practice
MICHAEL L. FREE
0471 981443   September 1999   196pp   Paperback

Cognitive Therapy for Bipolar Disorder
A Therapist's Guide to Concepts, Methods and Practice
DOMINIC HUNG LAM, STEVEN HUNTLEY JONES, PETER HAYWARD AND JENIFER A. BRIGHT
0471 979392   July 1999   320pp   Hardback
0471 979451   July 1999   320pp   Paperback

Treating Complex Cases
The Cognitive Behavioural Therapy Approach
Edited by NICHOLAS TARRIER, ADRIAN WELLS and GILLIAN HADDOCK
0471 97840X   December 1998   456pp   Hardback

Beyond Diagnosis
Case Formulation Approaches in CBT
Edited by MICHAEL BRUCH and FRANK W. BOND
0471 975257   August 1998   238pp   Hardback
0471 982229   August 1999   238pp   Paperback